LABOUR IN THE SOUTH AFRICAN GOLD MINES
1911–1969

AFRICAN STUDIES SERIES

General Editor : DR. J. R. GOODY

LABOUR IN THE
SOUTH AFRICAN GOLD MINES
1911–1969

by FRANCIS WILSON

Senior Lecturer in the Department of Economics
University of Cape Town

CAMBRIDGE
AT THE UNIVERSITY PRESS 1972

Published by the Syndics of the Cambridge University Press
Bentley House, 200 Euston Road, London NW1 2DB
American Branch: 32 East 57th Street, New York, N.Y.10022

© Cambridge University Press 1972

Library of Congress Catalogue Card Number: 77-161290

ISBN: 0 521 08303 6

Printed in Great Britain
by Alden & Mowbray Ltd
at the Alden Press, Oxford

CONTENTS

APPENDIXES

TABLES

PLATES

FIGURES

I have tried, in writing . . ., to limit myself to a bare description of the facts and of their inevitable connections and I have not – so I honestly believe – either allowed my own political opinions to colour that description or made covert propaganda for any cause, or race, or party. If, then, any reader disagrees with me he disagrees about what the facts and their connections really are.

GODFREY WILSON, to whose memory this work is dedicated

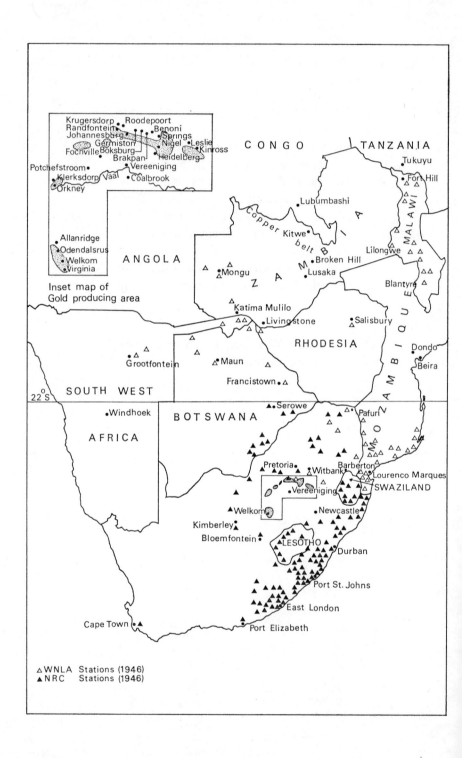

Inset map of
Gold producing area

△ WNLA Stations (1946)
▲ NRC   Stations (1946)

PREFACE

In his writings Père Teilhard de Chardin suggested that man's development consists chiefly in a growing awareness and understanding of himself.[1] It has been further suggested that this idea is equally true of collective man.[2] The development of society may itself be measured by the extent to which men understand, and are conscious of, the community in which they live. To this growing awareness of society the economist, along with the sociologist, the psychologist, and the historian, has a contribution to make. Essentially his job is to analyse the nature of the economic forces which operate in society, to show whence they derive their power, and to demonstrate their effect both on the individual and on the society at large. In this book I have focused on one sector of a complex and fascinating economy in the hope that, from the depths of a detailed case study, some useful insights may emerge which would enable us to understand this particular society a little better than we did before.

The choice of the gold mining industry for detailed analysis was dictated mainly by the fact that more information is readily available about it than about any other sector of the South African economy. Not only has the necessary background to the behaviour of the labour market in that industry already been filled in by Dr. Sheila van der Horst in her classic study, *Native Labour in South Africa* (O.U.P., Cape Town, 1942), but the annual reports of the Chamber of Mines and of the Government Mining Engineer provide a great deal of raw material. Indeed there can be few industries in the world that have published so much valuable statistical information which can be used for purposes of comparison over so long a period of years. Furthermore, as we shall see in the first chapter, the development of the gold mines has probably done more than any other industry to shape the structure of the whole South African labour market into the form in which it exists today.

[1] T. de Chardin, *The Phenomenon of Man* (Collins, London, 1959), pp. 147 ff B.
[2] M. Wilson, *Religion and the Transformation of Society* (C.U.P., Cambridge, 1971), pp. 18–23 and 130–3 B.

Preface

The facts on which this study is based were collected from three main sources. First, there is the published statistical and descriptive information available from government reports, publications from the gold mining industry, and data published in books, journals, and newspapers. The second major source of information came from direct observation in particular mines. Altogether I visited six gold mines and was able to see all stages of production, from the stope face to the smelter in both old and new mines. Material was also drawn from field work in the Transkei early in 1963. The third source flowed from discussions with those involved in mining gold. I talked not only with administrative officials in the Chamber of Mines and in the individual mining finance houses, but also with those at work on the mines, including white managers, shift bosses, and miners, as well as black clerical workers and migrant labourers. No method of systematically interviewing a cross-section of the labour force was employed. The study did not aim, and cannot claim, to give a scientific assessment of individual attitudes within the industry, nor of the patterns of behaviour which vary from person to person.

In addition to the existing body of economic theory, a further source of ideas, which assisted not only the selection of facts to be collected but also their subsequent analysis, came from comparisons. This study has made use of parallels, and important differences, between the South African labour market and the role of race in the American economy, the existence of migrant labour in other parts of Africa, and the breakdown of the colour bar in the copper mines of Zambia. In the case of the copper mines the opportunity of a short visit to Zambia, which included discussions with officials and visits to two mines, was extremely useful. For the American parallels and contrasts, a year of reading and discussion in that country was invaluable.

It is always necessary for those writing about South Africa to explain their terminology. Because of objections by those to whom they refer I have avoided the use of such classifications as 'non-white', 'native' or 'Bantu'. For simplicity I distinguish the four racial groups as black, Coloured, Indian and white. The word 'tropicals' refers to the men who come to work on the mines from those parts of the continent lying north of latitude 22°s. All countries are referred to by their present names.

One of the major problems facing scientists today is how to communicate the results of their work in a form that is intelligible to an audience wider than the small group that has learnt to use the essential tools of mathematics, statistics, and shorthand jargon. Part of the difficulty is that in translating one's results into a language that more people understand a certain precision can get lost. Yet the attempt must be made: it is a fundamental principle of economics, as Kenneth Boulding has remarked in this context, that specialisation without trade is useless. Moreover the immense power of knowledge to shape our world cannot be left in the hands of a few. If mankind is to achieve a more democratic society then all knowledge must surely be made available for the winnowing process of public debate. For this reason I have tried to relegate jargon to footnotes and appendices. For those parts of the text that remain obscure the reader may blame the writer.

F.W.

University of Cape Town
November 1971

ACKNOWLEDGEMENTS

The generous co-operation of many people in the gold mining industry made field work both informative and enjoyable. In particular I am grateful to the numerous officials in the mining houses, in the Chamber of Mines (including the recruiting corporations) and in the office of the Government Mining Engineer, for their help both in answering my many questions in the head offices and for arranging my visits down mines. Also most helpful were mining officials in Zambia and in the United States Bureau of Mines.

It is a moot point whether anybody working in a university community can claim sole authorship of a book. So much of one's thinking is moulded by others, and so many ideas are derived from teachers, colleagues and students that it is impossible to document fully all one's debts. But there are a number of people whose teaching and criticism have, I know, been incorporated into this book. Needless to say they cannot be held responsible for my interpretation of the points they have made. The supervisor of the thesis on which this book is based, Dr. Malcolm R. Fisher, read and criticised an entire draft, portions of it several times, and he more than once suggested a fruitful line of approach, particularly on the analytic side. Mr. Michael J. Farrell first taught me economics; his insistence on the importance of thinking rigorously has, I hope, borne fruit. Professor D. Hobart Houghton not only suggested that I study some aspect of the labour market in South Africa but also criticised and encouraged much of the early work. Professor Gary Becker helped me enormously in discussions as to how his work on the economics of discrimination and on human capital might be applied in a South African situation. Mr. Colin Leicester gave me much patient advice about the use of multiple regression analysis. Professor James Meade and Mr. Leo Katzen, the examiners of the thesis on which this book is based, gently eliminated a number of bad mistakes. Others who read large chunks of early drafts and whose criticism was most valuable include Dr. Richard Jolly, Mr. J. B. Knight, Professor H. M. Robertson, and Dr. Sheila van der Horst. I learnt a lot of useful facts from Mr. Charles Diamond whilst supervising his work on *African Labour Problems on South African Gold Mines with Special Reference to the Strike of 1946* (unpublished M.A. thesis, Cape Town, 1969).

xv

Acknowledgements

The opportunity to present papers to seminar groups at the Universities of Cambridge, Cape Town, Columbia, and Virginia was most helpful. Despite their protests, I must acknowledge publicly my debt to my family whose various members gave me ideas, criticised drafts, checked tables, threw out bad writing, and provided support when the going was rough.

Without financial support this study would have been impossible. I am indebted to numerous bodies including the Relm Foundation for two H. B. Earhart fellowships; the Thomas Jefferson Center for Studies in Political Economy for a senior research fellowship and the facilities for a year's quiet reading; the Ernest Oppenheimer Memorial Trust for a grant to do field work in South Africa; the Inter-University Study of Labor Problems in Economic Development for two grants; Gonville and Caius College for a grant; the Cambridge African Studies Centre for the provision of working facilities during a year of writing; and, finally, to the University of Cape Town for a grant and for leave from teaching during the final months of writing.

I am grateful to Miss Judith Elton for drawing the original maps, to Mr. Miles Marsh for checking some of the statistical tables, to Mrs. Annette Thom, Miss Norma van Vrede and Miss Anne Robertson who did all the typing; to Miss Peta Jones for drawing the original diagram on page 17; to Miss Brenda Lichtman and Miss Beulah Goldie for help in constructing the index; to the mining industry for the various photographs; and, last but not least, to my publisher for waiting patiently long beyond several deadlines.

AUTHOR'S NOTE

References in the text, as well as other writings on which I have drawn for facts and for ideas, are listed in the bibliography, which is subdivided into four parts:

A Official and other institutional reports   c Articles
B Books and pamphlets   d Unpublished material

The single letter at the end of each footnote indicates in which section of the bibliography the reference is to be found.

Were it not for the fact that they are banned, and so may not legally be quoted in South Africa, a number of excellent historical works listed in the bibliography would have been cited in the text. I regret that in order that the book may circulate in South Africa, it has not been possible to quote Mary Benson, Alex Hepple, Ezekiel Mphahlele, Edward Roux and H. J. and R. E. Simons. I trust that scholars in other lands will understand – and forgive – the omission.

For simplicity a number of abbreviations have been used. The most common are:

A.M.W.U.   African Mine Workers' Union
C.C.T.A.   Commission for Technical Co-operation in Africa South of the Sahara
F.M.P.W.   Federation of Mining Production Workers
F.M.U.   Federation of Mining Unions
G.M.E.   Government Mining Engineer
G.M.T.S.   Government Miners' Training Schools
G.P.C.   Gold Producers Committee
I.M.F.   International Monetary Fund
M.U.J.C.   Mining Unions' Joint Committee
M.W.U.   Mine Workers' Union
n.a.   not available
N.I.P.R.   National Institute for Personnel Research
N.R.C.   Native Recruiting Corporation
O.F.S.   Orange Free State
p.t.m.   per ton (of 2,000 lb) milled
S.A.I.R.R.   South African Institute of Race Relations
S.A.T.U.C.   South African Trades Union Congress
T.C.M.   Transvaal and (after 1953) Orange Free State Chamber of Mines
W.N.L.A.   Witwatersrand Native Labour Association

For most of the period with which this book deals South African currency was measured in pounds, shillings, and pence. However, in 1961 measurement changed to rands and cents. In order to facilitate comparison all figures in this book have

B

been converted to South African rands. Until November 1967, R2·00 was equal to £1 sterling and it is at this rate of exchange that the conversions for the pre-1961 figures have been made. At the time of writing (December 1970) R1·00(S.A.) = £0·58(U.K.) = $1·39(U.S.).

A word of warning is necessary concerning the use of index numbers. The official retail price index which I have generally used to deflate current figures (i.e. expressed in terms of the value of money at the time to which the figure refers) into real terms is based on the expenditure patterns of the average white family. Possible errors arising from the lack of a retail price index based on what Africans, with a far lower average income, buy, must be borne in mind.

CHAPTER I

FOUNDATIONS

The subject matter of economics is essentially a unique process in historic time. Nobody can hope to understand the economic phenomena of any, including the present, epoch who has not an adequate command of historical facts and an adequate amount of historical sense or of what may be described as historical experience ... The historical report cannot be purely economic but must inevitably reflect also 'institutional' facts.

Joseph A. Schumpeter, *History of Economic Analysis*

Labour problems go back a long time in South African history.[1] Within the first decade of his arrival at the Cape in 1652, van Riebeeck was faced with a labour shortage which he alleviated – temporarily – by importing slaves. But the existence of slavery was to give rise to other problems, not the least of which was the development of a colour consciousness which made whites unwilling to do menial work.

Nearly two hundred years later it was a combination of the abolition of slavery and a shortage of labour which sparked off the Great Trek from the eastern Cape into the interior.[2] And a central issue of South African politics for at least a hundred years before the National Party came to power in 1948 was the organisation of adequate supplies of black labour in such a way that it would not compete with white. 'Having pushed the native possessors off the soil,' writes Sir Keith Hancock, the whites 'felt the need of pulling native labourers back onto it.'[3] The discovery of minerals in the second half of the nineteenth century, while marking a new stage in the country's development, intensified the push-pull dichotomy. The perennial labour shortage, which Natal sugar planters had alleviated in 1860 with the introduction of indentured Indians, was aggravated. By 1874, only eight years after the discovery of the first diamond, the Kimberley diggings were employing no less than 10,000 blacks, and farmers throughout the country were complaining bitterly of

---

[1] For the detailed historical background, readers are referred to Sheila T. van der Horst, *Native Labour in South Africa* (O.U.P., Cape Town, 1942) B.

[2] M. Wilson and L. Thompson (eds.), *The Oxford History of South Africa* (Clarendon Press, Oxford, 1969), I, 292 B.

[3] W. K. Hancock, *Survey of British Commonwealth Affairs* (O.U.P., London, 1942), II, pt 2, 25 B.

the developments which were drawing off their labour.[1] But things were to become still more difficult for farmers when, with the discovery of gold in 1886, the demand for labour grew rapidly. By the turn of the century the black labour force on the mines of the Witwatersrand was little short of 100,000 men. Such radical changes in the economic structure over so short a period of time were not achieved without difficulty, and the restructuring of the labour market that took place during this period was to provide the pattern for much of the economy during this century. Of this structure there are four features which, because of their peculiar nature, and because they were to remain at the centre of the South African labour market for so long, need to be examined in some detail. They are the organisation of the supply of unskilled labour, the migrant system, the colour bar, and the pattern of industrial relations.

ORGANISATION OF LABOUR SUPPLY

The mineral magnates developed and refined two instruments to ensure adequate labour supplies: the law and recruiting organisation. Amongst the laws enacted specifically to push blacks into the service of white employers were those relating to taxation. Although they did not prove very successful in increasing the supply of labour they are significant as demonstrations of the power of the mining financiers to make laws in their favour.[2] For example, the Glen Grey Bill which incorporated a labour tax of 10s. a head on selected 'male natives' was introduced to the Cape Parliament by the chief of the magnates, Cecil Rhodes, who was also Prime Minister:

You will remove them [the Natives] from that life of sloth and laziness, you will teach them the dignity of labour and make them contribute to the prosperity of the State, and make them give some return for our wise and good government.[3]

The Bill was passed.

Legal curbs on the geographic mobility of labour in South Africa go back as far as 1760 when slaves were first required to carry passes in moving between urban and rural areas. Slavery was abolished in 1834, but during the nineteenth century numerous laws controlling movement were enacted in all parts of what was to become the Union of South Africa. The power of the mining magnates to push through legislation that would help control their black labour force was amply demonstrated by the Transvaal Volks-

---

[1] A. Trollope, *South Africa* (Chapman and Hall, London, 1878, 2nd. edn.), I, 83–128, 146, 301; II, 80 B. M. Wilson and L. Thompson (eds.), *The Oxford History*, II, 117–20 B.
[2] van der Horst, *Native Labour*, pp. 133–4 B.
[3] Cape of Good Hope, *Hansard*, 1894, p. 362. Cited by van der Horst; see van der Horst, *Native Labour*, pp. 148–52, for an analysis of the various provisions of the Act.

raad's enaction, in 1895, of a pass law drafted by the Chamber of Mines.[1] The thinking behind the mass of nineteenth-century legislation which had been designed to dishearten cattle rustlers and to discourage labourers from breaking their contracts, took a new – and prophetic – turn in 1921 when the Transvaal Local Government Commission reported that:

the native should only be allowed to enter the urban areas, which are essentially the white man's creation, when he is willing to enter and to minister to the needs of the white man and should depart therefrom when he ceases so to minister.[2]

The Natives (Urban Areas) Act of 1923 tightened white control over the movement of Africans to the cities. The legislation was amended numerous times, tightened in 1936, consolidated in 1945 and again in 1952, until with the passage of the Bantu Laws Amendment Act in 1969 the whites had created all the machinery necessary to carry out the policy enunciated half a century before. The advantages which the pass (and passport) laws gave to the mining industry over other sectors of the economy will be explored in a later chapter.

A third arm of the law used to augment the supply of labour was that relating to land. The Glen Gray Act contained important provisions restricting ownership, but it was the Land Act of 1913 that was decisive. Although pressure for the legislation came primarily from farmers its effects were to prove even more beneficial to the Chamber of Mines which drew so large a proportion of its black labour force from the overcrowded 'reserves' created by the Act.

Besides legislation, the other weapon in the hands of the mining industry was the organisation of recruiting. In 1893 the Chamber of Mines established a Native Labour Department with the two-fold objective of assuring an adequate and regular supply of black labour by opening up sources of supply within the Transvaal and by arranging for the recruiting of labourers from Mozambique, and of taking 'active steps for the gradual reduction of native wages to a reasonable level'.[3] However, the pass law of 1895 was ineffectively administered and failed to achieve its purpose of controlling the movement of black mineworkers; and so, towards the end of 1896, perturbed by the fact that 'a great deal of trouble and money were being thrown away by the competition for natives',[4] the Chamber formed its own recruiting organisation, the Rand Native Labour Association, to bring workers to the mines.

[1] *Ibid.* p. 133.
[2] Transvaal Province, *Report of the Local Government Commission* (Stallard) (T.P.1, Pretoria, 1922) para. 267 A.
[3] T.C.M., *Fifth Annual Report* (1893), p. 4 A.
[4] T.C.M., *Tenth Annual Report* (1898), p. 455 A.

Labour in the South African gold mines

Countering criticism from mine managers about the costs of recruitment a spokesman of the Association, at the annual general meeting in 1898, pointed out that employment on the mines had risen from 14,000 in 1890 to 88,000 at the end of 1897. Were it not for the Association 'they would have had a continuation of the cut-throat competition which then existed, and they would have had each mine touting for its own labour'.[1] As it was the increase in employment by over 500% in eight years was achieved 'without any appreciable rise in wages'. The establishment of the Labour Association in 1896 was accompanied by an agreement to reduce wages and, unlike the agreement of 1890 which had succeeded only temporarily in reducing wages by 25%, this was enforced by means of inspection of wage sheets. Thus by 1899 the Chamber of Mines had succeeded in raising a black labour force of 99,000 men at a wage rate considerably lower than it had been ten years previously when the mining industry had only just begun. In 1900 the mining magnates approached the government of the Transvaal with a request that the recruiting of labour be a state enterprise, but the proposal was turned down.[2] And so, the employers reorganised their recruiting arrangements and formed the Witwatersrand Native Labour Association in order to monopsonise recruiting, by preventing mines from competing against each other for labour. At first it was planned that the W.N.L.A. should recruit all black labour for the industry, but it took a few years for the mines to stop competing for South African labour. Meanwhile the W.N.L.A. was the only body allowed to recruit in Mozambique.

The first decade of the twentieth century was a very difficult one for the mines. The Anglo-Boer war had disrupted production and then, when hostilities had ceased, the mines found themselves critically short of black labour. There were a number of reasons for the shortage, not the least of which was the fact that, in setting up the W.N.L.A., the Chamber of Mines had lowered the wage rate from the pre-war average of R5.00 to R3.00 a month.[3] Except for work on farms, where there were generally better fringe benefits, this was probably the lowest cash wage for black labour in the whole of Southern Africa.[4] Moreover working conditions were deplorable: the death rate of recruited workers in 1903 was 80 per thousand, and black workers were frequently assaulted by whites. Faced with a crippling shortage of labour, the mining industry began, in 1904, to bring indentured labour from the north of China where, due to the Russo-Japanese war, men who normally went to work as farm labourers in Manchuria were no longer able

---

[1] T.C.M., *Tenth Annual Report*, p. 462 A.
[2] D. J. N. Denoon, 'The Transvaal labour crisis, 1901–6', *J.A.H.* VII (1967), 482 C.
[3] Denoon, *J.A.H.* (1967), p. 482 C.
[4] B. Kidd, 'Economic South Africa', *Christian Express* XXII (1903), 58, 77 C.

to do so.[1] The use of Chinese labour was controversial and, after the 1905 Liberal victory in Britain, pressure to repatriate the 50,000 men was exerted. Further recruiting was prohibited at the end of 1906. By 1910 there were few Chinese left on the Witwatersrand and, in 1912, the Chamber of Mines established the Native Recruiting Corporation (N.R.C.) to organise the recruitment of black labour from within South Africa and the three 'Protectorates' as the W.N.L.A. was doing in Mozambique. Because of the appalling pneumonia death rates, recruiting from any area north of latitude 22°S was prohibited in 1913. It was to be twenty years before the industry was to be allowed north again.[2] Despite the loss of these areas, the industry was by this time sufficiently well organised to maintain its monopsony power over the labour market by means of a maximum permissible average agreement.[3]

OSCILLATING MIGRATION

Closely related to the organisation of supply was the second notable feature of the labour market; namely the pattern of oscillating migration whereby unskilled black workers came to the mines for a limited time and then returned to their rural homes. During the early stages of industrialisation in any country, the evidence suggests that many people, moving from rural areas to the new centres, do not commit themselves immediately to permanent residence in town, but that, after a good deal of movement between old and new homes, people gradually settle near their place of work. The common pattern at first repeated itself in South Africa; however the oscillations of workers backwards and forwards did not gradually diminish as elsewhere but became established by means of the compound system.

During the early years of the diamond diggings it appears that, despite Trollope's rosy description of the effect of money on 'civilised kaffirs', Kimberley was a sordid place.[4] Robert Moffat of Kuruman describes it as it was in 1881:

It was a mining camp, in the process of solidifying into a town. It was a dangerous place to walk about after dark, drunkenness and violence were rampant. The mortality was portentous among natives. A dead 'nigger' lying in some nook or corner or on the open veldt at break of day was so ordinary an event as to be scarcely worth a paragraph in the newspapers. The native labourers herded in the vilest

1 Denoon, *J.A.H.* (1967), p. 490 C.   2 See p. 69.
3 van der Horst, *Native Labour*, pp. 166, 192–3 B. It was not until 1919 that the Robinson group of mines joined the N.R.C., thus giving the Corporation the complete monopsony of gold mine recruiting in South Africa and the 'Protectorates'.
4 Trollope, *South Africa*, II, 185 B.

shanties, and drank the vilest Cape dop, which they bought with the diamonds they stole during the day from the mines they worked in.[1]

The losses which employers incurred from illicit diamond buying and from absenteeism after week-end drinking led them to establish the closed compounds which by the late 1880s were a universal feature of the diamond fields and which were to remain essentially unchanged for the next eighty years. Despite Moffat's approval of the system which had 'saved thousands of [natives] from untold misery and degradation', the South African Native Races Committee stated in 1901 that, even when well managed, it regarded the closed compound system 'with very qualified satisfaction, and as exceptional and, in its present form, a temporary expedient...its application to gold-mining or other industries does not now appear to be probable or desirable...The family life of the natives, however different from that of civilised white men, ought to be treated with consideration and respect. It would be unfortunate if the breaking up of tribal organisations and the free movement of natives in search of work were to create a large mass of men without local or family ties.'[2] Despite this view, and despite the 'growing wish' of African workers to bring their families to the mines, the early pattern whereby men came to work for periods of eighteen months or less became entrenched on the gold mines.[3] On some of the coal mines, by contrast, as much as 50% of the labour force was, by the 1930s, housed in married quarters.[4] And in secondary industry compounds were the exception rather than the rule.

Why did the diamond and gold mines perpetuate the system? In a later chapter we shall analyse the economic forces which continue to undergird the pattern of migrant labour in the gold mines, but it is worth noting that the reasons for the establishment of compounds on the Witwatersrand were not the same as in Kimberley. On the diamond diggings the primary reason for the building of closed compounds which black workers were not allowed to leave during their entire period of contract was the prevention of illicit diamond buying. On the Witwatersrand, however, the possibility of miners finding ingots of pure gold was remote and so the system of *closed* compounds was never adopted. Unlike the diamond mines which seldom were short of labour, the gold mines went out to recruit men from all over southern Africa.

---

[1] The South African Native Races Committee (ed.), *The Natives of South Africa* (John Murray, London, 1901), p. 142 B. See also G. Tyamzashe, 'The Natives of the Diamond Fields', *Kaffir Express* (January, 1874), reprinted in F. Wilson and D. Perrot (eds.), *Outlook on a Century; South Africa 1870-1970* (Lovedale Press, 1972), p. 19 B.

[2] South African Native Races Committee, pp. 145, 220 B. Cf. 'The Kimberley compounds' in Wilson and Perrot (eds.), *Outlook on a Century*, p. 297 B.

[3] van der Horst, *Native Labour*, p. 187 B.   [4] *Ibid.* p. 188.

And in doing so they were committed to housing them in bachelor compounds both because fewer men would have been willing to come without knowing that they would have somewhere to stay and because neighbouring governments were unwilling to let several thousand able-bodied men leave permanently. Compound housing was much cheaper for the mines than family quarters. Some of the earliest compounds were built for the Chinese indentured labour, and so were later available for black recruits.

COLOUR BAR

As we shall see in a later chapter, the pattern of migrant labour is reinforced by the colour bar. The use, by whites, of skin-pigmentation as a means of discriminating against potential competitors in the labour market did not originate in the gold mines nor, indeed, on the diamond diggings, but the mineral discoveries did much to entrench it in the South African economy. At first there were plenty of unskilled men able and willing to dig, but artisans were not so readily available. Those who were not willing to gamble their future on a lucky strike had to be enticed out of Europe by high salaries. Thus began the enormous differential between skilled and unskilled earnings. The situation was not unique but the peculiarity of the South African case was that the skilled men happened to be white and the unskilled happened to be black. What had begun as a classical example of the free interaction of supply and demand gradually hardened into a rigid caste system. This process of ossification as it took place in the gold mines is worth examining in some detail for it was to have far-reaching consequences in the country's political and economic development.

White miners saw themselves as a labour aristocracy: as early as 1893 the Volksraad enacted the first legal colour bar in the economy. A clause in the Transvaal republic's first mining law stipulated, in effect, that only whites might do the actual blasting. Amended regulations in 1896 dropped this particular prohibition (although the *de facto* position did not change) but introduced two more. One of these was dropped at the insistence of the employers and the industry entered the Anglo-Boer war with one statutory colour bar which reserved the job of engine drivers for whites only. However, with the importation of Chinese labour in 1904, the regulations were tightened up again. The Chamber of Mines agreed that white labour must remain an aristocracy but the Imperial government, in endorsing this view, went a step further and insisted that before Chinese could be brought in white opinion in the Transvaal should favour such a policy. This proviso made it necessary for the Chamber to make elaborate concessions to the white artisans

7

who opposed importation. The most important of these concessions was, as D. J. N. Denoon has pointed out: 'the prohibition of the employment of Chinese in an enumerated list of capacities, which obviated the risk of their ever competing with skilled or semi-skilled whites'.[1] Denoon suggests that the mining magnates had not intended this legislation to be applied against Africans nor had they considered it to be final. However the prohibition on Chinese doing these jobs was seen by the artisans as reserving the jobs exclusively for whites. The timing of this enactment was important, for it came at a moment when the proportion of white workers in the mining industry was larger than usual. Had the line been drawn either five years earlier or five years later, the number of reserved jobs would probably have been considerably smaller.[2] Nor was it only the Chinese who were a threat to the white miners: in 1907 there was a strike to prevent blacks doing skilled jobs. Although the strike was lost it had the effect of 'causing the government to insist upon a definite ratio in mining of "civilised labour" to indentured natives'.[3] Thus in the troubled years between the ending of the Anglo-Boer war and the Act of Union, the white miners on the Witwatersrand were able to entrench themselves firmly in their position of privilege. Their status was further reinforced by the Mines and Works Act of 1911. In terms of this law, the Governor General was empowered to make regulations requiring certificates of competency for the performance of different kinds of work. In the Transvaal and Free State such certificates were granted only to whites and by 1920 more than 7,000 white men in 32 mining occupations were protected by these regulations. The law itself was buttressed by the force of custom, backed up by trade union action: in 1920 a further 4,000 men were protected by the customary colour bar.[4]

INDUSTRIAL RELATIONS

It was the growing power, both relative and absolute, of the white colour-bound unions that formed the fourth institutional peculiarity of the labour market as it developed during the early decades of gold mining. In 1897 the Chamber of Mines attempted to cut the wages of all its employees. The white miners went on strike and were able to prevent a reduction in their rates of pay. Black wages however were sharply reduced. White miners struck again in 1907, this time to protect themselves against competition by their black

[1] Denoon, *J.A.H.* (1967), p. 490 C. [2] *Ibid.*
[3] I. L. Walker and B. Weinbren, *2000 Casualties* (S.A.T.U.C., Johannesburg, 1961), p. 24 B. In 1903 it was estimated that, up until that time, the ratio of black–white employees on the mines had been approximately 8:1 (Kidd, *Christian Express* (1903), p. 76) C. See Appendix 26.
[4] van der Horst, *Native Labour*, p. 179 B.

fellow-workers, and in July 1913 the white miners came out on a massive strike. After riots and bloodshed they won recognition from the Chamber of Mines for their trade unions. As soon as this was accomplished there was another, larger, strike in January of 1914 whose purpose was, in C. W. de Kiewiet's words, 'to testify to the common purpose of all white labour to protect its interests'.[1] What was at issue was 'the whole immense problem of social and economic relationships between industry and labour, between skilled and unskilled worker, between white and black. Thus did the desire of the mines to make the most economical use of their labour become a problem that touched the life of the country at every point.'[2] Nor was the unrest confined to whites. Following the successful strike in 1913, Africans on several mines 'rose in protest against their conditions of employment'.[3] Their fundamental grievance was, as the Commission appointed to investigate the disturbances found, 'the colour bar which blocks practically all opportunities of promotion'.[4] But nothing was done to remove the barrier. With the outbreak of the First World War there was an uneasy truce until 1918 when, under pressure from the white trade unions, the Chamber came to an agreement that the existing *status quo* on each mine, with regard to the relative scope of employment of white and black employees should be maintained.[5] The purpose of this agreement was to prevent any further crumbling of the colour bar which the legislation, in the face of labour shortages, could not effectively prevent.

The post-war years saw an astronomical increase in the cost of living with prices rising by almost 50% between 1917 and 1920. As a result of pressure from the unions white wages were increased so that, in real terms, average earnings fell by only 4% between 1916 and 1921. The black workers, however, were not so successful. During eleven days in February 1920 some 71,000 men came out on strike for better pay, for lower prices in the compound stores, and against the colour bar.[6] From the beginning police and troops from the S.A. Mounted Rifles surrounded the striking compounds, arresting leaders and protecting strike breakers. There was one violent clash in which three men were killed and nearly 50 men (including about a dozen on the government side) injured. But, in general, the demonstration of force

[1] C. W. de Kiewiet, *A History of South Africa* (O.U.P., London, 1941), p. 168 B.   [2] *Ibid.*
[3] C. R. Diamond, *African Labour Problems on South African Gold Mines with Special Reference to the Strike of 1946* (M.A. thesis, Cape Town, 1969), p. 211 D.
[4] South Africa, *Report of the Native Grievances Inquiry* (Buckle) (U.G. 37, Cape Town, 1914), para. 280 A, cited by Diamond, *African Labour Problems*, D.
[5] It is worth noting that, on the outbreak of war, African mineworkers had pledged themselves to withhold all action to redress their grievances for the duration of the war.
[6] See Diamond, *African Labour Problems*, ch. 3, D, for details of the strike. The maximum number of men on strike at any one time was estimated to be 42,000.

brought about a peaceful return to work. Apart from a reorganisation of trading methods the strike achieved nothing. In 1921 black wages, in real terms, were 13% lower than they had been in 1916. It was another quarter of a century before African mineworkers were to strike again. With the support of the state and backed up by the Native Labour Regulation Act of 1911, which made it a criminal offence for blacks, under contract, to strike, the employers were in a powerful position to crush any attempts at collective bargaining. But for white mineworkers, despite the Chamber's hostility, the strike was to prove a more potent weapon. Already, as we have seen, it had won recognition for their trade unions. But the main showdown was still to come.

In 1921 the Chamber of Mines, alarmed by the sharp drop in the price of gold from 130s. per fine ounce in February 1920 to 95s. per fine ounce in December 1921, took hasty steps to reduce working costs in the belief that if they failed to do so a further drop in the price to 84s. per fine ounce would render 24 of the 39 mines on the Witwatersrand unprofitable. On 10 December 1921 the Chamber brusquely gave notice to its white workers of the termination of certain wage agreements and of its intention to withdraw the *status quo* agreement as from the end of January. It proposed to increase the black:white employment ratio to 10·5:1. The white workers were equally alarmed: not only were they deeply suspicious of the Chamber's motives as a result of the long bitterness of previous strikes and the Chamber's uncompromising attitude in dealing with the unions, but also the time was one of great depression and the mineworkers were afraid of losing their jobs.[1] They went on a strike which developed into a full-scale rebellion. There were several days of fighting, property was destroyed, and between 230 and 250 people were killed.

In his study of the causes of the rebellion, Bernard Hessian places a great deal of emphasis on the mutual suspicion between the Chamber of Mines, whose attitude was 'autocratic', and the labour leaders. The chances of a negotiated settlement were prejudiced 'because the Chamber of Mines' representatives were not prepared to accept the workers as equals in the negotiating room'.[2] The motives on both sides were very confused. The Chamber saw itself not only as fighting for the very existence of the gold mining industry but also as trying to reduce racial discrimination caused by the white workers. These same workers on the other hand saw the issue not as one 'between white and black labour, but between free labour and

[1] B. Hessian, *An Investigation into the Causes of the Labour Agitation on the Witwatersrand* (M.A. thesis, Witwatersrand, 1957), pp. 16–21 D.
[2] *Ibid.* p. 112.

cheap slave labour'.[1] Both sides felt morally justified while the success of either would not have given blacks equal economic opportunities with whites: depending on which side won, blacks were to be faced either with the pass laws alone or with a combination of pass laws and colour bar.

Although the miners lost the battle, as the Chamber of Mines did in fact lay off a number of white workers and reduce white wages, they won the war. The impact of the rebellion entrenched the colour bar more firmly than ever before not only in the mines but in the economy as a whole. For fifty years fear of provoking another Rand rebellion was to be a potent force in preventing employers from attempting to breach the colour bar. In 1923 the Mines and Works Act was declared *ultra vires* but, after a Mining Regulations Commission had 'reported alarmingly on the introduction of machinery capable of being worked by semi-skilled natives, a development which, unless checked, would lead to the "elimination of the European worker from the entire range of mining occupations" ',[2] the Mines and Works Amendment Act of 1926 was passed. In terms of this Act, blacks and Indians were specifically barred from jobs as mine managers, mine overseers, mine surveyors, mechanical engineers, engine drivers, miners entitled to blast, and various others. The Act remains the basis of the colour bar in the mining industry.

In 1924 the Smuts government, in an attempt to prevent any repetition of violence, rushed through the Industrial Conciliation Act for the creation of machinery to deal with industrial disputes. Black mineworkers, however, were not amongst those declared to be employees within the meaning of the Act and were thus excluded from the industrial self-government which was to prove so successful in reducing conflict between employers and their white workers.

Another result of the rebellion was to bring to power a coalition formed between the National and Labour Parties. Together they adopted a 'civilised labour' policy whose objective was subsequently explained by the Secretary for Labour as being:

to ensure that the class of workers described above [white unskilled workers] is not denied entry into unskilled occupations by reason of the fact that the lower standard of living to which the Native is accustomed has hitherto kept the rates of pay and their conditions of employment for work of this nature at a level which will not enable such workers to live in accordance with the standard generally observed by civilised persons. The policy is in no way associated with any question of racial segregation.[3]

[1] Transvaal Strike Legal Committee, *The Story of Crime* (Johannesburg, 1924), p. 39 B.
[2] H. M. Robertson, '150 years of economic contact between black and white', *S.A.J.E.* III (1935), 21 C.
[3] Letter from the Secretary for Labour and Social Welfare to the Advisor of the Institute of Race Relations, 14 November 1935, *Race Relations Journal* II (1935) C.

Labour in the South African gold mines

The policy was applied primarily to state enterprises and in the case of the railways was most successful. Between 1924 and 1936 the proportion of whites employed rose from 9·5% to 28·9% while blacks fell from 75% to 57·8%. The proportion of Coloured people remained constant at 11·3% but Indians fell from 4·2% to 0·8%. In the depression year of 1933 it was the black railway workers who lost their jobs. They fell to 48·9% while whites rose to 39·3% of the total force.[1]

Besides the Mines and Works Amendment Act of 1926 and the civilised labour policy, there were no other direct measures to protect white workers; but there were several laws which indirectly limited the economic progress of non-whites. One of these which affected the Coloured people, particularly, was the Apprenticeship Act of 1922 which imposed no colour bar but in terms of which conditions for apprenticeship were set. By March 1939 in all 41 trades for which conditions had been laid down, the level of entry required was at least Standard VI, but as the majority of schools for Coloured pupils did not go beyond that level and many, indeed, not even so far, the effect of the Apprenticeship Act, subsequently re-enacted in 1944, was to bar Coloured people from the skilled trades which they had traditionally occupied in the Cape.[2] The educational barrier was reinforced by the tacit acceptance, by employers, that only white youths were to be trained.

Another law which indirectly barred the advance of blacks was the Wage Act of 1925 which was re-enacted in 1937 and 1957. Although it had been set up to improve the conditions in industries employing unorganised, unskilled labour, nevertheless during the 1930s the Wage Act was not used primarily to help black workers but rather to protect and improve the position of whites. Before the Second World War the Wage Act was an instrument of the civilised labour policy. However with the movement of whites out of unskilled occupations, and the disappearance of the poor-white problem, the Act has been increasingly used as a means of raising the minimum wage of blacks in various sectors of the economy.[3]

By 1936 the United Party government led by Generals Hertzog and Smuts was able not only to complete the Land Act of 1913 which effectively limited black land ownership to 13% of the country, but also to pass the Representation of Natives Act which removed the last black South African voter from the common voters' roll. Seen in its historical perspective, the election of the

---

[1] Hancock, *Survey of British Commonwealth Affairs*, p. 52 B. This was not the first time that black railway workers had been sacked to make room for more highly paid whites. A similar policy had been pursued twenty years before. Wilson and Perrot (eds.), *Outlook on a Century*, p. 330 B.
[2] Hancock, p. 53.
[3] W. F. J. Steenkamp, 'In quest of aims and norms for minimum wage fixing in terms of the wage Act (1925)', *S.A.J.E.* XXXI (June 1963) C. D. E. Pursell, 'Bantu real wages and employment opportunities', *S.A.J.E.* XXXVIII (June 1968) C.

National Party in 1948 marked not so much a turning point in South African history as the intensification of a process which had been going on for three hundred years. The increased economic co-operation during the Second World War, when thousands of blacks moved into manufacturing industry, once again had its counterpart in the increased conflict made visible by ensuing legislation which, focusing on the colour bar and the supply of unskilled labour, added further barriers to occupational and geographical mobility.[1]

In the years that followed the four features which had been built into the structure of the South African labour market by the development of the gold mining industry became, as we shall see, yet more firmly entrenched. Indeed, for their labour policy in all sectors of the economy, the architects of Apartheid have taken the gold mining industry as their model.

[1] For the original analysis of South African economic history in terms of co-operation and conflict see H. M. Robertson, '150 years of economic contact between black and white', *S.A.J.E.* II (1934), III (1935) C.

CHAPTER 2

GOLD MINING

In a way it is even humiliating to watch . . . miners working. It raises in you a momentary doubt about your own status as an 'intellectual' and a superior person generally. For it is brought home to you, at least while you are watching, that it is only because miners sweat their guts out that superior persons can remain superior. You and I and the editor of the Times Lit. Supp., and the poets and the Archbishop of Canterbury and Comrade x, author of *Marxism for Infants* – all of us *really* owe the comparative decency of our lives to poor drudges underground . . . with their throats full of . . . dust, driving their shovels forward with arms and belly muscles of steel.

George Orwell, *Down The Mine*

Nobody knows how long gold has been mined in Southern Africa for in 1867 old workings were found on the banks of the Tatie river which flows through Botswana.[1] This rediscovery led to further prospecting and in 1871 gold was struck in the eastern Transvaal. But it was not until 1886 that the main reef was found on the farm Langlaagte on the outskirts of what is, today, Johannesburg. For the next sixty years most of South Africa's gold came from the area of the Witwatersrand, though small pockets were mined in the Eastern Transvaal round Pilgrim's Rest, Sabie, and Barberton, whilst the districts of Pietersburg, Lichtenburg, and Pretoria also yielded enough to excite diggers. As early as the turn of the century gold was found in the Orange Free State but it was not until the sharp price increase in 1933 that prospecting again took place there. The outbreak of the Second World War delayed the opening up of the new field until 1946, when development of the first large gold mine in the Orange Free State began. Simultaneously further intensive prospecting took place and in the same year the Geduld strike provided spectacular evidence of the wealth that lay far below the maize. The post-war years saw a major shift in the geographical sources of supply. In 1936 no gold at all was produced south of the Vaal and by 1960 the Orange Free State accounted for almost one-third of the country's total output. At the same time discoveries of previously unknown deposits led to the development of new mines both to the east and west of the central Witwatersrand.

[1] J. Mackenzie, *Ten Years North of the Orange River, 1859–1869* (Edmonston and Douglas, Edinburgh, 1871), p. 453 B.

The known gold-bearing ore is to be found roughly in the shape of a great horseshoe, stretching some 300 miles from Kinross in the east to Virginia in the south-west.[1] The gold itself lies in a number of different reef leaders whose average width is a mere twelve inches, sometimes thinner and occasionally thickening to eight feet. The main reef leader itself, stretching east from Roodepoort, forms an unbroken strip of gold forty miles long. Although varying from horizontal to vertical the reefs tend to dip, commonly at an angle of 23°, from west to east.

Contrary to popular belief, most of the South African gold-bearing ore is not very rich. But its comparatively low grade is balanced by a number of favourable factors.[2] The most important of these is the sheer volume of ore concentrated in a remarkably small area. For the gold goes very deep and rock temperatures, although high, do not make deep-level mining impossible. As a result of this, not only are individual mines large but also they are clustered together in a way which enables them to achieve considerable economies of scale.[3] Furthermore, the grade of ore has a comparatively uniform distribution over a wide range; in other words, the amount of gold per unit quantity of ore generally varies fairly smoothly in any given mine from high to low values. The importance of this, as Jeppe has pointed out, is that if either the price of gold increases or working costs decrease, ore that was previously unpayable now becomes worth mining.[4] But it also means that a small rise in costs can cause a considerable reduction in the volume of payable ore reserves.

Despite the volume of ore and the regular distribution of gold within it, the reefs are often disjointed and broken. This unevenness is a major obstacle to increased mechanisation. As one miner explained: 'When one has a thin gold sandwich scattered at anything up to two miles below the surface there is no better way of mining than sticking one's finger in and scratching it out.' But this drawback was, after the Second World War, mitigated for many mines by the discovery of uranium oxide (U_3O_8). The exploitation of this by-product, which was found in the ore of nearly half of the gold mines, did much to inject new life into the industry. In the first year of production, 1952, the revenue from sales of uranium was a mere 0·1% of the revenue derived from gold, but by 1960 the proportion had risen to 20%.[5] Thereafter demand fell sharply but is expected to rise again in the 1970s. Other by-products, which the industry has produced for many years, are sulphuric acid and silver.

[1] See map on p. x.
[2] E. B. Jeppe, *Gold Mining on the Witwatersrand* (T.C.M., Johannesburg, 1946), p. 64 B.
[3] A 'large' gold mine is defined as one which employs at least 1,000 persons.
[4] Jeppe, *Gold Mining*, p. 64 B.   [5] T.C.M., *Seventy Seventh Annual Report* (1966), p. 64 A.

C

Labour in the South African gold mines

In addition to the favourable characteristics of the ore itself, the development of the South African gold mines has been facilitated by the proximity of abundant coal resources and by the enormous supplies of relatively cheap, unskilled labour. Indeed it has often been argued that without the cheap labour the gold mining industry would never have been able to develop as it did. Whether or not the earnings of unskilled labour could have been significantly higher without unduly reducing the reserves of payable ore is one of the questions which we seek to answer in this book. But in order to do this it is necessary to consider first the way in which gold is mined and to examine the organisation and financial structure of the industry.

DOWN THE MINE

Once a given site has been prospected and the decision to develop a mine has been taken, work begins by sinking a shaft through the reef. From this vertical shaft horizontal tunnels, or haulages, are driven towards the reef. From the end of the main haulages, which extend until they lie just under the reef, further haulages are then driven at right angles in both directions. These north and south haulages run, as shown fig. 1, just under the reef and from them cross-cuts are made to reach the ore itself. Fig. 1, a highly simplified diagram, shows the basic lay-out.[1]

Once in the reef another tunnel, the strike gully, is excavated along the plane of the reef parallel to the north and south haulages. The gully is normally wider than the reef and permits fairly free movement of both men and machines. It is from the strike gully that work begins on removing the gold-bearing ore at the stope face. This is done by driving a centre gully up inside the reef from the strike gully. Working from the centre gully men drill the reef on either side. Where the reef is only twelve inches wide or less the stope itself has to be wider to permit men to work but it is kept as narrow as possible to minimise the amount of waste rock that has to be broken and transported. The usual width of the stope is thirty-six inches. The importance of lay-out, which varies from mine to mine, is that once it has been executed it is prohibitively expensive to alter and it places a rigid constraint on the techniques of production, particularly the transport of ore.

In the gold mines there are two methods of conveying the ore from the stope face to the shaft; one considerably more labour intensive than the other. In the newer mines the broken ore is pulled by a mechanical scraper from the stope face down into the gully; there a second scraper, at right angles to the

[1] For a detailed explanation and diagram of a rather different layout see T.C.M., *Gold in South Africa* (T.C.M., Johannesburg, 1969), p. 11 B.

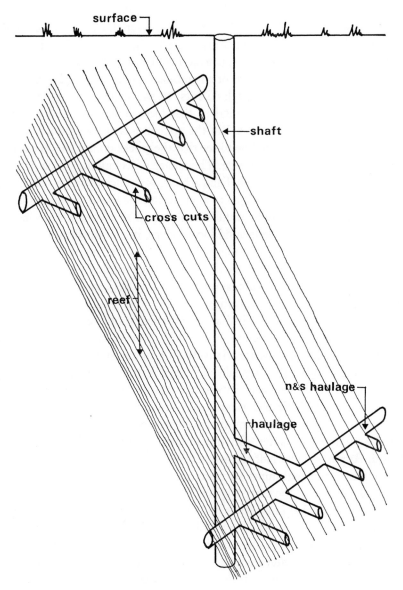

Fig. 1   Simplified layout of a gold mine

first, pulls the ore along the strike gully to a box-hole through which the ore falls into a hopper which stores it until a truck is pulled underneath the hopper. From there the ore is hauled by an electric locomotive to the shaft where there is another box-hole into which the ore is poured. At the bottom of the shaft it is fed into skips which bring it up to the surface. The alternative method, used in the older mines, is to scrape the ore directly into the trucks which are then pulled, by means of an endless rope haulage (pulley), operating on the same principle as teleski lifts, to the shaft. The newer system requires considerably more capital in that locomotives are used which in turn necessitate larger haulages. But the system uses far less labour, as men are not needed all along the line to see that the trucks do not fall off as is the case with the endless rope haulage. The choice of technique, which depends upon the relative prices of capital and labour, is a crucial one for once it has been made it is almost impossible to alter during the life of the mine.[1] Thus, although East Daggafontein could have operated more cheaply during the 1960s by using more underground locomotives, it continued to use endless rope haulages because, given the expected life of the mine, the costs of transition were too great to make the change worthwhile.

Besides transport and rockbreaking, which involve jobs of sinking shafts, developing haulages, and excavating reef, the mining of gold requires its extraction from the ore. This is done by crushing it on the surface and processing it through a reduction plant. The process is a straightforward chemical one and the mines use relatively little labour in this stage of production. Ancillary to the primary taks of breaking, transporting, and reducing the ore are the miscellaneous jobs which, underground, involve the laying of pipes through which air and water is taken to the stope face, the support of workings to prevent caving, provision of electric power, maintenance of tools, and the pumping of water. On the surface the ancillary jobs are mainly clerical. Approximately half the whites and three-quarters of the blacks in the services of the gold mines work underground; an analysis of the various underground jobs in the early 1940s is shown in table 1.

Of the total number of Africans underground on 17 February 1943, nearly 8,000 (3·5%) were in supervisory positions as 'boss-boys', men who were, in effect foremen serving as intermediaries between white gangers and black workmen. A much greater number, which is difficult to estimate precisely, were operating jack-hammer drills and doing other semi-skilled work. There has been some change in the distribution of the labour force over time. On old mines, which started producing gold before the Second World War,

[1] See R. B. Smart, 'Mechanisation applied to mining in relation to Native labour on Sub Nigel', *Papers and Discussions of the Association of Mine Managers of the Transvaal 1937–1938* (T.C.M., Johannesburg, 1939), pp. 315–30 c.

approximately one-third of the black underground labour force was employed on transporting ore from the stope face to the shaft; on the newer mines, using different techniques, the proportion on transport was approximately 15%. But the proportion of the total mine labour force working underground has remained remarkably unchanged: in 1936 78% of the blacks and 56% of the whites worked underground; in 1964 the figures were 78% and 57% respectively.[1]

TABLE I. *Distribution of jobs underground, 1940/1943*

Whites (1940)

	Officials %	Day's pay men %	Total %
Mining	19·8	66·7	86·5
Engineering	0·8	10·3	11·1
Miscellaneous	1·0	1·5	2·5
Total (percentage)	21·6	78·5	100
Total (absolute)	4,600	16,700	21,300

Blacks (1943)

	%
Rockbreaking	15·6
Shovelling and tramming	38·5
Mechanical scraping	4·1
Sweeping	4·3
Support of workings	15·2
Mining department general	16·0
Engineering departments	6·4
Total (percentage)	100
Total (absolute)	226,500

SOURCE: C. B. Jeppe, *Gold Mining on the Witwatersrand*, pp. 1734 and 1750 B.

Running a mine has been likened to captaining a great ship; tight organisation is essential to minimise the ever present risk of things going wrong. The men going down one of the two or three shafts of a typical gold mine include an underground manager, an engineer, four or five mine captains (overseers), and thirty shift-bosses. These are the officials. Below them are the 'day's pay

[1] T.C.M., *Annual Reports* A.

men'. They include half a dozen shaft timbermen; ten assistant miners (A.M.T.s); thirty 'P.T. & T' men who work on pipes, tracks, and timber; twenty general shaft personnel (including onsetters, banksmen, and skipmen); some sixty artisans (electricians, boilermakers, fitters, riggers, handymen, and pumpmen); and approximately forty contract miners – the men whose earnings depend largely on the amount of ore that the gangs of labourers under their charge can extract from the stope face or the development end. Each white official has his own 'boss-boy' to assist him in general supervision, and most day's pay men have their gangs of black workers, one of whom is the 'boss-boy' and responsible for seeing that the orders given by the white miners are properly carried out. But this hierarchy is not entirely correlated with experience and skill. Although difficult to document, there is little doubt that, because of the rigidity of the South African caste system, many 'boss-boys' are considerably more skilled in mining than some of the men above them.

It is easy to describe the process of mining gold without conveying adequately the immense difficulties which those involved have had to overcome. The sort of problems encountered by managers and engineers are perhaps best summarised in the following passage from the public relations department of the Chamber of Mines:

Imagine a solid mass of rock tilted . . . like a fat 1,200-page dictionary lying at an angle. The gold bearing reef would be thinner than a single page, and the amount of gold contained therein would hardly cover a couple of commas in the entire book. It is the miner's job to bring out that single page – but his job is made harder because the 'page' has been twisted and torn by nature's forces, and pieces of it may have been thrust between other leaves of the book.[1]

And the analogy says nothing about the dangers and difficulties added to the extraction of this single page by the existence, in some mines, of highly explosive methane gas; of the ever present possibility of a stope face, two miles below the surface, bursting under pressure; or of unexpected flooding where, as in the case of West Driefontein mine in 1969, 85 million gallons of water can rush into a mine in a single day.

For someone who has never been down a mine to get some idea of the working conditions with which those actually mining the gold have to cope, it is perhaps easiest to start by thinking of a road labourer digging up a pavement with a jack-hammer drill. Now imagine him doing that work thousands of feet underground, in intense heat, where he cannot even begin to stand upright, and where the drill is not going with the aid of gravity into the ground beneath, but where it has to be held horizontal and driven into the

---

[1] T.C.M., *Gold in South Africa*, p. 10 B.

wall in front.[1] Add to this picture the noise of a road-drill, magnified several times by the confined space;[2] dust which, despite strenuous efforts to control it with water, invades the lungs; and the possibility that the roof of the mine might suddenly cave in under the pressure, or that a spark from the drill or a careless cigarette might ignite a pocket of methane gas, and one has some idea of the work of a 'machine-boy'.[3] Echoing Orwell's thoughts about coal miners in Britain it is impossible to watch such men at work without feeling a pang of envy for their toughness. It is 'a dreadful job . . . an almost super-human job by the standard of an ordinary person'.[4] And yet, like Orwell's miners, they look and work as though they are made of iron. As a mine man-ager remarked in 1946 when describing how the 'machine-boy' usually lay on his back or side and provided pressure to the machine with his legs, 'In other lands few men would be able to carry out this arduous operation for many days.'[5]

Over the period 1936–66, no less than 19,000 men, 93% of them black, died as a result of accidents in the gold mines.[6] And there is evidence for the assertion that the black jobs were somewhat more hazardous than white jobs; for, over this period, the white death rate averaged 0·97 per 1,000 men per annum in service whilst the average rate for blacks was 1·62 per 1,000.[7] During 1968, 491 blacks and 18 whites were killed whilst 25,000 blacks and 2,000 whites were disabled for at least 14 days by accidents in the gold mines. More than 98% of these accidents were estimated to have been due to the inherent danger of the work. The major cause of death was falling ground, including rock bursts. The non-fatal accidents were due to a variety of reasons of which rock-falls, trucks and tramways, falls of mining materials, and men slipping and falling were the most important. And 1968 was the year in which the fatality rate reached an all time low of 1·20 per 1,000 per annum. Nevertheless, despite determined efforts by the Chamber's Prevention of Accidents Committee to inculcate safety mindedness into all

[1] After the Second World War, legs, standing on a cushion of air, were developed to bear the weight of the drill once it has been shifted into place.
[2] A survey in Europe in 1968 found that 80% of people who worked in a noise with a level of 116 decibels or more could become permanently deaf. The pneumatic drill is not only one of the noisiest of the compressed air tools, but the sound that it makes is in the more dangerous higher frequency ranges. Early in 1969 a number of mines began to issue ear plugs. There is no record of the number of men whose hearing may have been impaired by the noise during the previous decades of drilling.
[3] On 25 March 1969 the *Star* reported that it had been proved beyond doubt that someone must have tried to smoke on the President Steyn mine when a methane gas explosion killed some twenty men. The Mine Workers' Union was reported to be 'perturbed about the many [white] miners charged with smoking in dangerous mines'.
[4] Orwell, *Selected Essays* (Penguin, Harmondsworth, 1957), p. 52 B.
[5] Association of Mine Managers of the Transvaal, *Papers and Discussions, 1946–1947*, p. 9 B.
[6] An average of three deaths a shift.
[7] T.C.M., *Seventy Seventh Annual Report* (1966), p. 72 A.

mineworkers, the overall accident rate (including fatalities) for the year was 64 per 1,000 persons in service, a rate that was more than twice as high as that in the coal mines, and seven times that in the diamond mines.[1]

ORGANISATION OF THE INDUSTRY

Because of the depth to which they work, the high cost of prospecting and the necessary expenditure of as much as R60 million on development, the gold mines have to be very large to ensure an adequate return on capital sunk into a particular spot.[2] A measure of their size is given by the fact that the average mine, in 1969, employed 8,400 people and milled 1·7 million tons of gold-bearing ore.[3] This size enables individual mines to achieve considerable economies of scale in such diverse activities as training of labour and buying of equipment, but the nature of mining is such that, large though they are, individual mines are not big enough to achieve alone some of the more important economies. Thus, almost from the very beginning, pressures were generated forcing mines to group themselves into still larger units.

The first mining was done on outcrops of gold-bearing ore but, as time went on, it became necessary to mine at deeper and deeper levels. Besides the pressure this exerted to reduce working costs, a pressure which was partly responsible for the Jameson raid,[4] this deepening demanded more specialised technical services and required the risky investment, for prospecting and development, of large sums of money with a lag of several years before any returns began to accrue. These factors led to a rapid change in organisation. In 1893 there were in the Transvaal some 183 gold mining companies of which 104 produced no gold at all, but by the end of the next seven-year period there was a marked clustering of mines and the basis of the modern group system had been laid.[5]

Under this pattern the individual gold mine exists as a separate corporate entity but it contracts with one of the mining houses to provide various services to the company. These include staffs of consulting engineers and

[1] Department of Mines, *Mining Statistics 1968* (R.P. 34, Pretoria, 1969), pp. 19–22 A.
[2] In 1959 the Anglo American Corporation and de Beers Consolidated Mines together spent an annual average of R5 million on prospecting alone (C. S. Menell, *The Changing Character of the South African Mining Finance Houses in the Post-War Period* (M.B.A. thesis, Wharton, 1961), p. 69 D). For a breakdown of the costs of development see Appendix 1. The R60m. in 1969 compares with R25m. in 1952 and the R1·3m. needed to sink a mine to the depth of 3,000 feet in 1887 (Cartwright, *The Gold Mines*, p. 104 B).
[3] See Appendix 2.
[4] G. Blainey, 'Lost causes of the Jameson Raid', *Economic History Review* XVIII (1965) C.
[5] Cartwright, *The Gold Mines*, p. 105 B. J. Martin, 'Group administration in the gold mining industry of the Witwatersrand', *Economic Section of the British Association for the Advancement of Science* (Johannesburg, 1929) C.

others, research laboratories, the organisation of bulk buying, legal advice about such matters as taxation and medical compensation, secretarial services, and, most important of all, finance. Over and above the natural endowments which have facilitated the growth of the gold mining industry in South Africa, there has been its ability to attract large amounts of capital from more developed economies. Political factors, such as the British connection and South Africa's location in the sterling area, have certainly eased the flow of funds, but the role of the groups has been crucial. The first financial house was formed in 1887, to bring the Rand goldfields before the British public.[1] The success of the different finance houses in tapping the capital markets of the world has owed a great deal to the fact that the group system helps to spread, and so to minimise, the risks of investment.

Investment in a gold mine has been likened to betting on a horse race.[2] Carrying the analogy a stage further, one may think of a group as the stable which develops several horses in the knowledge that, although some may fail, others will probably do well enough to make the whole enterprise profitable. The size of a stable will depend partly on its ability to obtain financial backing from outside, partly on its skill in developing its internal resources, and partly on sheer chance. A horse may break a leg; a gold mine may flood. In the Orange Free State, for example, of the fifteen mines developed by the end of 1960 no less than eight had failed. When in the late 1930s, one of the groups had the opportunity of acquiring three new mines it felt the risks too high to procure more than two; the one it rejected ultimately proved to be the most profitable.[3] Only three mines in the Orange Free State proved unqualified successes but their combined working profit, R92 million in 1966 alone, would suggest, at first glance, that the failure of some mines could be borne without undue hardship. In 1969 the five wealthiest mines – four of them in the Anglo American stable – alone accounted for more than half the total working profit of R306 million earned by the industry's forty-eight producing mines.[4] However, as Frankel has pointed out, the degree to which the profits of wealthy gold mines were taxed was such as to reduce considerably the ability of successful mines to counterbalance the inevitable failures.[5]

Despite the high level of taxation and despite the fact that, between 1935

[1] S. H. Frankel, *Capital Investment in Africa* (O.U.P., London, 1938), p. 79 B.
[2] M. R. Graham, *The Gold Mining Finance System in South Africa : with special reference to the financing and development of the Orange Free State Gold Fields up to 1960* (Ph.D. thesis, London, 1964), p. 321 D.
[3] *Ibid.* p. 40.
[4] The five mines (and the years in which they started production) are: Free State Geduld (1956), Western Holdings (1953), Western Deep Levels (1962), West Driefontein (1952) and President Brand (1964).
[5] S. H. Frankel, *Investment and the Return to Equity Capital in the South African Gold Mining Industry 1887–1965* (Basil Blackwell, Oxford, 1967), p. 9 B.

TABLE 2. *Relative size*[a] *of mining finance houses, 1936/1969*

Name	Date of establishment	No. of mines[b]		Employment (black labour) (%)		Gold production (fine oz) (%)		Approximate proportion of group's funds invested in gold and uranium 1960
		1936	1969	1936	1969	1936	1969	
The Consolidated Gold Fields of South Africa Ltd.	1887	9	11	12	17	11	17	55
Johannesburg Consolidated Investment Company Ltd.	1889	7	4	23	4	24	3	13
Rand Mines Ltd.	1893	14	7	36	17	34	12	50
General Mining and Finance Corporation Ltd.	1895	2	3	4	10	5	7	86
Union Corporation Ltd.	1897	6	8	6	13	8	13	n.a.
Anglo American Corporation of South Africa Ltd.	1917	5	12	13	29	14	41	40
Anglo-Transvaal Consolidated Investment Company Ltd.	1933	1	5	2	10	1	6	50
Sundry companies		4	1	4	0	2	–	–
				100	100	100	100	
Total		48	51	302,000	337,000	11·0m.	30·9m.	

[a] This table is no more than a rough guide as it does not show the involvement of each group with mines under the control of other groups.
[b] Including non-producing mines.
SOURCES: W.N.L.A. Annual Reports, 1936 and 1969.
T.C.M. Annual Reports, 1936 and 1969.
C. S. Mennell, thesis (1961), p. 50.

and 1963, the average rate of return from investment in the gold mines was 4·3% compared with 7% for United Kingdom equities, the mines were remarkably successful in raising their capital requirements.[1] In 1960 it was estimated that, since the Second World War, the industry had made a capital expenditure of approximately R940 million, of which three-quarters was new money from the public.[2] Of this R700 million, approximately half came from overseas. Most of the R240 million not drawn from the public came from within the industry itself, but R40 million was drawn, to the temporary annoyance of De Beers shareholders, by Sir Ernest Oppenheimer from diamond profits in order to finance the development of the Free State fields.[3] When they first started, the groups had few internal resources. However, as time went on, the groups began to build up financial reserves from jobbing and from the services they provided to individual mines. Some of the profits from this were invested and the groups acquired a third source of income in the form of dividends. Over the seven years which began with the declaration of the first Orange Free State dividend in 1954, the investment income of the Anglo American Corporation alone trebled from R5·2 million to R16·4 million.[4] Another seven years later, by 1967, the figure had risen to R28·6 million.[5] For all the groups together the average annual income over the period 1954–60 was R52 million, of which nearly two-thirds came from investments, more than a quarter from various services provided to the mines, and the remaining 9% from jobbing profits.[6] Not all this income was from gold. For although all the groups had originally been formed in order to develop gold mining they were essentially finance houses specialising in the provision of capital (and technical services) to any enterprise that seemed to be a worthwhile investment. Consolidated Goldfields, for example, was a London-based group which had long had interests in South America and elsewhere. The Anglo American Corporation, which had never been solely concentrated on gold, began in the 1960s to diversify still further into areas as far afield as Mauretania and Canada, and into sectors as varied as agriculture and steel. Important though these developments were, it was estimated in 1968 that of Anglo American's total attributable income of R60 million, no less than R25 million came from South African gold mines. Indeed the

---

[1] Calculated in current terms. After allowing for inflation, the figures were 0·2% and 2·1% respectively, Frankel, *Investment and the Return to Equity Capital*, p. 8 B.

[2] W. J. Busschau, 'The world's greatest goldfield', *South Africa Today* (September 1960) C.

[3] Financial Mail, 'Inside the Anglo power house', *Financial Mail* (Supplement, 4 June 1969), p. 7 Menell, *Mining Finance Houses*, p. 131 D.

[4] Graham, *Gold Mining Finance System*, p. 18 D.

[5] Financial Mail, 'Inside the Anglo power house', p. 19 C.

[6] Graham, *Gold Mining Finance System*, p. 70 D. These figures were queried by someone within the industry who read an earlier draft of this book. He suggests that investment income, and revenue from services were, in 1966, more nearly equal, each accounting for approximately 46% of income.

twelve gold mines directly administered by the Corporation were alone responsible, in 1968, for more than 3% of the country's gross national product.[1]

CONCENTRATION OF POWER

One of the fascinating questions that emerge from the most cursory glance at the organisation of the gold mining industry concerns the concentration of economic power.[2] Largely because of its successful developments in the Orange Free State, after the Second World War, the Anglo American Corporation became the banker to the gold mining industry. By 1958 the assets of this one group comfortably exceeded the combined resources of all the other South African finance houses.[3] From a detailed investigation by the *Financial Mail* as well as from an earlier analysis by Graham, it is clear that different groups, but particularly Anglo American, were able to forge strong financial links which bound the whole industry together.[4] At the group level, Anglo American interests, in the late 1950s and early 1960s, acquired potential control over Johannesburg Consolidated Investment Company (J.C.I.) as well as the Rand Mines group. In addition Anglo American, in partnership with Federale Mynbou, acquired a substantial, although not controlling, stake in General Mining and Finance. These financial links are reflected in the interlocking directorships of the four groups as illustrated in table 3 which shows the names of directors who, in 1965, were on the board of more than one group. Besides this the Anglo American 'family' was, via Charter Consolidated, the largest single shareholder in Union Corporation and also had a 20% interest in the most important South African asset of the Consolidated Gold Fields group, namely its mines around Westonaria and Carletonville.[5]

This interlocking of the gold mining industry at group level was reinforced and extended by the ties between boards of the individual mines. Table 4 lists the men who, in 1965, were directors of gold mines in more than one group. The dominance which Anglo American had acquired by then is

1 Financial Mail, 'Inside the Anglo power house', p. 41 C.
2 See J. A. Hobson (*The Evolution of Modern Capitalism* (Allen and Unwin, London, 1926, 4th edn.), pp. 265–72 C) for a discussion on the concentration of economic power in South Africa at the turn of the century.
3 *Financial Mail* (29 May 1959) cited by Menell, *Mining Finance Houses*, p. 137 D.
4 Financial Mail, 'Inside the Anglo power house' C. Graham, *Gold Mining Finance System*, p. 63 D. Menell (*Mining Finance Houses*, p. 51 D) makes the point that unlike other countries (e.g. the U.S.A. since the 1930s) South Africa does not compel businesses to make public their investment portfolios. Until this is done a thorough analysis of the power of capital in South Africa will be almost impossible.
5 Financial Mail, 'Inside the Anglo power house', p. 23 C.

perhaps best illustrated by the fact that of the twenty-eight mines that had started producing gold in the twenty years after the Second World War only one did not have an Anglo American nominee on the board of directors.[1]

But it is not only finance and interlocking directorships which bind the industry together; there is also the Chamber of Mines. Beginning as the Diggers' Committee in 1886, and reconstituted into its present form in 1889, the primary purpose of the Chamber is to deal with matters concerning labour. It is through the Chamber that black labour for all large gold mines and for the coal mines of the Transvaal is recruited; it is with

TABLE 3. *Interlocking directorships: mining houses, 1965*

Anglo American Corporation Ltd.	Rand Mines Ltd.	Johannesburg Consolidated Investment Company Ltd.	General Mining and Finance Corporation Ltd.
H. F. Oppenheimer			H. F. Oppenheimer
C. S. McLean			C. S. McLean
R. B. Hagart	R. B. Hagart	R. B. Hagart	
C. W. Engelhard	C. W. Engelhard		

SOURCE: Walter R. Skinner's *Mining Yearbook* (1965).

the Chamber that white trade unions must bargain when pressing for higher wages, and it is by the Chamber that much of the training of white workers is organised. The relative importance of the Chamber's different functions may be gauged from the breakdown, by an official commission, of its main items of expenditure in 1948. Out of a total budget of R912,000, 31% was spent by the two African labour recruiting organisations. Training and education, predominantly for whites, absorbed 14%, research into new methods of mining 11%, general administration (which included the formulation of policy with regard to legislation and other government action) 10%, publicity 9%, contributions to public appeals 8%, and other services, including the running of the Rand refinery and the phthisis sanatorium for whites, absorbed the remaining 15% of the budget.[2] The Chamber is run by an executive committee whilst matters

[1] Cf. P. C. Dooley, 'The interlocking directorate', *A.E.R.* LIX (1969) C.
[2] South Africa (van Eck), *Report of Commission on Conditions of Employment in the Gold Mining Industry* (U.G. 28, Pretoria, 1950), p. 40 A.

pertaining specifically to the gold mines are handled by the Gold Producer's Committee (G.P.C.), which consists of seven men each of whom represents one of the seven groups. Normally one of these seven is elected president of the Chamber of Mines at the annual general meeting. By 1969 the Chamber of Mines, which in 1968 had broadened its constitution so as to include not only gold and coal mines in the Transvaal and Orange Free State, but all types of mines in all four provinces, had, in the words of its president, 'a membership of 16 financial companies and 108 mining companies, including gold, uranium, coal, diamond, platinum, antimony, asbestos, and copper mining companies.'[1] Its gold mines alone employed more than 400,000 men and produced a record total of 31·28 million fine ounces of gold which formed 7·5% of the gross national product for the year.[2]

To summarise, the lines of control within the industry are as follows: when an individual mine is formed by one of the finance houses it contracts with the same group in order to obtain various services. Under this contract, as a president of the Chamber of Mines explained, 'The financial corporation itself holds the appointment as managers, consulting engineers, buyers and secretaries, and it then delegates members of its staff to carry out those respective functions for the company. All the subsequent work of planning, developing, operating, maintaining and managing the company in every respect is then done by the financial corporation or controlling house through those officials, and subject to the board of directors of the company. The board of directors will not consist exclusively of members of the staff of the controlling house, but they will be in the majority ... The "control" of the company thus rests upon contract and not necessarily, as some people imagine, upon a majority shareholding.'[3] In practice, as another president explained, 'The control which any one of these corporations exercises is exercised by virtue of the support of the general body of shareholders of the individual companies, and not by the weight of its own share interest.'[4] Theoretically this may have been so, and Graham is doubtless right when he suggests that shareholders would not willingly acquiesce in this way unless the groups were successful and reputable organisations, but in practice the reins of power rest in the hands of the parent group whose officials possess, in effect, a monopoly of financial and mining expertise and it would be well-nigh impossible for any other body of shareholders to wrest them away.[5]

---

[1] T.C.M., *Eightieth Annual Report* (1969), p. 12 A.
[2] See Appendix 3 for statistics of employment over the period 1911–69.
[3] H. C. Koch, *The Organization of the South African Gold Mining Industry* (revised version of lecture in Stellenbosch, 1957) C.
[4] Martin, *British Association for the Advancement of Science*, p. 11 C.
[5] R. Marris, *The Economic Theory of Managerial Capitalism* (Macmillan, London, 1964), p. 17 B.

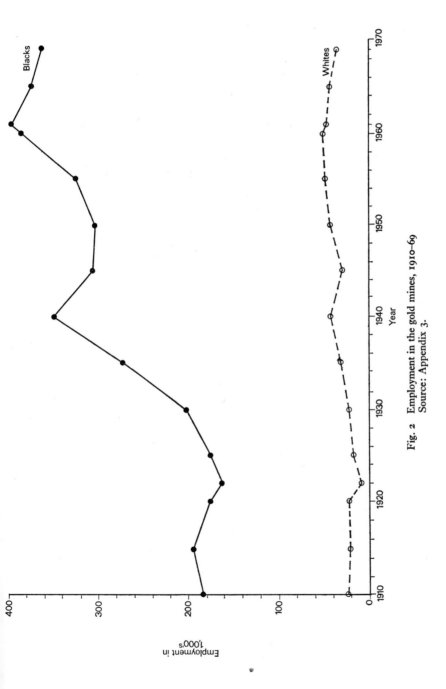

Fig. 2 Employment in the gold mines, 1910–69
Source: Appendix 3.

TABLE 4. *Interlocking directorships : mines, 1965*

Director	Anglo American	Rand Mines	J.C.I.	General Mining	Anglo-Transvaal	Union Corporation	Consolidated Gold Fields	Total No. of mines
No. of mines in each group	12	8	4	3	5	9	14	55
				No. of mines in which individual was a director				
H. C. Koch	11	2		2	4	4	7	31
P. H. Anderson	2	5	1	1	1	4	2	15
T. Reekie	2	6			1	4	4	17
R. M. Strachan	1	1	1			1	6	10
F. S. Berning	10				4	2	2	19
S. G. Menell	3	1	1	2	5		1	12
C. B. Anderson	5	1				9	1	16
J. M. M. Ewing	1	2				1	6	10
D. B. Hoffe	5			1	2		5	13
C. S. McLean	1		1	3	2			7
W. M. Walker	1	1	1			1	3	6

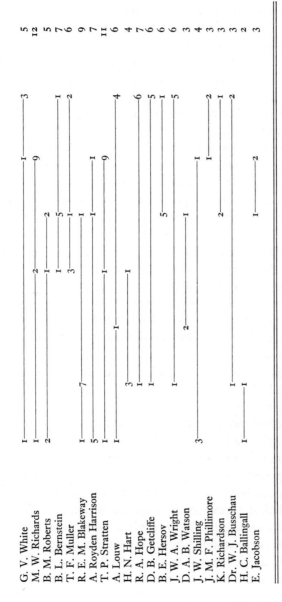

SOURCE: *Beerman's All Mining Yearbook*, 1965.

Thus the seven groups effectively control all, except one, of the large gold mines in South Africa.

Considerable though the concentration of power is, there has been debate as to its effectiveness. For example, J. A. Hobson writing in 1926, maintained that 'nowhere in the world has there ever existed so concentrated a form of capitalism as that represented by the financial power of the mining houses in South Africa, and nowhere else does that power so completely realise and enforce the need for controlling politics'.[1] A generation later, however, the chairman of Anglo American, Mr. Harry Oppenheimer, questioned the view. Big business, he suggested, did not really have much power anywhere.[2] 'The days when big business had any political power in this country are gone forever', he said. In South Africa it is certainly true that, in the year after Hobson's analysis, 'capitalist power' was not the only force in political life. Even within the mining industry itself the power of the white trade unions to enforce policies that were contrary to the economic interests of the Chamber of Mines was considerable. The struggle between the two power groups, with the trade unions still (in 1969) dominant, is examined in greater detail in a later chapter (p. 114). However a general assessment of the extent to which the Chamber of Mines or the Anglo American Corporation is, or is not, able to influence affairs in Southern Africa lies beyond the scope of this book. Nevertheless the organisation of management power within the gold industry itself must be examined to see whether or not it affects the behaviour of the mines, particularly with regard to its labour force.

In a much quoted assessment, a former economic adviser to the Bank of England argued that the industry was the epitome of rationalisation. 'Through the group system of control of the separate mining companies, and the close co-operation of the whole industry through the Chamber of Mines and its subsidiary services, it has substituted for the blind selection by competition of the fittest to survive, a conscious and deliberate choice of methods, equipment, areas and personnel.'[3] One of the most notable features of the industry has been the willingness of individual mines and groups to share their technical discoveries and expertise with their rivals. This unusually free flow of knowledge is due primarily to the fact that the product of the industry is homogeneous and, during most of the period under consideration, was in infinitely elastic demand by the Federal Reserve Bank of the United States of America. In such circumstances there is nothing to be gained by

---

[1] Hobson, *Modern Capitalism*, p. 267 B.
[2] Financial Mail, 'Inside the Anglo power house', pp. 10, 17 C. *Cape Times*, 24 March 1970.
[3] Sir Henry Clay in preface to Martin, *British Association for the Advancement of Science* C.

hiding new methods of producing the good more cheaply, for nobody could capture markets by undercutting anybody else.

Despite this technical co-operation there is one sphere in which competition between groups is always acute.[1] Under South African law the mineral rights are vested in the state which leases them in the first instance to the landowner. Thus groups compete vigorously with each other in order to buy, from the landowner, the option which then entitles them to apply for the mining lease. Landowners, of course, are likely to be aware of this and so great guile has to be displayed by a group if it wishes to get the mineral rights on an area that might contain very rich deposits without letting other groups in on the secret and so driving up the price against itself. Indeed, to prevent competitive bidding going too high, it happens quite often that two groups agree to run a mine as a joint venture. But even where they do not so agree, once the matter as to which group is going to control a particular mine is settled, the pattern of brotherly co-operation reasserts itself.

Contrasting with the competition for land has been the collusion over labour. Indeed it is with regard to the wage structure that the centralisation of control has had most effect on the behaviour of the mines. For, by organising the recruitment of African labour through the Chamber of Mines, the industry as a whole has gained a significant degree of monopsony power over the market for unskilled labour. Furthermore, as we shall see (p. 107), one important reason why, for many years, wealthy mines chose to collude rather than raise wages despite an acute shortage of labour lay in the fact that they were not independent of the finance houses.

REVENUE, COSTS, AND PROFIT

Having looked briefly at the organisation of gold mining in South Africa, it is now necessary to consider the financial structure of the industry, for it is not possible to analyse the pattern of earnings until we have seen how it fits into the overall framework of income and expenditure.

Fig. 3 shows the breakdown, over the period 1911–69, of revenue, costs, and profits. It shows also the phenomenal growth of the industry during the 1950s and 1960s. Between 1955 (when production was slightly higher than the previous maximum in 1941) and 1969, South Africa's gold output, measured in fine ounces, more than doubled from 14·6 million to 31·3 million. The three factors determining the revenue of a mine are the total amount of ore that is broken, hoisted, and milled, the grade of the ore milled, and the price of gold.

---

[1] Menell, *Mining Finance Houses*, p. 63 D.

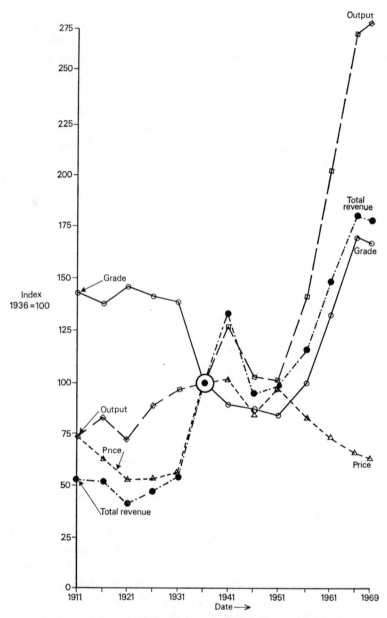

Fig. 3a   Determinants of revenue, 1911–69
Source: Appendix 4

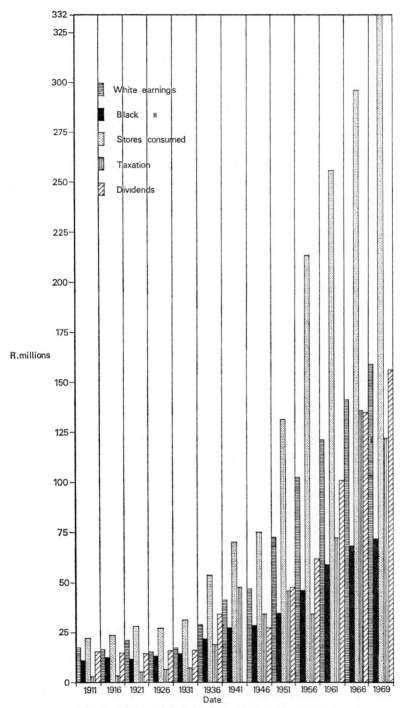

Fig. 3b   Major components of costs and profits, 1911–69
Source: Appendix 4

35

Labour in the South African gold mines

Gold is bought primarily to be used as money; that is both as a medium of exchange and as a store of value.[1] It is valuable because men want it and men want it because, in the last resort, it is still almost the only material which they are confident will be accepted by others as money. Thus the price of gold depends mainly on the workings of the monetary systems of the world. From the birth of the gold mining industry in South Africa until 24 July 1919, Britain was on the gold standard and bought all gold offered for sale at a fixed price of £4·24773 (R8·49546) per fine ounce. When she abandoned the gold standard, at the end of the First World War, gold was sold at a premium above the standard price until Britain returned to the gold standard, at pre-war parity, in April 1925. Thereafter gold was again bought at a price of just under R8·50 until the end of December 1932, when South Africa devalued her currency by abandoning the gold standard. This devaluation was of great benefit to the country for the price of gold rose sharply and yet retail prices of consumer goods actually declined slightly. In January 1934 the United States of America announced her intention to raise, by more than two-thirds, the price at which she would buy all gold offered for sale. From that date until March 1968 the Federal Reserve Bank was willing to pay $35 a fine ounce for all gold not already taken off the market by private buyers.

The actual price which South Africa received for her gold was thus determined mainly by the dollar–sterling exchange rate as South African currency was, until the British devaluation in November 1967, maintained at a parity with sterling. After 1934 the price continued to rise until the beginning of 1940, when it was fixed at 168s. (R16·8) a fine ounce for the duration of the war. Thereafter it continued to rise slowly but steadily until September 1949, when the depreciation of sterling by the British Government increased the price of gold by over 40% from R17·25 to R24·825 a fine ounce. In 1954 the London Gold Market, which had been closed since the outbreak of the Second World War, was re-opened and South African gold was once again sold in a manner so British that perhaps only an American journal could have described it as graphically:

Every weekday morning at 10.30 sharp, five men stride briskly into the Bank of N. M. Rothschild in St. Swithin's Lane, London. They enter an ornate room carpeted in green velvet, furnished with green leather chairs and an old grandfather clock. On the walls hang glowering portraits – an Emperor of Austria, King Frederick William III of Prussia, Tsar Nicholas II of Russia. Each man seats himself at a small desk equipped with a telephone open to his trading room, a calculating machine and a small Union Jack, the flag placed downward on his desk. Then

---

[1] Except when, as in the 1960s, the possibility of monetary authorities raising the price causes a huge speculative demand. F. Machlup, 'The price of gold', *The Banker* CXVIII (1968), 784 C. The increasing industrial use of gold is analysed in the *Financial Mail*, 20 March 1970.

36

the day's spirited bidding in gold begins. The moment a trader raises his Union Jack and calls, 'Flag up!' all trading stops, while he gets an opportunity to ponder the exchange – perhaps to call the home office – before making another bid. Once he is ready, the flag is lowered again and trading resumes.[1]

The ritual, which was first started in 1919 when Rothschilds were named official gold brokers to the Bank of England, determines the market price of gold not only for five banks but also, in effect, for buyers and sellers around the world.[2]

In South Africa the gold produced is sold by the industry to the country's Reserve Bank at average weekly prices relating to the London daily quotations less a small amount for shipping charges.[3] Thus, apart from times of financial crisis such as the great depression and the aftermath of world wars, the price of gold has been fairly stable. Indeed one of South Africa's many economic good fortunes has been the fact that the price stabilisation scheme[4] for the primary commodity that was her main major export was remarkably successful in preventing the sine curves which have characterised the prices of other commodities like cocoa, copper, rubber, sugar, or tin. The only time that the price of gold fell sharply South Africa came, as we have seen (p. 10), very close to revolution.

However, by the 1960s, it was becoming apparent that the stability of the gold price was something upon which South Africa could no longer rely. For private speculators, hopeful that United States balance of payments difficulties would lead to a substantial rise in the price of gold, increased their demand enormously so that by 1967 the private demand for gold was twice as much as new supplies; and stocks held by monetary authorities of the western world declined by over 1,500 million dollars, which was considerably more than the value of the 31 million fine ounces produced by the entire South African industry in that year.[5]

But whilst these pressures seemed likely to pull up the official price of gold there were other forces at work which, in the long run at least, suggested that the price of gold might fall below the level at which it had been supported for so long. There were signs that the factors which had previously both

[1] D. L. Thomas, 'Trading in gold', *Barron's* (2 June 1969), p. 3 C.
[2] W. M. Clarke, *The City in the World Economy* (Pelican, Harmondsworth, 1967), ch. 4 B.
[3] For a few years, 1949–54, a small proportion (4% in 1951) of gold produced in South Africa was sold in places other than the official London money market. The premium obtained offset, almost entirely, the increase in working costs over the period (*S.A. M. and E. J.*, 8 January 1955). The premium which South Africa obtained on the free market after 1968 (and possibly also from undisclosed buyers during the poker game that was played by the different monetary authorities after the establishment of the two-tier price system) did much to ease the pressure of rising costs during this period (see p. 154). During 1969 the industry received a total premium of R57m., R37m. of which was included in the industry's total working revenue of R817m. (T.C.M., 1969).
[4] Clarke, *The City*, pp. 82–5 B.　　　　　　　　　[5] Machlup, *The Banker*, p. 784 C.

prodded and enabled individual nations to replace gold with paper were liable to bring about the same transmutation at an international level.

Trade was being hampered by the shortage of liquid assets to finance it,[1] but at the same time the increase in scale due, amongst other things, to increased communication, was making international co-operation more possible.[2] The tentative steps taken by the International Monetary Fund in the late 1960s to create special drawing rights, culminating in the agreement to create $9,500 million worth of such rights during the first three years of the 1970s, were seen by many people as the beginning of the process whereby gold would be replaced by a much cheaper substitute. Others, however, argued that the separation, in March 1968, of the official and the private markets for gold with the consequent two-tier price system was a stop-gap measure which would not save the United States from having to devalue the dollar by raising the price at which she was prepared to buy gold. What was going to happen in the future was, at that time, anybody's guess. The extent of uncertainty is illustrated by the fact that, in 1968, an expert paper was published containing no less than six possible 'plots' as to what might happen.[3] These varied from a tripling of the official price, to a decline far below $35.

The possibility, however remote, that the price of gold might actually fall, combined with the tantalising glimpses of it doubling or more, added a new and substantial risk factor which had to be taken into account when the opening of new mines was being considered. However the agreement at the end of December 1969 between South Africa, the United States, and the I.M.F. was seen as a step towards greater stability in the gold market.[4]

The primary task of a gold mine is to dig the ore from the earth and to bring it to the surface where it may be crushed and the gold extracted. Thus the total gold output, and hence revenue, of a mine depends to a large extent on the amount of ore that is dug out. There are three measures of this output: the tonnage broken, hoisted, and milled.[5]

Not all the ore that is broken contains gold of a sufficiently high grade to warrant treating, and there is a considerable amount of waste rock that never goes to the reduction plant but is either stored underground, or hoisted and sent to a dump. In some of the Orange Free State mines, for example, the layer of hard quartzite separating the reef from the soft shale is so thin

[1] The ratio of gold to the world's imports declined from 111% in 1938 to 17% thirty years later.
[2] Cf. G. and M. Wilson, *The Analysis of Social Change* (C.U.P., Cambridge, 1945), ch. 2, for a discussion of change in scale.
[3] Machlup, *The Banker*, pp. 789–90 C.
[4] B. S. Kantor, 'The Gold Agreement and the future of gold', *South African Banker* LXVII (February 1970) C.
[5] 1 ton = 2,000 lb = 900 kilograms.

Plate 1. Only the white man is allowed to 'charge up' by driving the explosive into the hole; he is assisted by a 'chisa boy'

Plate 2. Hand lashing into a truck

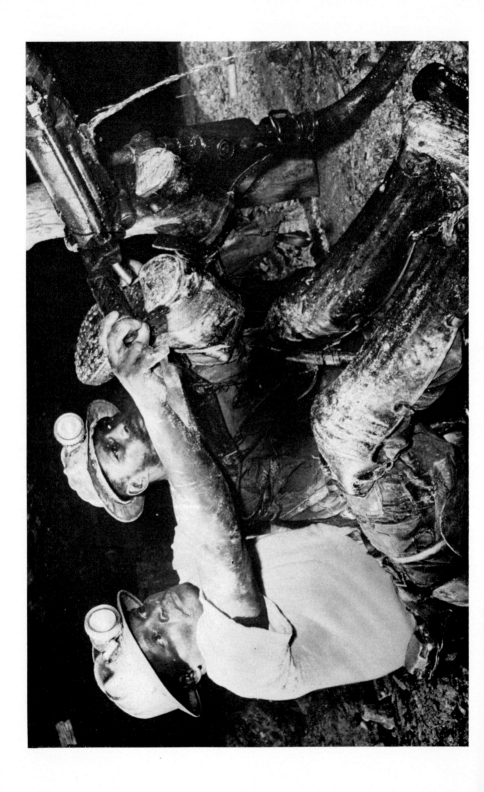

Plate 4.   A mechanical scraper

Plate 5. Old compound

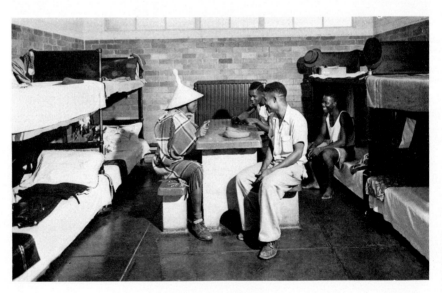

Plate 6. New compound

that *resue* stoping is employed, whereby blasting is done twice: first, above the reef to clear the shale, which is then packed underground, and a second time to break the reef itself. In other mines, however, no waste can be stored. For at very deep levels the pressure is so great that the roof of the stope is pushed to the floor within two months. In such conditions the packing of waste in the area that has already been worked prevents it from closing and so places extra pressure on the stope face, thus increasing the likelihood of dangerous pressure bursts. Hoisting waste rock is costly and the extent to which any mine can increase the ratio of tonnage milled to tonnage hoisted affects its profitability appreciably. In 1936 less than 80%, and in 1969 69%, of the tonnage broken by the large producing mines was milled; of the remainder, approximately half was packed underground and the rest hoisted but discarded before milling.[1]

The amount of ore milled is, however, not itself an accurate measure of output, for the amount of gold in a ton of ore varies widely. There are two levels of grade, both measured in pennyweights per ton milled: the pay limit, and the average ore reserve. The concept of the pay limit is crucial in the economics of gold mining. A government commission called it the 'temperature chart' of policy and defined it as being of sufficient value to cover all the costs of developing, mining, milling and extracting the gold from the ore, including all overhead charges, rates, licences, insurances and head office costs, but not including any allowance for interest or amortisation of capital.[2] An increase in working costs raises the pay limit and so lowers the amount of payable ore reserves of a mine. Thus the pay limit is determined both by the ability of management to reduce working costs, and by characteristics of the ore: a wide unbroken reef near the surface would obviously have a much lower pay limit than scattered concentrations of ore 10,000 feet down.

By law each mine has to work to the average grade of its declared ore reserves. It is not allowed to pick the eyes of a mine by removing only the high grade ore and make a quick profit at the expense of leaving behind ore which would, if mined, contribute to the national income. One paradox of this is that as working costs rise the average grade of the reserve that remains payable may also rise and so enable a mine to increase its profits in the short term. But in the long run, the rise in costs will, by transferring some of the ore reserves from the payable to the unpayable range, lower the total revenue of the mine over its working life. In 1934, for example, there was a sharp drop in the average grade of ore milled; because the higher price for

[1] Figures supplied by the Chamber of Mines.
[2] South Africa, *Conditions of Employment*, p. 26 A.

gold made it possible for mine managers to lower their pay limits and so increase their ore reserves, thus prolonging the life of mines. The rise in the grade of ore milled from 4·6 pennyweight in 1936 to 7·8 pennyweight in 1969 was due partly to the increase in working costs which raised the pay limit, and partly to the discovery and exploitation of the very rich gold deposits in the Orange Free State and western Transvaal.

The significance of the relation between the pay limit and the average grade may be seen most clearly in the case of marginal mines, whose average grade of ore reserves is so close to their pay limits that the working profit would vanish with a marginal increase in costs. Because a mine, once closed, cannot readily be re-opened there have always been strong pressures on both the industry and government to hold down working costs or even to subsidise marginal mines so as to postpone for as long as possible the closure of a mine. Whether or not the state should subsidise such mines has been a matter of considerable debate in South Africa. Clearly, if there is an expectation that the price of gold may rise in the near future a strong case can be made for keeping mines artificially alive. In 1963, the government began subsidising marginal mines, and in 1968 it introduced a more comprehensive scheme to assist all mines likely to close down before 1975 if not subsidised. By June 1969 no less than 19 of the country's 48 producing gold mines were being granted assistance by the state. Nine of them failed to cover even their working costs during the year.[1] However the argument that even if the price is not expected to change all mines should be kept going, because of foreign exchange they earn or the employment they provide, rests on a much flimsier foundation. Although, in the short run, the subsidisation of marginal mines may be the cheapest method of providing employment for a large number of unskilled workers who might otherwise be unemployed, it encourages the maldistribution of resources and provides no mechanism for the establishment of new self-sustaining industries which could later absorb such persons. A further important consideration with regard to any assessment of marginal mines is the fact that their existence has been, as we shall see (p. 108), the major factor in the industry-wide collusion to hold down black wages.

Labour costs form one of the two main components of the working costs of any mine; the other component is made up of stores and equipment. In 1936 the cash wage bill was no less than 31% of total revenue; by 1969 it had fallen to 28%. Significantly, while the cash wage bill for Africans fell from 13·7% of total revenue in 1936 to 8·9% in 1969, the white cash wage bill rose from 18·6% to 19·4% of total revenue. This despite the fact that the

---

[1] T.C.M., *Eightieth Annual Report* (1969) pp. 12 and 52. A. The annual cost of the subsidy was approximately R9m.

proportion of blacks to whites in the service of the industry changed only slightly from 8·4:1 to 9·1:1 over the period. Exactly what happened to the wage structure, and why, is examined in the next two chapters. Stores consumed by the industry absorbed 34% of revenue in 1936, and 30% in 1968.[1] It is worth noting that the foodstuffs supplied free to employees accounted for 8% of the total stores consumed both in 1936 and 1969. Other major items were machinery, electric power, explosives, iron and steel, buildings, transport, and timber.[2] In addition to labour and stores there were various miscellaneous costs which, between 1928 and 1948, averaged a little less than 6% of total working costs. During the 1940s, when these figures were examined by an official commission, a major component of these miscellaneous costs was for recruiting African labour.[3]

The difference between the revenue and the working costs of a mine is its profit, some of which is retained and ploughed back into future development. The rest is declared as 'working profit' and goes either to the government in the form of taxation or to shareholders, as dividends. The state, as S. H. Frankel has pointed out, developed a scheme that effectively leased the right to exploit gold resources to the highest bidder.[4] Most mines were granted their mining rights subject to an agreement whereby they would share their profits with the government. The share which varied with the particular circumstances of each mine was set according to a general formula:

$$Y = a - \frac{b}{X},$$

where Y was the percentage of profits payable to the state, X profits as a percentage of the value of gold produced, and a and b were real numbers varying from mine to mine. President Steyn mine, for example, had to pay the state a share of profits:

$$Y = 12 \cdot 5 - \frac{75}{X}$$

whilst the share of East Geduld was

$$Y = 50 - \frac{1,200.}{X}$$

Again depending upon the mine, there was an arrangement whereby the share of profits paid to the government could not fall below a certain minimum; in the case of President Steyn the minimum was 0% and for

[1] T.C.M., Annual Reports A.   [2] For detailed figures, see tables in T.C.M. Annual Reports A.
[3] South Africa, *Conditions of Employment*, p. 40 A.
[4] Frankel, *Investment and the Return to Equity Capital*, p. 104 B.

East Geduld 10%. Approximately 20% of the government's revenue from gold between 1946 and 1966 was derived from this lease consideration.[1] The other 80% came, in the main, from income tax which, after 1946, was based on a similar formula:

$$Y = c - \frac{d.}{X}$$

But in this case c and d, in any one year, were the same for all mines.[2]

In spite of various plans by both Afrikaner and African nationalists the gold mines had, by the end of the 1960s, not been nationalised. It has already been shown (p. 25) to what extent the industry relied upon the capital market for raising the necessary funds to develop itself. In order that this spring should not run dry it was necessary for the industry to use a major portion of its working profit for the payment of dividends to shareholders, both large and small. Yet, despite the increasing capital intensity of mining, dividends as a proportion of total revenue were reduced, by taxation, from 22% in 1936 to 19% in 1969. But, of course, by 1969 the industry was getting back a substantial amount of the tax in the form of subsidies to the marginal mines, so that even some of the mines that failed to cover their working costs were able to declare a dividend.

Besides the general picture (see p. 35) of the changes in relative importance of the various components which make up the revenue of the gold mines, it has been possible, by means of multiple regression analysis, to get some idea of the significance of the different factors influencing the profitability, costs, revenue and output of mining.[3] As might be expected, the chief determinant of profitability is the average grade of ore with which a given mine is endowed. Nevertheless, taken together, the five independent variables (employment, grade, capital, output, and vintage) had a multiple correlation co-efficient of 0·94; in other words 94% of the variation of profitability between mines in 1936 could be attributed to these five variables, of which grade was far and away the most important. By 1966 the picture had changed considerably. The correlation co-efficient had fallen to 0·27, and although grade remained significant, its own correlation with profitability was far lower than it had been. Moreover both the age of the mine and capital invested in it had become significant variables with even higher partial

[1] G.P.C., *The Outlook for Gold Mining* (T.C.M., Johannesburg, 1966) p. 56 A.
[2] Over the years 1946 to 1966 c varied between 60 and 70, whilst d varied between 360 and 420. For further details about the intricacies of gold mining taxation and its effects the reader is referred to D. Black, *The Incidence of Income Tax* (Macmillan, London, 1939), ch. 8 B; Busschau, *Measure of Gold*, ch. 6 B; Frankel, *Investment and the Return to Equity Capital*, pp. 9–12 B; and G.P.C., *The Outlook for Gold Mining*, pp. 55–60 A.
[3] See Appendix 5 for the table of regression results.

correlations than grade. This makes sense. In 1936 the new mines, stimulated by the price rise of 1933, were not yet in production, but by 1966 not only were these mines operating but also some very rich deposits, unknown before the end of the Second World War, had been discovered and exploited. As a result there were a number of new, highly profitable, mines operating in 1966. What remains unexplained however is the sharp fall in the multiple correlation co-efficient from 0·94 to 0·27. This decrease may reflect the fact that the newer mines were more capital intensive, and that the variations of capital equipment from mine to mine are difficult to measure accurately.

Some interesting results emerge from an analysis of the factors influencing the costs of mining. In 1936, 28% of the variations in cost between individual mines could be attributed to differences in employment, grade, capital, output and vintage. But of these five variables only grade was significant. By 1966 the multiple correlation co-efficient had risen from 0·28 to 0·38 and grade had ceased to be a significant variable. Moreover employment, capital, output and the age of the mine were now all significantly affecting the costs of mining. The sign of the regression co-efficient shows that, in 1966, the older mines produced at lower cost than the newer ones. This suggests that the profitability of the newer mines was due not to lower working costs but rather to the fact that their ore was of higher grade. The strong positive correlation between costs and labour in 1966 compared with its relative insignificance in 1936 suggests, as a possible explanation, that managers were more conscious of the importance of using labour efficiently than they had been. A further fact that emerges is the importance of economies of scale particularly in later years. In 1966 the correlation between costs and output was significant and the sign of the regression co-efficient was negative. In other words, the larger the number of tons milled the smaller was the average cost of production. The factors influencing the output (still measured in tons milled) of the mines were also assessed. It was found that in 1936 81%, and in 1966 76%, of the variations of output could be attributed primarily to the differences in the numbers of Africans employed from mine to mine. The capital invested in each mine was not significant in 1966, although it was in 1936. An attempt to fit a Cobb–Douglas production function to the data was reasonably successful, particularly in 1966 where a multiple correlation co-efficient of 0·94 was obtained for the following equation:[1]

$$Q = AE^{\alpha}G^{\beta}K^{\gamma}$$

[1] Q = output (tons milled); E = employment (number of blacks on 31 December); G = grade of ore (equivalent, in a sense, to fertility of soil); K = capital invested (Frankel, 1967, p. 88, col. 4); $\log A = -2\cdot15$; $\alpha = 1\cdot06$; $\beta = -0\cdot09$; $\gamma = 0\cdot03$. The fact that $\alpha + \beta + \gamma = 1\cdot00$ implies constant returns to scale, which contradicts the finding of economies of scale.

Having glanced briefly at the organisation of the gold mining industry and at the inter-relationships between the various components that comprise it, let us turn now to consider in more detail that aspect on which this book is focused, namely the determination of wages.

CHAPTER 3

EARNINGS

Almost every student of the labor market complains at one time or another about the inadequacy of wage data and the ambiguity of their interpretation.

George J. Stigler, *Domestic Servants in the United States, 1900–1940*

The most striking feature of table 5, which shows the average annual cash incomes of blacks and whites working in the gold mines over the period 1911–69 is the evidence it provides of the extent to which the distribution of earnings in the industry has apparently become less equitable over time. We have already seen (p. 4) how, by means of monopsonistic recruiting, the labour organisations of the Chamber of Mines during the 1890s were able to lower the annual wages paid to the black mine workers from R78 in 1889 to R58 in 1897, notwithstanding the enormous increase in the demand for labour as the gold fields were opened up. During the Anglo-Boer war wages were reduced still further to R36 a year, but the shortage of labour became so acute that, despite the arrival of indentured Chinese, this level could not be maintained.[1] By 1905 cash wages for Africans had risen to an average of R54; Chinese wages however were considerably lower, R39 for the year. By 1911 the Chinese experiment had drawn to an end and the industry was reconciled to the fact that the major source of its labour force would be within Africa. Black cash wages had, by this time, risen from the war-time rate to R57 a year, a level that was slightly lower than it had been in 1897 and considerably below what it had been in 1889. Details of white wages are not available but the evidence suggests that they did rise between 1889 and 1911.[2] It seems likely that the ratio of average cash earnings between white and black widened from approximately 7·5:1 in 1889 to approximately 10·5:1 in 1898 and to 11·7:1 in 1911. Thereafter it continued to widen, particularly after the First World War, until it reached 15·0:1 in 1921. It was the size of this gap, combined with the fall in the price of gold, that induced the mining industry to try to make the colour bar a little less rigid. The attempt led (p. 10) to the Rand rebellion with its Pyrric victory for the Chamber of

---

[1] Monthly wage rates have been multiplied by twelve for purposes of comparison (sources, see pp. 3-4).
[2] T.C.M. Annual Reports.

Mines. However, although it failed to crack the colour bar, the Chamber was able to reduce white wages substantially and the ratio between average cash earnings of the two colour groups narrowed to 11·2:1, the smallest it had been for a quarter of a century. For the next ten years the cash earnings of both white and black remained almost stationary, although in real terms, due to falling prices, wages rose during the 1930s. However, with the outbreak of the Second World War, the earnings gap started to widen again. By 1946 it was 12·7:1. Five years later it was 14·7:1, and by 1956 the gap was wider even than it had been at the time of the Rand rebellion in 1922. But things

TABLE 5. *Annual cash earnings on gold mines, 1911–69*

Date	Current rands[a]		Index of real earnings[b]		Earnings gap Ratio W:B
	White	Black[c]	White	Black	
			(1936 = 100)		
1911	666	57	102	100	11·7:1
1916	709	59	94	90	12·0:1
1921	992	66	90	69	15·0:1
1926	753	67	85	88	11·2:1
1931	753	66	90	92	11·3:1
1936	786	68	100	100	11·5:1
1941	848	70	94	89	12·1:1
1946	1,106	87	99	92	12·7:1
1951	1,607	109	113	89	14·7:1
1956	2,046	132	119	89	15·5:1
1961	2,478	146	129	89	17·0:1
1966	3,216	183	149	99	17·6:1
1969	4,006	199	172	99	20·1:1

[a] Divide by 2 to obtain the value of wages in pounds sterling for all years prior to 1968.
[b] Using Retail Price Index calculated from 1938 as the base year. Real earnings were then converted to an index taking 1936 = 100.
[c] This category includes coloured persons and, for 1911 and 1916, a small proportion of Indians. For discussion about the wages of these groups see Appendix 6.
SOURCES: G.M.E., Annual Reports 1911–61.
　　　　Department of Mines, Mining Statistics 1966–9.

were not to stop there; five years later, in 1961, the gap had widened to 17·0:1. And during the 1960s, a decade that had started with political unrest and a re-appraisal, by businessmen, of African wages, the gap continued to widen until, by 1969, it was no less than 20·1:1.

Another striking feature of the table is the fact that, in real terms, using 1938 as the base year, black cash earnings in 1969 were no higher and possibly even lower than they had been in 1911. For whites, on the other hand, real cash earnings increased by 70%. And, although there is no price index with which to adjust figures before 1911, it is worth noting that, between 1889 and 1911, white cash earnings probably rose whilst those for blacks fell by more than 25%.

However the above table provides an incomplete picture of the structure of earnings in the mining industry. It contains none of the substantial wages in kind that are provided to both black and white workers on the mines. Moreover the figures are averages which tell us nothing about the distribution of wages within each racial group; and they provide no information about possible changes in skill which might have affected the pattern of earnings. Thus before being able to determine the possible reasons for the massive shift in the distribution of incomes to which table 5 points, it is necessary to break down the overall averages into their component parts, to make due allowance for earnings in kind, and to consider the problems inherent in any comparison between black and white incomes.

CASH EARNINGS

The cash-earnings structure, over much of the period under consideration, was first established in 1927 by the Mining Industry Arbitration Board which was asked to examine certain wage demands made to the Gold Producers' Committee by the Mineworkers' Union and the Reduction Workers Association.[1] This Lucas award (named after the chairman of the Board) laid down the minimum rates of wages of employees in occupations covered by the two unions, and in the same year arbitrators laid down the minimum rates for mechanics, engine drivers, and associated workers. After 1927 there were considerable changes in the minimum rates, but much of the subsequent increase in white earnings was through the introduction and increase of allowances such as those for leave and the cost of living. White miners, the men responsible for supervising gangs of black workers at the stope face, were in a special position. Some of them were employed at daily rates of pay but others were paid by results.[2] The earnings of these contractors depend, as we have seen, on the amount of ore that the gang of men under them extracts on the frontiers of the mine.[3] The significance of the contractors lies in the fact that this method of payment-by-results has enabled them to capture the rewards of increased labour productivity without sharing them

---

[1] South Africa, *Conditions of Employment*, p. 3 A.

[2] In stoping, development, and shaft-sinking, earnings per shift of contract workers in 1911 were 29%, 75% and 102% higher, respectively, than earnings of day's pay men in similar jobs. By 1957 (the last year for which figures were published) the proportions were 20%, 48%, and −27% respectively. Numbers are not available for 1911 and 1957 but in 1936 89% of the 3,612 developers, stopers, and shaft sinkers in the gold mines were contract workers (sources: G.M.E., Annual Reports).

[3] See p. 55.

E

with the other (black) men who help to achieve the results. Furthermore, the earnings of the contractors set the pace for miners being paid at daily rates, and hence for all whites in the industry. Less is known about the structure of cash earnings for blacks, but it too was built upon a foundation of minimum rates which varied, although less widely than white rates, according to a few broad categories of jobs. But the structure was far simpler than for whites: there were few of the allowances and other benefits which raised white earnings far above their minimum levels.[1]

Of the various allowances to white workers, that awarded for the cost of living was, during much of the period under consideration, the most important. Following the Rand rebellion in 1922, the cost of living allowance which had previously been paid to officials on the gold mines was withdrawn, with a few minor exceptions. In spite of repeated efforts by the unions no cost of living allowance was granted by management until 1941 when, following a request by the Mining Unions' Joint Committee (M.U.J.C.), the Gold Producers' Committee (G.P.C.) of the Chamber of Mines agreed that an allowance of one penny (0·8 cents) per shift qualifying for leave should be made for each six-point increase in the retail price index number for food, light, fuel, rent and sundries, on the Witwatersrand. The G.P.C. followed this up later in the same year by recommending that the cost of living allowance be paid to all mine officials in receipt of salaries between R30 and R170 per month at the rate of 25 cents per month for each six-point rise of the price index. Juniors, earning less than R30 a month, were to receive half the allowance. And in the same year, following a request by the M.U.J.C., the cost of living allowance was increased by 15%. Much of the increase in white earnings after that date was due to further increases in this allowance. By 1949, only eight years after it was introduced, it formed no less than one-fifth of white cash earnings. And in 1955, by which time the allowance formed more than a quarter of cash wages, part of it was consolidated into the basic wages. For black mine workers, on the other hand, despite the recommendation of a government commission in 1944, there is no cost of living allowance.[2]

Paid leave for white mine employees was first introduced with effect from the beginning of 1934. Underground workers on completion of 312 qualifying shifts (i.e. a working shift exclusive of overtime) were granted 18 week-days leave on full pay.[3] After 624 qualifying shifts their leave was 24 week-days;

1 See Appendixes 7 and 18 for detailed statistics.
2 South Africa, *Report of the Witwatersrand Mine Natives' Wages Commission on the Remuneration and Conditions of Employment of Natives on Witwatersrand Gold Mines 1943* (Lansdown) (U.G. 21, Pretoria, 1944) para. 287 A.
3 For black mineworkers one year is generally taken to be 313 working shifts.

on completion of 936, and every subsequent 312 shifts, they were granted 24 week-days leave with pay for 30 days. Surface workers, except those in dusty occupations where pneumoconiosis was a danger, were granted 18 week-days leave for every 312 shifts completed. In subsequent years the annual amount of leave pay increased substantially, as did the length of leave. But the proportion of total cash earnings paid for leave remained fairly constant at approximately 10% throughout the period. For black mine workers, excluding only the tiny minority who are not migrant labourers, there is no paid leave.

Payments in the Witwatersrand Gold Mines Employees Provident Fund, which was established for white workers in 1934, are made only by employers, both in the form of occasional lump sums as well as by means of a monthly contribution according to the number of white employees in service. During 1938 a new branch of the provident fund was inaugurated whereby employers deposited, monthly, into the savings branch a sum of money that varied with the number of shifts worked by each employee. It was originally intended that the benefits paid out in lump sums by the provident fund should, as from 1939, be converted into pensions and the payout spread over the years of retirement. However, the unions opposed the Chamber's plan which was dropped, and in 1946 a pension fund for mine officials was established; both employers and employees agreed to contribute 5% each of basic salaries. Following the gold price rise in 1949 a second pension fund was established for all day's pay men on the same contributory basis. Once again, blacks are excluded from these advantages. Although it is organised somewhat differently, medical care for black mineworkers is in general as good as it is for whites, although in the case of Africans the care does not include their families left behind in the rural areas.[1] No medical benefit allowance is paid but the cost of all treatment, both preventative and curative, is borne by the industry.[2] By law every mine has to have a properly equipped hospital for its black employees and there is, in addition, the W.N.L.A. hospital which deals with more serious operations and rehabilitation work of those crippled by accidents at work.

The medical benefit allowance was introduced in 1936 with the purpose of assisting white mine employees, including officials, to pay their subscriptions to the Mines Medical Benefit Society of which they were all members. This allowance (which was begun at the rate of R15 a year for each white employee)

---

[1] It should be noted that much of the money accruing to the deferred pay interest fund is made over, in the form of grants, to hospitals working in the rural areas from which migrants come (see p. 136). Further details about the grants made by the fund are to be found in the *Report of the Witwatersrand Mine Natives' Wages Commission*, p. 61 A.

[2] See pp. 68, 95.

49

was equal to the cost of complete health insurance for employees and their families. In 1969, for example, the Chamber of Mines increased the allowance by a total of R1·3 million[1] and it has been raised several times to meet increased costs. Minor ailments are treated by one of a panel of private doctors. For more serious operations there is the Cottesloe hospital built just before the Second World War by the Chamber of Mines. After the sterling devaluation in 1949 and the rise in the gold price the medical allowance was consolidated into the minimum rate of wages. In 1955 the G.P.C. assisted the Medical Benefit Society by buying a nursing home at a total cost of R300,000. At the same time mines in the Orange Free State paid R10,000 for the additional costs of medical services during the year.

There had been some form of compensation for mine workers injured on the job ever since the first Workers' Compensation Act was passed in 1911. A new Act in 1941 formed the basis of subsequent legislation under which compensation paid to an injured man or his dependants was calculated according to his earnings at the time of the accident. Under the rules, compensation for an average worker totally and permanently disabled by a mining accident was a lump sum of approximately R1,228 if he was black and an annual pension (paid monthly) of R1,800 if he were white.[2]

A great deal of feeling amongst both white and black mineworkers was generated over the years about the industry's responsibility for one particular hazard of mining, pneumoconiosis. The disease is caused by dust getting into the lungs, which then become more vulnerable to tuberculosis. It was not until after the First World War that adequate steps were taken to reduce the amount of dust in the mines. Before the development of water-fed drills and the introduction of hoses to spray water in areas that had just been blasted, the concentration of dust was so high that the men working on the drills were likely to get bad silicosis within five or six years. The problem was aggravated for whites by the fact that many of the miners during the early years came from mines in Cornwall where they had already inhaled a lot of dust. During the first 25 years after Union no less than eleven Acts were passed dealing with pneumoconiosis compensation. By 1936 a total of 5,200 white miners had been granted monthly allowances for secondary silicosis or for silicosis with tuberculosis; 3,500 of these miners had already died by 1936; their average life expectancy from the time they received their certificates from the Phthisis Board being no more than five years. In

[1] *Star*, 20 October 1969.
[2] Figures, supplied by Rand Mutual Assurance Co., are based on average cash earnings for 1969. Whites might also be granted a constant attendance allowance; for blacks, once the compensation had been exhausted, there would probably be 'a small extra-statutory allowance' for life.

addition to these monthly payments the Board also made lump-sum awards, varying between approximately R600 and R1,700 for ante-primary and primary silicosis.[1] To meet these costs the mining companies were, by this date, paying an annual levy of R2 million into the miners' phthisis compensation fund.[2] Black mineworkers at this time received some compensation for lung diseases caused or aggravated by their work. But in 1943 the Miners' Phthisis Acts Commission reported that the evidence it had received disclosed 'a disquieting state of affairs in regard to the compensation, the medical examination and the after-care of Native employees who have contracted compensatable lung diseases'.[3] The Commission recommended the immediate establishment of a country-wide system for the adequate compensation and medical treatment of all Africans suffering from such diseases. By 1967 the compensation fund was paying out an annual total of approximately R10 million, mainly in the form of pensions or lump-sum benefits. Of this total approximately two-thirds went to white (including some Coloured) employees or their dependants and the remaining one-third to blacks.[4] Between 1964 and 1967 the average number of whites – working in all types of mines – who were certified each year as having a compensatory lung disease was 605; the average number of blacks was 5,930.[5] In 1967 the average compensation for men suffering from pneumoconiosis combined with tuberculosis was, in the case of whites, a pension equivalent to R1,230 a year, and in the case of blacks a once and for all payment of R576.[6] In addition to the cost of compensation the Chamber of Mines bears approximately half the costs of the pneumoconiosis research unit which was established in 1956. During the three years 1966–9 the annual cost to the Chamber was R100,000.[7]

It is difficult to quantify precisely the relative extent of care which the industry took with regard to blacks and whites suffering from pneumoconiosis and from tuberculosis caused by it. For apart from differences in the amount of compensation paid, the method of treatment is not the same for the two groups. White miners who develop tuberculosis have access to the Springkell Sanatorium where they are looked after for several months until they are cured. The costs of maintaining the sanatorium, which rose from

1 Department of Mines, *Report of the Miners' Phthisis Board for the Period 1st April, 1935 to 31st March, 1936* (U.G. 18, Pretoria, 1937), pp. 13–15 A.   2 *Ibid.* p. 8.
3 South Africa, *Report of the Miners' Phthisis Acts Commission, 1941–1943* (U.G. 22, Pretoria, 1943), p. 24 A.
4 South Africa, *Report of the Pneumoconiosis Commissioner for the year ended 31 March 1967* (R.P. 20, Pretoria, 1968), p. 20 A.   5 *Ibid.* p. 10.
6 *Ibid.* pp. 14, 20 A. Mine Labour Organizations (Wenela) Ltd., *Report of the Board of Directors for the Year Ended 31st December, 1967* (Johannesburg, 1968) p. 8 A.
7 T.C.M., *Seventy Seventh Annual Report* (1966), p. 33 A.

R40,000 in 1939 to R254,000 in 1962, are borne by the Chamber of Mines. Africans on the other hand used to be sent home as soon as the tuberculosis had been checked[1] but it was found that, with the lack of food at home, tuberculosis often recurred and the ex-miner infected others. Thus, Africans who develop tuberculosis on the mines are now kept in bed for three or four weeks before being sent home armed with antibiotics and the address of a rural clinic where they can obtain more. Unfortunately, however, many men fail to keep taking the antibiotics regularly and so tuberculosis recurs.

Another important fund – which has remained largely unused – was established in 1939 by the Minister of Labour to provide incomes for white mineworkers should they ever find themselves unemployed. Contributions were made both by employers and employees, but by 1969 the fund seemed to have lapsed. There was no similar fund for the black labour force.

In addition to the various allowances outlined above there were a number of *ad hoc* payments to whites. For example, in May 1943, the Mineworkers' Union submitted to the G.P.C. a demand for a 30% increase in wages. This was not granted but the following year an agreement was signed whereby the industry agreed to provide R200,000 a year for five years for housing and co-operative or other schemes designed by the union for the benefit of its members.[2] An additional sum of R50,000 was made immediately available to the union for use in connection with these schemes. However in 1948, a year before the 'lump sum payments' were due to cease, a new executive committee of the M.W.U. estimated that, because of corruption and mal-administration, less than one-third of the R680,000 so far paid by the G.P.C. had been of any benefit to the actual rank and file members of the union.[3] As a result of this lump-sum agreement the M.U.J.C. requested the industry to pay to the individuals of the other unions a sum equivalent to that paid to the M.W.U. – but in the form of an additional medical benefit allowance to individuals. This allowance was due to cease at the end of October 1949, but, in view of the sterling devaluation in mid-September, the G.P.C. agreed to continue paying it out on a month to month basis (to M.W.U. members as well) until the van Eck Commission, appointed to enquire into white conditions of employment in the gold mining industry, had submitted its report.[4] An 'active service allowance', introduced soon after the outbreak of the Second World War, was also applicable only to whites. After 1945 ex-servicemen who returned to the mines received a

---

[1] That is, as soon as three sputa had been found negative.
[2] T.C.M. *Fifty Fifth Annual Report* (1944) A.
[3] See South Africa, *Reports of the Mine Workers Union Commission of Enquiry*, U.G. 36 of 1946 and U.G. 52 of 1951.
[4] South Africa, *Conditions of Employment* (U.G. 28, Pretoria, 1950). A.

gratuity calculated at the rate of R60 for each year of full-time military service. For Indian and 'Eurafrican' (Coloured) employees the gratuity was calculated at the rate of R24 a year. For blacks there was nothing.

So much then for the breakdown of the component parts of the average cash wage. We must turn now to consider the distribution of wages about the average.[1] Full details of white cash earnings were published annually in the Reports of the Government Mining Engineer up until 1949. Thereafter, for one of those mysterious reasons known only to the keepers of statistical records, an invaluable source of information suddenly dried up. In 1936, when the mean white cash wage per shift was 252 cents the median wage was 225 cents. For officials alone the median was R78·8 a month (265 cents a shift) and for day's pay men it was 224 cents a shift. By 1946 the overall mean had risen to 354 cents a shift, and the median to just under 250 cents a shift. The reason for the wide difference between the mean and the median in 1946 was not due to a greater skewness in the distribution of white earnings as much as to the fact that the figures from which the means were calculated included all allowances, which the median figures did not. Between 1936 and 1946 white basic rates of pay did not increase very much but allowances became a substantial proportion of overall earnings. A measure of the internal changes in the white wage structure may be taken from table 6 which shows earnings for particular jobs between 1936 and 1956 when another source in the Government Mining Engineer's annual report disappeared. When measured in real terms it appears that, apart from apprentices, the incomes of all these workers actually declined slightly between 1936 and 1946. Thereafter they rose substantially.

Little is known about the distribution of black wages on the mines. Far less information than for whites was published, even before 1949, in the Government Mining Engineer's reports. The Chamber of Mines, although most helpful about other material, refused to make available unconditionally to me any information on this particular topic. Thus, only for 1943, when the Lansdown Commission was investigating the conditions of black mine-workers, is there any detailed information. In that year the mean cash earnings of the total black labour force of 300,000 men was 23 cents a shift and the median was 20 cents. In 1954 earnings for all underground workers other than 'boss-boys' varied from a minimum of 30 cents per shift to a maximum of 44 cents for underground police. 'Boss-boy' earnings varied from 36 to 59 cents a shift. In addition to these wage payments the average piecework bonus per man per underground shift varied from zero to 2 cents. There were other bonuses such as that for first aid (averaging 2 cents a shift).

[1] See Appendix 8.

TABLE 6. *Wage rates for selected white jobs, 1936–56*

	Current cents/shift		
	1936	1946[b]	1956[c]
Shift-bosses, underground[a]	351	366	731 (n.a.)[d]
Contract miners machine stoping, underground	299	356	622 (738)
Fitters and turners, surface	233	243	451 (692)
Trammers, underground	206	258	549 (722)
Clerks, surface[a]	202	237	446 (n.a.)
Apprentices, surface	56	93	178 (258)

[a] Paid monthly: shift rate worked out by dividing by 26.
[b] Including allowances but excluding overtime, savings fund allowances etc. To be more directly comparable with 1936 the figures for 1946 would have to be raised by about 10% to take into account various allowances which did not exist in 1936 and which were excluded from the 1946 figures.
[c] Excluding overtime, leave pay, medical benefit allowances, savings fund allowances and cost of living allowances, but including bonus.
[d] Figures in parentheses include the components excluded under note c.

SOURCES: G.M.E., Annual Reports, 1936–56.

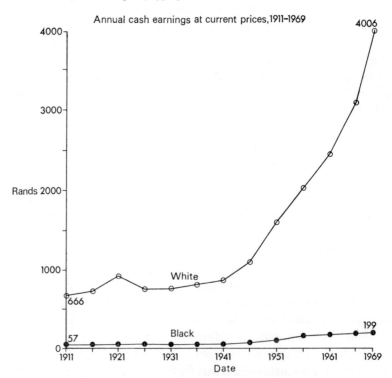

Fig. 4 Annual cash earnings at current prices, 1911–69
Source: Table 5, p. 46

The total underground rate, including overtime and all bonuses but excluding the additional half shift for Sundays, varied from 37 cents on one mine to 40 cents on the highest paid mine.[1] By 1961 the mean had risen, in current terms,[2] to 47 cents a shift. On one mine for which figures were made available most of the workers earned a basic 32 cents plus a bonus of 7 cents, whilst for 'boss-boys' the basic rate was 42 cents and the bonus 22 cents.

There were two important changes in the wage structure during the 1960s. The first came as a result of the disturbances in Langa and Sharpeville in 1960 when one of the mining groups decided that it should raise black wages (see p. 106). Thus the group took active steps to raise the productivity of black workers in the mines under its control. Under the scheme, jobs were graded into five main unskilled or semi-skilled categories and four supervisory ones. On the three mines in which the scheme was first introduced the average skill distribution of the black labour force into the different categories was approximately as follows: unskilled 67%, semi-skilled 20%, supervisory 11%.[3] The new rates of pay for these jobs varied between 25 and 167 cents a shift; the median being 64 cents. These substantial pay increases (between 35% and 45% for most of the mines of the group) were not achieved in one jump but were introduced over a period of three years by means of successively higher scales.[4]

The expectation that these increases would contribute to a narrowing of the gap between black and white earnings was not fulfilled, for in 1967 after prolonged negotiation and numerous strikes by white miners, the second major change in the industry's wage structure was introduced. This was the concept that all white wage increases be based explicitly upon improved 'productivity'. In terms of the new agreement the 22,000 members of the gold mining unions were upgraded from 'day's pay men' and put onto a monthly salary basis at a considerably higher rate than they had been earning before.[5] In return for an 11% increase in earnings the unions agreed to the elimination of various restrictive practices in order to allow better use of labour. The increases in productivity were to come not, as one might have expected, from harder work by those benefiting from the agreement, but from the fact that blacks were to be allowed to do jobs that they had not been allowed to do legally before. The white mining unions were in a unique bargaining position and the agreement of 1967 was a striking demonstration

---

[1] Based on a cross-sample of black workers in four mines. N.I.P.R.D., tables 4–6.
[2] 'Current terms' refers to the value of money on the specified dates.
[3] See Appendix 9.
[4] See Appendix 10.
[5] The concept, of course, was not new. Implicitly it had been built into the white wage structure for years. See p. 47.

of their ability to use this power to obtain a high price for even the smallest upward shift of the colour bar (see p. 116).

One important service provided for blacks but not for whites is the system of deferred pay under which migrant workers are able to save part of their earnings until they get home where they can draw it from the local recruiting office. The system is voluntary for South Africans but in terms of the agreements with Mozambique and Malawi the workers from there are compelled to wait until they get home for up to one-half of their wages. The cost of administering the system is met out of the interest which accrues to the deferred pay interest fund from investment, at call, both of the deferred pay itself and money which workers deposit for safe-keeping with the compound managers. The bulk of the fund is given to hospitals and medical missions in the areas from which the migrant workers come. From the inception of the system in 1918 until 1943 the annual amount available for distribution was approximately R12,000. It has probably increased considerably since then.[1]

WAGES IN KIND

It has been argued by the mining industry that although the cash wages of black mineworkers might seem to be abnormally low, if one takes into account the wages paid in kind, the gap between black and white earnings is not as high as it appears at first glance.[2] To assess this claim it is necessary to examine in detail the earnings in kind of both blacks and whites.

Discussion about the cash equivalent of wages in kind has long been bedevilled by dispute as to the difference between the *cost* of such earnings to the industry and their *value* to the recipient worker. The figure used can so easily depend upon what one is wanting to prove. From an analytical point of view, however, it is clear that it is *cost* which is important when considering the demand for labour, and *value* which influences the supply. In practice the figures generally available are those relating to the cost to the mines of providing these wages; it is more difficult to obtain estimates of their value to employees. For example, it is argued that the cost of food supplied by the industry to a black worker is considerably lower (because of the difference between wholesale and retail prices) than the worker would have to pay for the same food in the market. This is true: but at the same time it is necessary to bear in mind that a man who has come to town to earn money to feed and clothe his family might, in order to save more, prefer to buy less food for

1 South Africa, *Witwatersrand Mine Natives' Wages Commission*, pp. 32–3 A.
2 T.C.M., *Gold in South Africa*, p. 25 A.

himself. It is arguable that, faced with the choice of free food or the cash equivalent of its *cost* to the industry, men might choose the cash – provided that there were adequate food shops near the mines. It is worth noting that on the diamond mines, which have never found it necessary to recruit labour, African workers are not provided with food but buy it for themselves. In 1960 it was estimated that diamond workers spent an average of 13 cents a day on food compared with the 12 cents per man which it cost the gold mines to feed their men. Moreover the diamond workers saved or sent home 36% of their wage bill, compared with 18% by gold miners.[1] One of the main reasons why the gold mines feed their black workers rather than pay extra wages is to ensure that the men remain fit enough for the hard physical work involved in deep underground mining. Between 1936 and 1969 the cost of foodstuffs supplied free to black miners rose in current terms from 3 to 15 cents a day (including Sundays) for each man,[2] an increase in real terms of approximately 50%. Generally speaking very little food is supplied to white workers whose wages are high enough and whose wives live near enough to ensure that they are fed properly. However for officials, most of whom are on the surface at lunch time, some mines have subsidised canteens. No information is available as to the exact size of the subsidy but I have had a meal on one of the new mines at a price approximately one-third, if not one-quarter, the cost of a similar meal in a café. Also all mines provide tea, twice daily to white surface workers, and in unlimited quantities to underground workers when they come up from their shifts into the changing rooms.

Another major form of wages in kind is housing. The vast majority of black workers are housed in compounds or hostels where the men live in dormitories. For the 1% who are allowed to bring their families with them, small houses and gardens are provided until the men leave or retire. The pattern of compound housing for the migrant labourers differs little from mine to mine, although there is considerable difference in quality between the older and the newer mines. The number of men in a single compound or hostel varies from 2,400 to 7,000, and the numbers in each room vary from 12 (in mines built after the Second World War), to 20 on mines built during the 1930s, to between 60 and 90 in those mines developed before the First World War.[3] Washing facilities are available in the form of showers with hot

[1] E. J. B. Sewel, 'Native labour and payment on Premier Diamond Mine', *Papers and Discussions of the Association of Mine Managers of South Africa* (T.C.M., Johannesburg, 1960–1), pp. 841 ff. A. Gold mine remittances exclude money not sent home through official channels.
[2] See Appendix 11.
[3] T.C.M. and W.N.L.A., Annual Reports A. In 1968 the Johannesburg City Council agreed to lease the old compounds from disused mines (Robinson Deep and Crown Mines, No. 17 shaft) as a 'temporary solution' to the problem of finding 10,000 beds for single African men working in Johannesburg (*Star*, 28 August 1968).

and cold water, and there are large sinks for washing clothes. On the newer mines there are dining rooms and, in some mines, better quality bedrooms for more senior men. In compounds built before 1939, beds are not supplied and men either sleep on the concrete bunks or they have to make, or buy from their predecessors, wooden beds specially designed to fit the short bunks. In some compounds the bunks have concrete sides and tops as well so that men can only enter them by crawling in at one end. On the older mines there are no dining rooms and men eat either outside or in their dormitories which generally have a coal stove for heating purposes. The photographs between pages 38 and 39 give some impression of the difference in quality between the older 'compounds' and the newer 'hostels'. At the end of 1964, 51% of the black labour was living in hostels built after 1945 while 19% was living in compounds built before the First World War. By 1969 the proportions were 71% and 15% respectively.

To an outside visitor the most noticeable feature of the compounds, apart from the sheer number of men in each, is the fact that no women are allowed into them. An examination of the full social implications of the migrant labour system lies beyond the scope of this study, but a visit to any of the compounds impresses one forcefully with the extraordinary nature of an industry, whose demand for labour is not seasonal, and which has relied for many decades on workers who are not allowed to settle with their wives and children near their place of work.[1] Mining officials have been known to describe the method of organisation in a compound as one which preserves the traditional tribal pattern of authority. In reality it most resembles an all-male boarding school of the Thomas Arnold tradition with its system of housemaster (compound manager), prefects (indunas), seniors (izibondo) and boys ('boys').

The cost of the compound housing was estimated in 1943 to be 2 cents a man shift, exclusive of 0.8 cents for the capital cost of compound and hospital buildings.[2] By 1960 this had risen, for one group, to 5 cents; an increase in real terms of 45%. That fraction of the black labour force which lives in family housing on the mines works mainly in secretarial and administrative posts. Their housing was estimated, by one group in the 1960s, to cost R110 a year for each family. R86 of this was for the amortisation, over 20 years of the capital cost of R1,000, and R24 for the cost of fuel which is also free.

For whites the situation is somewhat different. In the older mines, the

---

[1] See pp. 137–9. Cf. also D. Hobart Houghton, *The South African Economy* (O.U.P., Cape Town, 1964), ch. 4; N. Robb, 'Apartheid's labour system', *South African Outlook* XCVIII (July 1968), pp. 103–7; and F. R. Mohlabi, 'Moral effects of the system of migratory labour on the labourer and his family', *Mapumulo Consultation*, 1971 C.
[2] South Africa, *Witwatersrand Mine Natives' Wage Commission*, p. 7 A.

mining companies have never attempted to house all their workers, most of whom, except for a few key men, live in the surrounding suburbs. But in the newer mines, situated far from the main urban centres, the companies found it necessary to build houses – indeed whole towns – for their white employees. Subsidised housing is one of the juiciest carrots used in trying to entice qualified miners from the established areas into the more rural surroundings of the West Rand and the Orange Free State. The exact nature of the subsidy varies from group to group and from mine to mine, but it is generally true to say that all the mines in the areas developed after 1945 provide housing for the great majority of their white employees at rentals far below the cost price. The quality of this housing was fully described by Mr. Harry Oppenheimer when replying, in 1950, to an accusation by the Minister of Labour that, although the mining companies took particular pains to have a satisfied black labour force, they did not consider it so necessary to do that for their white employees. According to Mr. Oppenheimer none of the houses on the new mines of his group were less than 1,150 square feet in size, which compared with an average of approximately 800 square feet for workmen's low rental houses in Britain and the United States. No house stood in a plot less than a quarter of an acre; nor did it have less than three bedrooms, a bathroom, a separate w.c., a lounge, a dining recess, and a kitchen. Houses all had servants' quarters, an enclosed back yard, and a garage. And they were all supplied with built-in cupboards, an electric stove, and a geyser providing hot water to both kitchen and bathroom. The minimum cost of building such a house had been R5,000.[1] By 1965 this group provided six main types of houses for their white employees in the Orange Free State, with a tax-free subsidy which varied between R41 a month for the cottages and flats available to day's pay men, and R330 a month for the mine manager's house. Similar subsidies were available on the new mines of all other groups. Rents actually paid by those living in the houses varied between R10 and R20 a month.[2] At a conservative estimate, the average housing subsidy for all white employees on the mines developed after the Second World War was R512 a year, tax free. An average of 164 cents a shift is a not insignificant perquisite for approximately half of all whites working in the industry.

The third major form of earnings in kind are the facilities provided for recreation. For whites there are club amenities available at heavily subsidised fees. In 1953, before many of the post-war mines had started production, there were 37 cricket fields, 63 football fields, 20 golf courses, 255 tennis courts, 83 bowling greens, and 38 swimming baths for the 46,000 whites

[1] *S.A.M. and E.J.*, 18 November 1950.　　　　　　　　[2] See Appendix 12.

employed by the industry.[1] For the 291,000 blacks the recreational facilities included a bar lounge in each compound and a total of 101 playing fields and 55 dance arenas. In addition, one or two of the newer mines had first-class cycle and cinder tracks on which some of the country's best athletes were produced. The most popular pastimes are soccer, cycling, athletics, and dancing, all of which draw crowds of spectators. For the select few with family houses on the mines facilities include tennis courts and, on a few mines, swimming baths. There are also voluntary literacy classes for one or two hours a week. In six mines of one group there were, in 1965, 1,000 pupils a week for a course which lasted three months. On the average some 60% of these men were expected to become literate in their own language. Having done this they were then allowed, if they wished, to become literate in English or Afrikaans. At this date it was estimated that between 40% and 50% of those who came to the mines were already literate in some language; this was considerably more than five years previously.[2] Once again it is difficult to quantify differences in the cost per man of recreational facilities provided by the mines for the two colour groups. But there is no doubt that the costs for whites are considerably higher than for blacks, not least because on the mines in the Orange Free State (which in 1964 employed 25% of the total labour force) recreational facilities for blacks are financed from the profits on the sales of sweets and cigarettes in the dry canteens in each compound.

Clothing issued either free or below cost price should, some might think, be included as part of wages in kind. However such clothing is more accurately classified as capital equipment without which men cannot perform their work efficiently. Indeed although boots, which in the 1960s cost the mines R2·50 a pair, were sold to workers for R1·45 (approximately one tenth of a month's salary), the subsidy was in fact doing no more than help the men to meet a cost that was primarily incurred during the course of their work.

PROBLEMS OF COMPARISON

Any attempt to compare the relative movement of black and white earnings in the gold mining industry involves a number of difficulties. At no stage in the production process do blacks and whites officially do the same jobs. Thus any comparison of earnings has to take into account the different skill distributions of the occupations filled by the two colour groups. This is more easily said than done, for although it is in general true to say that whites hold skilled and semi-skilled jobs while blacks do semi-skilled and unskilled work

[1] T.C.M. (P.R.D. Series No. 34, Johannesburg, 1953) A.   [2] *Rand Daily Mail*, 4 August 1967.

The structure of earnings

there are nevertheless many blacks, particularly in the supervisory ('boss-boy') class, who are considerably more skilled than many day's pay men who rank above them. No detailed information has been made available to enable a comparison of the relative earnings of the less skilled white workers underground and the highly competent senior 'boss-boys'. Nor is one able to find out the relative earnings in those few occupations where black and white do almost identical jobs such as driving locomotives (see p. 116). Changes in the relative average earnings of the two groups may have been due partly to changes in the distribution of skills within each. Few figures are available to measure whether or not any redistribution of skill occurred. In 1940, officials (including secretarial staff) constituted 22% of the white labour force in the mines on the Witwatersrand;[1] by 1946 the proportion had risen to 30%.[2] On the other hand the development of the economy had so increased the opportunities for skilled employment that in 1957 the *S.A. Mining and Engineering Journal* pointed out that 'far too many South African artisans cannot measure up to their counterparts in the major industrial countries'.[3] Indeed, one of the barriers to the full development of the mines in the Orange Free State was the poor quality of the white miners.[4] This suggests that the skill capacity of white mine employees at the bottom end of the ladder may actually have fallen over time. However without more information than is yet available, it is impossible to determine whether the relative skill distribution within the two racial groups working on the mines altered over time or not. But in view of the developments in the training of black workers which took place after the Second World War (see p. 93) it seems likely that the difference in skill between the 'average' white and the 'average' black worker narrowed rather than widened over the period under consideration.

The second major problem encountered in comparing average earnings is that wages in kind vary widely from mine to mine depending on their age and geographical location. Whites on the old mines between Johannesburg and Springs are not provided with the subsidised housing that is offered to miners in the new, more isolated, areas of the West Rand and Orange Free State. Similarly blacks are far more comfortably housed on the newer mines. Paradoxically both blacks and whites in general prefer to work on the old mines. The reasons for this have not been deeply probed but the scraps of evidence available suggest that for whites the reason may lie in the social disadvantages of living in a small mining town as compared with the area

[1] Jeppe, *Gold Mining*, p. 1734 B.
[2] G.M.E., *Annual Report including Reports of the Government Mining Engineer and the Geological Survey for the Year ended 31st December 1946* (U.G. 36, Pretoria, 1947) A.
[3] *S.A.M. and E.J.*, 23 August 1957.   [4] *Mining Journal*, 2 December 1955.

around Johannesburg. As for blacks, a friend who was a migrant worker over the decade 1954–64 explained to me that the mines in the Orange Free State were far too dangerous for him ever to want to go there.[1] A compound manager of an older mine on the East Rand thought the reason for its popularity was due partly to the fact that it was a shallower mine and thus cooler to work in, and partly that it had only one basic shift a day compared with the Free State goldfields where there are three shifts but no night bonus. Whatever the reasons, the fact remains that mineworkers of both colour groups discount, fairly heavily, the perquisites offered in the newer areas. Moreover, the fact that these variations apply to both groups means that comparisons of average black and white earnings is not significantly distorted by them.

For the comparison to be meaningful, it is also necessary to ensure that the earnings relate to comparable units of working time. The annual average earnings discussed (p. 46) were obtained by dividing the total wage bill by the number of persons 'in service'. But not all those in service were actually at work on any particular day. The reasons for this difference or wastage have remained much the same over the years.[2] For blacks the chief causes of wastage are sickness and, in the case of newly arrived recruits, physical unfitness for work due to the change of climatic conditions. For whites on the other hand, a large proportion of the wastage is accounted for by annual leave which has increased over time. Of the 110 shifts (per 1,000 possible) lost by whites in 1956, 87 were for leave, 13 due to absence with permission, and 10 due to absence without permission. Between 1936 and 1963 out of every 100 men in service the average number of whites at work was 88, and the average number of blacks was 98. In 1947 the number of shifts lost because of sickness was, for whites, 29 per 1,000 and for blacks 8.

Commenting on this difference, the Government Mining Engineer pointed out that the figures 'emphasise the benefits accruing to the industry from the control it enjoys over its native labour as a result of the "compound" system of housing'.[3] In addition to these differences is the fact that, in general, blacks worked longer hours than whites. By law each group is supposed to work a 48-hour week, but I was informed in 1965 that although this was true of whites, blacks spent approximately ten hours a day, six days a week,

---

[1] See Appendix 13.
[2] Wastage is a measure of the proportion of the labour force that is absent from work. It is defined as follows:

$$\text{Wastage} = \left(100 - \frac{\text{No. of persons at work}}{\text{No. of persons in service}} \times 100 \right) \%$$

See Appendix 14.
[3] G.M.E., *Annual Report* (1948) A.

between the time they got into a 'cage' to go underground and the time they got back to the surface. Not all this time was spent actually at the face or getting there and back to the shaft, for when they arrived underground most blacks had, until the 1967 productivity agreement (p. 176) to spend an hour or more at the foot of the shaft waiting for a white miner to arrive and examine the scene of blasting in the previous shift to check that it was safe. Having to wait as much as three and a half hours after work for a cage to take them to the surface was a major complaint of black miners to official commissions both in 1914 and in 1943.[1] Despite numerous requests by whites for a reduction of the working week to five and a half or five days, this has been consistently opposed by the Chamber, not only on the grounds of cost, but also because it fears that such a reduction would create unrest amongst the black labour force who would have too much idle time on their hands. 'One of the most important things in our welfare work', wrote one group in 1950, 'is to organise as much recreation for the African worker as possible in order to keep his mind occupied during his spare time.'[2]

Another factor to be taken into account is the distinction between what one might call consumption earnings and investment earnings. The former refer to all income which the employee receives for his own benefit; the latter refers to that part of income which, although it is part of the total earnings of an employee, may yet be regarded as a form of investment by the employer. For example, the free food supplied to black workers has long been regarded as a form of earnings in kind and is indeed an important factor in attracting labour to the mines. Nevertheless from the employer's point of view such expenditure may well be regarded as an investment, for better feeding of undernourished workers increases their productivity and, as we shall see in chapter 6, the rises in productivity are not necessarily followed by an increase in earnings but may accrue partly to the employers as a return on their investment. The same is true of education and training. Clearly it is impossible to draw a rigid distinction between consumption and investment earnings, but it must be realised that not all the earnings detailed in this chapter can be thought of as benefits accruing solely to the employees.

In correcting the comparative figures for these various differences, no account is taken of the fact that blacks generally spend longer underground than whites, nor of the fact that black jobs are considerably more dangerous and arduous than white. Also not taken into account are the costs of recruiting workers (see p. 73). Moreover it is impossible to make any quantitative comparisons over time of the costs of housing or of recreation. In 1960 the average

---

[1] South Africa, *Witwatersrand Mine Natives' Wages Commission*, p. 29 A.
[2] Rand Mines, *A Survey of African Welfare on Mines of the Group* (Johannesburg, 1950) B.

cost to one group, a number of whose mines were new, of housing black mineworkers was 3 cents per shift worked. This figure included maintenance of compound buildings, cleaning, heating, sanitation, and assessment rates to local authorities. For whites the housing subsidy on the new mines worked out at approximately 164 cents a shift at this date. With regard to recreation there are no figures for comparative costs, even for one year, but as already noted (pp. 59–60) there is no doubt that, as far as the mines were concerned, the cost of helping each white to relax was much higher than for each black.

Between 1936 and 1949 whites, for overtime work, were paid at time and a half; thereafter they have been paid at double time. For blacks there was no overtime pay until 1944, after which date the rate has been at time and a half.

Despite the difficulties in quantifying the wages in kind and in allowing for the differences in risk and working hours it is none the less possible to get a fairly accurate picture of the relative earnings of the two groups. There are figures which show that in 1961 the average underground wage paid to a black worker was 59% of the total cost – including recruiting expenses – of hiring him.[1] For whites it was estimated that, on three new mines in 1963, cash earnings varied between 51% and 59% of the total labour cost.[2] Given the similarity of these proportions it seems that it would be not unreasonable to compare relative earnings by contrasting the cash incomes (including allowances) of whites on the one hand with the cash incomes plus cost of food supplied to blacks on the other. Table 7 shows the relevant figures.

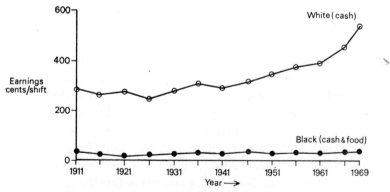

Fig. 5a   Earnings per shift worked (at 1938 prices), 1911–69

[1] In 1943 cash wages for black miners made up 68% of the total cost of hiring, including expenses of recruiting, housing, hospital and food. South Africa, *Witwatersrand Mine Natives' Wages Commission*, pp. 6–7.
[2] Figures kindly supplied by one of the mining houses.

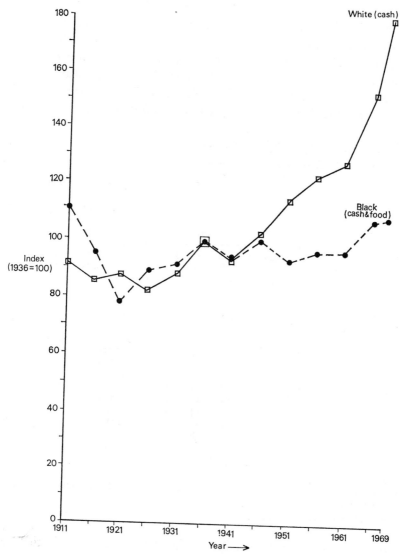

Fig. 5b Index of earnings per shift worked

Although the table does not include the considerable earnings in kind received by white mineworkers nor wages in kind other than food provided for black workers, there can be no doubt that the gap, or ratio, between average white and black earnings has always been large and that it increased rapidly during the 1950s and 1960s.

This movement is not only contrary to the pattern in other industrialised countries but was also quite different from what was happening in the South African industrial sector at the time. In the United States, for example, the gap between white and non-white median salary earnings fell between 1939 and 1953 from 2·4:1 to 1·7:1.[1] On the basis of the American experience, Reder suggested that the gap (or 'skill margin') between skilled and unskilled earnings tended to decline in periods of general labour shortage.[2] A similar narrowing of the skill margin occurred in Britain where, between 1880 and

TABLE 7. *Earnings per shift worked, 1911–69*

Year	White (cash including allowances) Cents	Black			Earnings gap	Index of real earnings[a]	
		Cash	Food	Total[b]	White : Black (cash) (cash and food)	White (cash)	Black (cash and food)
		Cents				1936 = 100	
1911	217	20	4	24	9·0:1	92	111
1916	233	20	4	24	9·7:1	86	96
1921	348	22	6	28	12·4:1	88	77
1926	263	22	4	26	10·1:1	82	89
1931	266	22	3	25	10·6:1	88	91
1936	283	23	4	26	10·7:1	100	100
1941	301	23	5	28	10·8:1	93	93
1946	411	29	9	37	11·1:1	102	100
1951	587	36	9	45	13·1:1	114	93
1956	760	43	13	56	13·6:1	123	96
1961	876	48	14	62	14·2:1	127	96
1966	1,170	59	17	77	15·2:1	151	107
1969	1,488	65	18	83	17·9:1	178	108

[a] Using retail price index calculated from 1938 as base year. Real earnings were then converted to an index, taking 1936 = 100.
[b] Due to rounding of figures this column is not always exactly equal to the sum of the previous two columns.
SOURCES: See Appendix 15, p. 168.

1950, the ratio of skilled to unskilled earnings fell substantially.[3] In the South African manufacturing sector the white–black earnings gap was not only much smaller than, but also moved differently from, that in the gold mines: between 1935 and 1946 it narrowed from 5·5:1 to 3·7:1 and then widened

[1] M. Zeman, *A Quantitative Analysis of White–Non-white Income Differentials in the United States* (Ph.D. thesis, Chicago, 1955), p. 25 D. The gap has not changed significantly since then. A. B. Batchelder, 'Decline in the relative income of Negro men', *Q.J.E.* LXXVIII (1964) C.
[2] M. W. Reder, 'The theory of occupational wage differentials', *A.E.R.* XLV (1955) C.
[3] K. G. J. C. Knowles and D. J. Robertson, 'Differences between the wages of skilled and unskilled workers, 1880–1950', *Bulletin of the Oxford Institute of Statistics* XII (1951).

The structure of earnings

again to 5·5:1 in 1962. By mid-1970 the gap was 5·7:1.[1] In order to understand both why the gap between black and white earnings in the gold mines was so large, and why it widened so much after the Second World War, it is necessary to turn to a detailed analysis of the forces operating in the labour market of Southern Africa.

[1] Office of Census and Statistics, *Census of Industrial Establishments 1935–6* (U.G. 24, Pretoria, 1938), Bureau of Statistics, *Statistical Year Book 1968* (South Africa, Pretoria, 1969). See Appendix 16.

CHAPTER 4

SUPPLY AND DEMAND

Nothing meaningful can be said about the particular wage level which will exist in a specific case unless we have knowledge of both demand and supply conditions.

Allan M. Cartter, *Theory of Wages and Employment*

At the simplest level, a man's earnings for a given unit of time may be thought of as the market price for his labour as determined by the interaction of supply and demand. Thus a necessary step in the deeper analysis of the wage structure is to clarify the different forces acting both on the supply of, and the demand for, labour. It is of course over-simple to assume that these forces act in isolation and do not affect each other, but before one can begin to understand the nature of their interaction one must examine each of them separately.

SUPPLY

By the 1930s, in spite of widespread recruiting in Southern Africa (see p. 3–5) the gold mining industry was still short of unskilled labour. Unwilling, for reasons that will be analysed in a subsequent chapter (p. 101), to augment the supply by raising wages, it sought to expand its recruiting services still further. There was little chance of doing this inside South Africa where the rise of manufacturing industries was providing the mines with stiff competition for labour; the only hope lay in increasing the number of labourers from Mozambique or in recruiting men from the tropics. Mozambique was difficult as the total number of recruits had been limited to a maximum of 80,000 a year under a new Mozambique Convention in 1928. However with regard to recruiting further north things had become more promising. As early as 1913 the W.N.L.A. had set up the South African Institute of Medical Research specifically to investigate the pneumonia which killed so many men when they came south to the mines. During the 1920s the Institute had begun to develop the Lister anti-pneumococcal vaccine which was to prove so effective in controlling the disease.[1] And it was just at this time that, following

---

[1] The Lister vaccine was replaced for some years by May and Baker's 693 sulphonamide drug which was discovered in Europe during the 1930s. However prevention is better than cure and the Lister vaccine is once again coming into its own.

68

devaluation in 1932, the mining industry was expanding rapidly and needing all the extra labour it could get. Thus at the end of 1933 the South African government, under constant pressure from the Chamber of Mines, authorised the engagement under prescribed conditions of 2,000 men from areas to the north of latitude 22°s.[1] The experiment was pronounced a success and, following the favourable report in 1937 of the Royal Commission appointed by the governments of the Central African territories to examine the desirability of men going south to work in the mines, the way was clear for the industry to tap this source of labour. Its importance to the industry may be seen by the fact that a former general manager of the Chamber of Mines, Mr W. Gemmill, relinquished his posts at the head of the two recruiting organisations in Johannesburg and moved to Salisbury in 1940 to organise Wenela's widening of the labour catchment area.

It was agreed that (Southern) Rhodesia was to be closed to the W.N.L.A., as was that area of Mozambique lying to the north of the Save river where cotton plantations needed manpower. But labour was available in Malawi, Tanzania, Zambia, Botswana (north of latitude 22°s), South-West Africa, and Angola. Recruiting stations were set up (see map, p. x) and agreements entered into with the governments concerned as to the number of men that might be engaged. The quotas varied widely according to country, and often changed from year to year. The annual number coming from Malawi fluctuated between 5,000 and 10,000 whilst the Barotse (Lozi) quota remained fairly constant around 3,500, as did the South-West African quota of 3,000. At first there was no agreement with Tanzania but Nyakyusa men from the Southern Province often walked across the Ndali hills to a recruiting station in northern Malawi.[2] There was never ever any formal agreement with the Portuguese authorities of Angola but the chief purpose of the W.N.L.A. outposts on the Okavongo and Zambezi rivers was to draw men from across the Angolan border. Similarly many men from northern Mozambique moved across to southern Malawi to sign on for the mines. In 1952, of the 31,000 'tropicals' recruited for the mines approximately 23% came from Malawi, 16% from Tanzania, 10% from South-West Africa, and 6% from Barotseland in Zambia. The remaining 45% came, presumably, from Angola, northern Mozambique, and northern Botswana.[3]

[1] South Africa, *Report of the Low Grade Ores Commission* (U.G. 45, Cape Town, 1919), p. 8 A.
[2] The men preferred going to the Copperbelt, where they could earn more if they were skilful and where working conditions were easier, but the copper mines did not provide a transport subsidy and jobs were scarce. M. Wilson, *Communal Rituals among the Nyakusa* (O.U.P., London, 1959), p. 203 B.
[3] W.N.L.A., *Annual Report* (1952) A. H. R. G. Hurst, 'A survey of the development of facilities for migrant labour in Tanganyika during the period 1926–1959', *Bulletin of the Inter Africa Labour Institute* VI (1959) C.

Labour in the South African gold mines

Besides the building of a 1,500 mile road from Grootfontein to Francistown, and the establishment of motor barge transport on the Zambezi as far north as Mongu, one of the major factors in the expansion of the tropical labour supply was the development after 1951 of an air service to bring men from the depots in northern Botswana, Barotseland, and Malawi to Francistown whence they were brought by train to the mines. By 1955 there were 32 flights in or out of Francistown every week, and a total of 72,000 men had been transported by air. By this time the industry clearly felt that the greatest obstacle to an improved labour supply lay in governmental restrictions. The president of the Chamber of Mines complained that:

The mines can offer more remunerative work to Natives from other territories in Africa than is generally available in their own countries where less industrial development has taken place. But for the restrictions imposed by various governments, these Natives would flock to the gold mines seeking work in even greater numbers; and the good relationships with our Native employees reflect the contentment of this very large body of workers with their conditions of employment.[1]

The relative importance of the various sources may be seen from table 8 which shows the geographical sources of black labour employed by the Chamber of Mines over the period 1896–1969.

TABLE 8. *Geographical sources of black labour employed*[a] *by the Chamber of Mines, 1896–1969*[b]

	1896–8 (%)	1906 (%)	1916 (%)	1926 (%)	1936 (%)	1946 (%)	1956 (%)	1966 (%)	1969 (%)
Transvaal	23·4	4·0	10·3	8·4	7·0	7·6	5·5	4·8	3·8
Natal and Zululand	1·0	4·8	5·3	2·6	4·9	4·4	3·8	2·4	1·9
Swaziland		0·7	1·9	2·1	2·2	1·8	1·6	1·1	1·4
Cape Province		13·7	33·0	29·8	39·2	27·8	24·4	24·8	23·6
Lesotho	11·1	2·6	7·9	10·9	14·5	12·5	11·9	16·8	17·5
Orange Free State		0·3	0·6	0·5	1·1	1·5	1·0	2·1	2·1
Botswana	3·9	0·4	1·8	1·0	2·3	2·3	3·1	5·0	4·0
Mozambique	60·2	65·4	38·1	44·5	27·8	31·5	30·8	28·4	26·9
North of latitude 22°s	0·5	8·0	1·1	0·2	1·1	10·6	17·9	14·7	18·8
Total (000s)	54	81	219	203	318	305	334	383	371

[a] As at 31 December. The figures include employment on the Transvaal coal mines which recruit labour through the Chamber of Mines.
[b] Apart from 1896–8, the Mozambique figures exclude men from north of latitude 22°s.
SOURCES: T.C.M. and W.N.L.A. Annual Reports.

[1] T.C.M., *Sixty Seventh Annual Report* (1956), p. 61 A.

Throughout its history the mining industry has been heavily dependent upon labour from Mozambique which before Union in 1910 supplied nearly two-thirds, and since then has regularly supplied more than a quarter of the total number of blacks employed by the gold mines and collieries of the Chamber of Mines. The second most important source of labour, particularly since the First World War, has been the Ciskei and Transkei. Lesotho was both in 1936 and in 1966 the third most important source of black labour, although in many of the years between it lagged behind the tropical areas. Although the total number of men employed by the Chamber of Mines rose from 318,000 to 371,000 between 1936 and 1969 the number of black South Africans fell from 166,000 to 131,000. The number of men from areas north of latitude 22°s rose from 3,000 to 70,000. In the peak year, 1961, when the gold mines and collieries of the Chamber were employing 414,000 blacks, the number of tropicals rose to 89,000, which was 21% of the total, whilst the number of men from the Cape Province was 105,000 (25%). By 1969, of the 371,000 blacks employed on the gold mines and collieries of the Chamber of Mines 27% came from Mozambique, 24% from the Cape Province, 18% from Lesotho, 19% from tropical areas, 4% each from the Transvaal and Botswana, 2% each from the Orange Free State and Natal, and 1% from Swaziland.

The northward shift in the geographical distribution of the mines' black labour force came about partly because of the expansion of manufacturing industry and the increasing competition for local labour, and partly because the Chamber of Mines achieved a situation where, in terms of the 1937 amendment to the Immigration Act, it alone was in a position to bring in contract labour from countries to the north of South Africa.[1] In passing, it is worth drawing attention to the parallel between the position of the Chamber of Mines with regard to 'tropicals' and that of the Californian farmers *vis-à-vis* Mexican Braceros who, until 1965, could be brought in under contract for harvest work.[2] In South Africa, given the political objections against attracting black labour to the cities, the men who made and enforced the laws were likely to favour those industries that were able to use temporary labour and which had an established method of controlling the entry and repatriation of such labour. The fact that the gold mines had an efficient recruiting organisation encouraged the government to permit them to draw

[1] Strictly speaking other sectors could equally well have recruited from the north but none of them were able to pool their resources in order to provide the necessary recruiting, transport and accommodation facilities. Nowhere have economies of scale been more important for the gold mining industry than in the organisation of its labour supply.

[2] Cf. L. H. Fisher, *The Harvest Labor Market in California* (H.U.P., Cambridge, Mass., 1953) B and United States' President's Commission on Migratory Labor, *Migratory Labor in American Agriculture* (Washington, 1951) A.

in foreign labour.[1] Subsequently the industry has remained in a strong position to oppose any attempt to curb the entry of 'tropical' labour.[2]

The search for adequate supplies of white skilled labour was pursued even further afield than that for black unskilled men. The main sources, after South Africa, were Western Europe and, to a limited extent, the white Commonwealth countries. Even before the Second World War the mining industry was short of artisans; a shortage that was aggravated by the restriction of skilled work to whites only. Efforts were made to recruit white South Africans but it was not until after the war that active steps were taken to widen the catchment area by setting up recruiting offices in Western Europe. Beginning in Britain in 1948, and later extending to Eire and the Continent, the results were disappointing. Of the 372 prospective trainees who arrived in South Africa in 1948 only 160 – less than half – were still in training at the end of the year. Forty-nine had failed to pass the silicosis medical test, while the rest had cancelled their indentures or absconded.[3] During 1952 recruiting began in Austria and Germany; and in 1956 a number of Hungarians were brought in. At the same time the Chamber of Mines created a new department to co-ordinate and intensify the search for white labour. Subsequently the mines had some success in persuading young South Africans to become learner officials, and a scheme was established whereby final-year engineering students in various European and Commonwealth universities were encouraged to work in the industry during their long vacations.

By widening the sources of supply, recruiting was clearly effective in holding down wages, particularly of blacks, but the costs of doing so were not insignificant. The vast majority of black recruits were transported at the industry's expense from their homes to the mines, but the workers themselves had to bear the cost of the return journey.[4] The minority who paid their own way to the mines were those who made use of the Assisted Voluntary Scheme (A.V.S.). In terms of this, men from South Africa and the Protectorates were allowed to choose their own mine and work for as little as four months at a time. But if they stayed for less than 9 months their rail fares, which were advanced to them by the N.R.C., had to be repaid. The scheme

1 In 1936, 157,300 of the 179,500 foreign Africans legally working in South Africa were on the mines. South Africa, *Industrial and Agricultural Requirements Commission* (U.G. 40, Pretoria, 1941), p. 9 A. By 1964 it was estimated that 294,000 of a total of 497,000 foreign Africans working in the Republic were in mining.
2 Cf. Statement by the Minister of Mines replying to criticism from his own party. Republic of South Africa, *Hansard* (Cape Town, 1964), cols. 6284-5, 6299 A.
3 T.C.M., *Annual Report* (1948).
4 In 1939 the Chamber decided to meet the costs of transporting (including food) black miners who were coming to work for 270 shifts or more. Thirty years later, in September 1969, the Chamber decided to meet the homeward costs as well. Diamond, *African Labour Problems*, p. 228 D; and *Rand Daily Mail*, 9 September 1969.

expanded during the 1930s but became less popular as time wore on; in 1942 49% of those recruited by the N.R.C. came on the A.V.S. but by 1969 the proportion had fallen to 5%.[1] The W.N.L.A. recruited from further afield than the N.R.C. and, naturally, its costs were higher. In 1938 the costs of recruiting were R6·2 per head for the W.N.L.A. and R3·4 for the N.R.C.; by 1969 the figures had risen to R36·4 and R23·6 respectively.[2] But these figures are not strictly comparable until allowance has been made for the differences in the average lengths of contract of men from the different areas. Precise figures are not available but, since all W.N.L.A. contracts vary between 12 and 18 months and since the usual N.R.C. contract is 270 shifts (about 10½ months), while 'assisted voluntaries' get a substantial bonus after 9 months' work, it seems reasonable to assume that the average man brought to the mines by the N.R.C. stays about two-thirds as long as the average W.N.L.A. recruit. This is confirmed by 1960 figures for the mines of one group. The average lengths of tour, measured in shifts worked, for men from the various regions were: South Africa 245; Botswana, Lesotho, and Swaziland 248; Mozambique 413; and north of latitude 22°S, 383.[3] A full year was generally taken to be 313 shifts. Thus the costs of recruiting from all areas worked out at slightly less than 9 cents for each shift worked in 1969. As a proportion of the total wage bill for blacks, recruiting costs in 1936 were 6% and, by 1968, 12%.[4] For whites, costs varied enormously. Recruiting whites within South Africa was generally not much more expensive than recruiting blacks, but there are no figures available on the average length of service of local white recruits, so strict comparison is impossible. Recruiting overseas was prohibitively expensive; not only was the turnover of these recruits very high (see p. 98), but the cost per head, starting at R196 in 1948, grew to R1,652 by 1959. By 1962 the cost was too high for the industry to continue such recruiting.[5]

The second major factor influencing the supply of both black and white labour to the gold mining industry over the period under consideration was the rapid expansion of other sectors of the economy, particularly manufacturing (see p. 148). This led to increasing competition for labour which previously had gone almost exclusively to the mines. Normally such an

---

[1] South Africa, *Witwatersrand Mine Natives' Wages Commission*, para. 46. N.R.C., *Annual Reports* (1942 and 1969) A.

[2] N.R.C. and W.N.L.A., *Annual Reports* A. Figures obtained by dividing total annual expenditure by number of recruits (including assisted voluntaries) obtained during the year ended, for N.R.C., 30 June, and for W.N.L.A., 31 December. In real terms the W.N.L.A. cost rose by 111% and the N.R.C. cost by 149%. In 1898 the average cost of recruiting was R6·40 a head (T.C.M., *Annual Report* (1898), p. 461 A).

[3] See Appendix 23.   [4] N.R.C. and W.N.L.A., *Reports Reports* A.

[5] G.M.T.S., *Annual Reports*.

'outbreak of competition' would have brought about an increase in the wages paid by the gold mining industry. However although this happened as far as whites were concerned, the pressure pushing up black wages on the mines was eased by the industry's successful venture into the tropical interior (see p. 69).

In addition there is one sector of the economy whose influence on mine wages is not competitive but complementary. There are two types of worker who come from the 'subsistence' sector of a developing economy. One is the man who takes the either–or decision; who has to choose whether he will stay where he is, or pull up his roots and move permanently to town. Making allowance for the attractions of living in a big city, he will decide to go only if his expected earnings there are at least as large (allowing for cost of living differences) as they would be on the land. In other words, his rural income sets the lower limit on what he must be paid elsewhere. It was this type of worker that W. Arthur Lewis implicitly analysed in his study of economic development with unlimited supplies of labour. But there is a second type of man, typified by those who work on the gold mines, for whom the subsistence sector has a different consequence. The oscillating migrant does not take an either–or decision, he goes to town primarily to supplement the income he is earning from the land. The more that the migrant can earn from farming, the less will he require from the city to supplement this income. Exactly the reverse is true, however, of the either–or man; the more he can earn on the land the *more* will he need to earn in town to induce him to go there.

Under a pattern of permanent movement to town the interests of the modern sector lie, as Lewis has pointed out, in ensuring that rural earnings are kept down so that men have to come to work even though wages in town are low.[1] But under a migrant-labour system, once employers have ensured that 'subsistence' earnings are lower than the worker requires to meet all his needs it is in their interests not to allow rural earnings to fall any lower.[2] For the smaller the gap to be filled, the lower the supplementary wage can be. In 1943, when the Lansdown Commission recommended an increase in black mine wages, the Chamber opposed this on the grounds that, although mine wages were lower than what was generally agreed to be a necessary minimum, they were in fact adequate because the Commission had, the Chamber maintained, underestimated the migrant's income from the land. In his annual address, the president of the Chamber of Mines, referring to the Lansdown Report, said:

---

[1] W. A. Lewis, 'Economic development with unlimited supplies of labour', *Manchester School of Economic and Social Studies* (1954), 149 C.
[2] See Wilson and Thompson (eds.), *Oxford History* II, 127–31, for an analysis of the 1913 Land Act.

In regard to wages we are naturally disappointed at the substantial nature of the recommendations, especially as we feel the Commission had neither the time nor the facilities for a full and satisfactory investigation into the complicated question of budgets in the Native territories, and the income derived in such territories.[1]

It is worth pointing out that the recommendations which seemed so substantial to the president of the Chamber were only adopted to the extent of raising the real level of black cash wages in 1943 to what they had been in 1941.[2] A more detailed analysis of the value of the mineworker's rural income will be made in a later chapter when the economics of the migrant system are being analysed; at this point it is sufficient to note that some, but by no means all, black mineworkers had rural incomes to supplement their mine wages.

Connected with the role of the subsistence sector is the question as to whether or not the blacks coming to the mines were target workers. One argument used by the mining industry against those who thought that black wages should be raised was that if the men were paid more they would simply work for shorter periods to earn what they needed before returning home.[3] In technical jargon the argument was that the supply curve of labour was 'backward sloping'; in other words that the higher the wage rate the *less* labour was available. Even in the early days of gold mining the argument was of dubious validity; as early as 1892 a recruiter in the Eastern Cape found that potential recruits were keenly aware of the different wage rates on the mines, railways, and farms and that they would not consider going to work where wages were lower than elsewhere.[4] Furthermore, as Berg has pointed out, although the supply curve of an individual migrant (in man hours per year) might be backward sloping, this by no means implied that the aggregate supply curve to a firm or industry sloped in the same direction.[5] Even where subsistence farming was the only alternative to working on the mines a higher wage would widen the geographical area within which men might find it worthwhile to make the journey to work. And where, as was certainly the case for black South Africans over the period 1911–69, the mines were not the only employers it is fallacious to argue that a higher wage rate would act to decrease the supply of labour. As the president of the Chamber himself recognised during the Second World War, 'the glamour of high rates of pay in other industries...adversely affected...recruiting efforts'.[6] This seems

---

[1] T.C.M., *Fifty Fourth Annual Report* (1943) A.   [2] See p. 46.
[3] See, for example, T.C.M., *Fifty Eighth Annual Report* (1947) A.
[4] Wilson and Thompson (eds.), *Oxford History* II, 121.
[5] E. Berg, 'Backward sloping labor. Functions in dual economies: the African case', *Q.J.E.* LXXV (1961) c. See S. Rottenberg ('Wage effects in the theory of the labor movement', *J.P.E.* LI (1953) c) for a discussion of the significance of job prestige as a determinant of the labour supply.
[6] T.C.M., *Fifty Fifth Annual Report* (1944), p. 57 A.

to have been true not only for that part of the labour force coming from inside South Africa, but also for those from outside who had fewer job alternatives. After an econometric analysis of the 'supply responses' of African tobacco farmers in Malawi, E. Dean concluded that they allocated their labour in ways that were consistent with economic theory, that they responded to high levels in foreign (i.e. South African) wage rates by migrating for employment, and that the supply curve of their own labour to their own tobacco farming was upward sloping.[1] The possibility of even individual labour supplies declining as wages rose was further reduced in the gold mines by virtue of the contract system whereby men were not accepted for work for less than a minimum period of time (see p. 73).

So far we have dealt with those factors which seem to have had a direct effect on the amount of labour coming forward at a given wage. Before turning to those factors which affect the demand side of the equation, it is necessary to examine three more on the supply side which are distinguished from those already discussed by their peculiarly artificial or restrictive nature. They are: the monopoly power of the white trade unions, the colour bar, and influx control.

In 1937, as a result of agitation led by the young Dr. Albert Hertzog, the Chamber of Mines reversed its trade union policy which, only a year before, it had publicly declared was to uphold the open shop principle and 'not to interfere with the liberty of the individual in deciding for himself whether he joins a union or not'.[2] The Gold Producers' Committee recognised seven white trade unions and demanded that every white employee, excluding officials, be a member of one of them. During the years that followed their recognition these bodies whose members were the only workers in the mining labour force to have the vote became extremely powerful and regained all the strength that they had lost as a result of their defeat in the 1922 Rand rebellion. By 1964 there were nine recognised unions, of which the Mine Workers Union, representing over half the day's pay men, was the most powerful.[3] Their power was used both to re-inforce the colour bar, in all its legal and customary ramifications, and to bargain for higher wages.[4] 'Pressure from white trade unions', wrote the *Mining Journal* in 1953, 'has led to an extension by custom of the range of occupations from which

---

[1] E. Dean, *The Supply Responses of African Farmers* (North Holland Publishing Co., Amsterdam, 1966), p. 32. A similar conclusion was reached by Norman Reynolds in his *Socio-Economic Study of an African Development Scheme* (Ph.D. thesis, Cape Town, 1969) D.
[2] Press statement issued by the G.P.C., 24 October 1936. T.C.M., *Forty Seventh Annual Report* (1936), p. 37 A. T.C.M., *Forty Eighth Annual Report* (1937)
[3] See Appendix 17.
[4] See Appendix 18 for a summary of the activities of the unions and of the responses made by the mining industry.

Africans are, in theory at all events, excluded.[1] Although individual unions, particularly the Mine Workers Union, approached the industry from time to time, most of the bargaining was done through the Mining Unions' Joint Committee (M.U.J.C.), an association of the different unions. In 1964 this body was formed into the Federation of Mining Unions, but in 1968 during the midst of a colour-bar crisis (see p. 117) the Mine Workers Union, together with the unions of drivers and stokers and of reduction workers, hived off from the Federation and formed a rival body, the Federation of Mining Production Workers. The reason for the split was that the production workers considered the policies of some of the artisan unions to be detrimental to the welfare of white employees. The split was followed by a declaration of war by the F.M.P.W. which announced, in mid-1969, that it would no longer abide by the 1937 agreement which specified to which union a particular type of worker must belong. Henceforth it would recruit members from all sections of the white labour force. Even the officials felt threatened by the aggressive tactics of the 20,000 strong F.M.P.W. and in August they approached the Chamber to prevent poaching by making membership of one of the two officials' associations a condition of employment for officials. The conflict between the F.M.P.W. and the rest of the whites working on the mines highlights the central economic dilemma of the white man in South Africa. Do his interests lie in maintaining a rigid colour bar and getting a large share of a small cake, or do they lie in raising the barrier and getting a smaller share of the larger cake that is thus produced? An attempt to answer this question is made in a later chapter (see p. 118).

Contrasting with the strength of the white trade unions was the powerlessness of black workers, which was most clearly demonstrated in the great strike of 1946.[2] The background to this was the events beginning in 1941 with the emergence of the African Mine Workers Union, after ten desultory years in which sporadic strikes and demands for better wages and conditions had been ignored. The government responded the next year by decreeing that all strikes by black workers were illegal in all circumstances. Following this up the A.M.W.U. demanded higher wages, to which the government replied by appointing the Lansdown Commission to investigate.[3] This naturally raised the expectations of the African mine labourers. However, writes Diamond, 'Its recommendations...were regarded as "miserable and

---

[1] A. G. Thomson, 'Shortage of Native labour in the South African gold mining industry', *Mining Journal*, 24 July 1953.
[2] In describing the strike I have drawn heavily on Diamond, *African Labour Problems* (especially ch. 11) D, to which readers are referred for further details.
[3] South Africa, *Witwatersrand Mine Natives' Wages Commission* A.

77

grudging", while Smuts's decision to cut these "to the bone" was scornfully condemned.'[1] The A.M.W.U. therefore organised protest meetings, whereupon the government under pressure from the Chamber of Mines prohibited such meetings on mine property and arrested the president of the A.M.W.U. and held him for a few weeks. Some months later, in May 1945, a large meeting of mineworkers asked the government to meet an A.M.W.U. deputation to discuss the implementation of *all* the recommendations of the Lansdown Commission, a general increase in wages, and the withdrawal of the emergency War Regulation No. 1425 which prohibited meetings of more than 20 persons on mine property without a special permit (a permit which was never granted to the A.M.W.U.). The acting Prime Minister, Mr. J. H. Hofmeyr, refused even to see the deputation. Meanwhile conditions on the mines were getting no better.

In 1945 there was a poor maize harvest which, quite apart from reducing the migrant workers' rural incomes (see p. 147), led the mining industry to reduce, with the government's permission, their beer and porridge rations. This caused much dissatisfaction and a number of disturbances and strikes occurred during the next few months. The response of the authorities was to hit back. On one mine, for example, a police baton charged killed two men and seriously wounded a hundred others. In April 1946 more than 2,000 delegates attended the annual conference of the A.M.W.U. where it was unanimously resolved that the Chamber of Mines and the government should take 'immediate steps to provide adequate and suitable food for the workers' and that, 'in accordance with the new world principles for an improved standard of living subscribed to by our government at U.N.O.', the minimum wage of all African miners should be raised to 10s. (R1·00) per day.[2] The Chamber of Mines did not reply to the various approaches made by the A.M.W.U. in seeking an interview to discuss its demands, presumably on the grounds that if one ignored a body that was not legally recognised one could pretend that it did not exist. However the Chamber did communicate once with the A.M.W.U.: in response to the above resolution a printed post-card was sent to the effect that the matter was 'receiving attention'. Whether it was or not is unclear, for nothing was done.

Some months and several small strikes later, the A.M.W.U. resolved to embark upon a general strike. This began on 12 August 1946 and lasted four days. 74,000 workers were involved, eight mines were brought to a total standstill and five others were partially affected. The government was not

---

[1] The improvements actually effected were 30% less than the Commission's recommendations. Diamond, *African Labour Problems*, pp. 206, 211 D.

[2] *Ibid.* p. 212.

slow to act; strike leaders on all the mines involved were arrested, police surrounded the compounds and, when stoned at one mine, fired on the miners. In another mine a baton charge was made and in another the men were driven underground from their compounds at bayonet point. Seventy men were dismissed, nine were killed, and more than twelve hundred injured. At no stage was the government or the Chamber willing even to discuss, let alone accede to, the demands of the strikers because, as General Smuts, who was Prime Minister at the time, put it, 'The native strike was not caused by legitimate grievances but by agitators.'[1] Four days later it was all over.

Shortly afterwards, the Chamber issued a statement making clear its attitude to collective bargaining by Africans. '. . . the Gold Mining Industry considers that trade-unionism as practised by Europeans is still beyond the understanding of the tribal Native; nor can he know how to employ it as a means of promoting his advancement. He has no tradition in that respect and has no experience or proper appreciation of the responsibilities arising from collective representation. No proper conduct of a trade union is possible unless the workers have that tradition and such a sense of responsibility.' After pointing out that the full recognition of, and cordial relations with, white unions showed that the Chamber was not opposed to unionism as such, the statement went on to add that 'the introduction of trade unionism among tribal Natives at their present stage of development would lead to abuses and irresponsible action'. The Chamber claimed that had the demand for a basic wage of R1·00 a day been met, 35 of the 45 producing mines would have been forced to close and some 240,000 blacks would have been thrown out of work. 'A trade union organisation,' the statement concluded, 'would be outside the comprehension of all but a few of the educated Natives of the urban type; it would not only be useless, but detrimental to the ordinary mine Native in his present stage of development.'[2]

The statement was an important one. It laid down explicitly the policy which the gold mining industry, with the full support of successive governments, pursued with respect to its black labour force not only prior to 1946 but in the decades that followed. Certainly the Chamber remains opposed to the unionisation of its black workers. And yet if black unions are never to be allowed to exist how will the workers ever acquire the 'tradition in that respect' which the Chamber consider a necessary prerequisite? The African Mine Workers' Union never recovered from its 1946 defeat; the combination of Chamber opposition and government legislation has effectively prevented

---

[1] *Ibid.* p. 218. See also A. Paton, *Hofmeyr* (O.U.P., Cape Town, 1964), for a discussion of the concern – and powerlessness – of African political leaders with regard to the government's attitude.
[2] T.C.M., *Tribal Natives and Trade Unionism* (T.C.M., Johannesburg, 1946) A.

its re-emergence and the black workers remain without countervailing weight to balance either the power of the Chamber of Mines or the bargaining strength of the white trade unions.[1]

Closely related to the power of the trade unions is the rigidity of the colour bar which affects both supply and demand. Apart from defining what jobs might not be done by blacks, the white unions also sought to prevent employers from using job fragmentation and alternative techniques of production in order to bend the colour bar by requiring that the ratio of blacks to whites employed on the mines should not rise above a certain maximum. From Appendix 3 it will be seen that, apart from the year of the Rand rebellion, 1922, the ratio of black to white employment in the gold mines between 1910 and 1969 never rose above 10·0:1 and never fell below 6·4:1. Indeed the average ratio over the period, excluding 1922, was 7·99:1 and the correlation between the levels of white and black employment was extremely high.[2] No less than 85% of the variance in the level of black employment in any year could be explained by differences in the level of white employment.

The background to this is that during the early years on the mines an employment ratio of eight blacks to one white rapidly became established as the 'normal' proportion. Writing in 1903, Benjamin Kidd pointed out that:

The natives employed in the mining industry in Johannesburg have hitherto outnumbered the white *employés* by eight to one, the former being employed on the rougher work and the latter principally in supervision and in the more responsible positions. There is nevertheless no work now being done by natives in the mines on the Witwatersrand which is not being done by white labourers in similar mines in America and other countries.[3]

By 1907 strike action by white miners had forced the government 'to insist upon a definite ratio of "civilized" labour to indentured Natives'.[4] In 1918, under pressure from the white trade unions, the Chamber of Mines came to an agreement that the *status quo* on each mine with regard to the relative scope of employment of black and white employees should be maintained. This ratio was the symbol over which the Rand rebellion was fought, for it was the announcement by the Chamber that it intended to withdraw the *status quo* agreement and to increase the black–white employment ratio to 10·5:1 that sparked off the bitter battle.[5] In 1931 the Trades and Labour Council submitted a memorandum to the Prime Minister gently reminding him of the importance of the ratio by drawing his attention to the employ-

---

[1] See discussion on pp. 150 ff.
[2] But no adjustment was made for auto-correlation. See Appendix 26.
[3] B. Kidd, 'Economic South Africa', *Christian Express*, May 1903 (reprinted from *The Times*) c.
[4] Walker and Weinbren, *2000 Casualties* (Johannesburg, 1961), p. 29 B.   [5] See p. 10.

Supply and demand

ment of whites in the mining industry and requesting that the ratio of black to white should not exceed 9·1 : 1.[1] The significance of this remarkably stable black–white employment ratio will be analysed in a later chapter.[2]

The third important restriction, affecting primarily the supply of unskilled labour, was influx control. The successive legislative steps necessary to maintain this control have already been described.[3] A measure of the increasing extent to which they were used is given by the figures of the total number of Africans convicted under the pass laws each year. Between 1940 and 1947 when, under the annealing power of war, the United Party government was deciding that it would have to adapt its policies to the reality of urbanisation, the number of convictions fell from 184,000 to 174,000. But with the election of the National Party the old policy was intensified. Between 1948 and 1962 the number of convictions soared from 176,000 to 384,000.[4] By 1969 some 632,000 Africans were being prosecuted annually – an average of more than one person every minute of the day and night.[5] Nor was the number merely a reflection of increasing population. Between 1936 and 1962 the percentage of convictions as a proportion of the total black population rose from 1·9% to 3·4%. From an economic point of view the chief beneficiaries of such control were farmers and the Chamber of Mines. In agriculture the effect of the laws was to make it more difficult for labourers to move to other farms or to town in search of better wages.[6] In the mining sector the legislation gave employers a decided advantage over their competitors for labour in manufacturing industry. No obstacles were placed in the way of men in the reserves wishing to go to the mines; to get permission to go to work in a factory was far more difficult.

In an attempt to assess the significance of various factors which might have affected the supply of black labour to the mines, a multiple regression analysis of such factors as could be quantified was made.[7] The results suggest, at first glance, that between 1936 and 1965 the level of employment in secondary industry and the intensity of the application of influx control were both highly significant variables in determining the number of men recruited from the Cape Province by the N.R.C. Furthermore the respective signs of the co-efficients confirm the hypothesis that, as manufacturing employment went up, so mine labour supplies fell. Also confirmed is the hypothesis that as influx control tightened so the supply improved. However the price of wool, the chief cash product of the reserves, does not appear to

[1] A. A. Moore, *Mining Problems* (1931, Ballinger Papers, University of Cape Town) D.
[2] See p. 111.   [3] See pp. 2, 71.
[4] *Union Statistics for Fifty Years*, F-4; Horrell, *Survey of Race Relations 1963*, p. 138 B.
[5] *Ibid.* 1970, p. 165.
[6] Wilson and Thompson (eds.), *The Oxford History* II, 142 B.   [7] See Appendix 19.

have been a significant factor, but in so far as it did increase it led, as might have been expected, to a fall in the supply of black South African labour to the mines. These results however are based on a time series in which there might well have been significant auto-correlation. To correct for this, a regression was run based on first differences. The value of the multiple correlation co-efficient fell to zero, which implied that none of the factors considered appeared to have had any influence in determining the supply of black labour. Nevertheless, although the *t* values of the co-efficients all dropped substantially, they are not altogether insignificant and the signs of all the parameters remain, albeit tentatively, consistent with the hypotheses.

No account has yet been taken of the variance in the basic food crop of the reserves. Figures for the maize crops are probably subject to a large degree of error as there was no direct method of measuring crops other than by going round from *umzi*[1] to *umzi* and asking how many bags were harvested. Nevertheless the maize figures do give some measure of the years when the rains were good and the harvest plentiful, and the years of drought. For the years 1947–62, excluding 1961, the results, when compared with those obtained earlier, suggest that employment opportunities in manufacturing and the intensity of influx control were considerably more significant in affecting mine labour supplies after 1947 than they were in earlier years. While the multiple correlation co-efficients remain insignificant the signs of the parameters for manufacturing employment, pass law convictions, and wool prices continue to be consistent with the hypotheses. However the result for maize[2] is surprising for it suggests that the larger the maize harvest was in the reserves the *greater* was the number of men who went to work on the mines. The result could be due purely to the (possibly large) error in the harvest statistics, but even if the figures were accurate a positive correlation between labour supply to the mines and maize output in the reserves might be obtained if the rate of population growth in the reserves was greater than the rate of increase of maize production. No test of this hypothesis was made but the increasing density of population in the reserves and the low level of agricultural techniques suggest that it may well be borne out by the facts.[3]

Summing up, we may say that, in so far as the results (when corrected for auto-correlation) failed to yield significant multiple correlation coefficients, they are inconclusive. Nevertheless they are consistent with the hypotheses that the mine labour supply was adversely affected by the growth of employment in secondary industry and that it was improved by tighter influx control. Furthermore it seems that these two factors were more important

[1] The Xhosa word for *homestead*.   [2] M in equation 5, Appendix 19.
[3] See Wilson and Thompson (eds.), *The Oxford History* II, pp. 55–68, for an analysis of the reasons for low agricultural productivity in the Bantustans.

after 1947 than before, and also that they were considerably more significant in influencing the supply of black labour to the mines than rural income from the production of maize or the sale of wool.

DEMAND

We turn now to an examination of those factors which affected the demand for mine labour. The most obvious of these was the expansion of the industry. Contrary to the expectations of the 1930s, the following three decades saw a phenomenal rise in the annual output of gold, due chiefly to the development of mines in new areas. Between 1936 and 1969 no less than 46 new mines came into production and the total annual output of gold rose from 11·3m. to 31·3m. fine ounces. One might well expect such a development to have been accompanied by a sharp increase in the demand for labour but in fact it was only during the 1930s that employment on the mines increased significantly – from a total of 241,000 men in 1933 to 365,000 in 1939. In 1941 and 1968, both years when the industry had an adequate supply of unskilled labour, the total number of blacks employed was constant at 368,000 although output more than doubled over the same period.[1] The reasons for this enormous increase in productivity included the discovery of higher grades of ore, greater mechanisation, better management, and more training of the labour force.

The choice of the best combination of labour and capital to use in any economic enterprise depends, as W. E. G. Salter has shown, not only on the relative prices of the two factors but also on the given state of technical knowledge. If labour becomes more expensive relative to capital, existing machines will be used for tasks that were previously done by hand and there will be pressure on the makers of machines to develop labour-saving techniques from the existing stock of knowledge. At the same time inventions, where they occur, make possible new methods of production that were not possible before. Where there is such technical progress capital goods become cheaper relative to labour and so the flow of inventions, or new knowledge, itself generates a pressure for the substitution of labour by capital. Applying Salter's analysis to the gold mines one would expect to find that there was over time a steady pressure towards mechanisation both because of the flow of new knowledge and because of the increasing risks of employing a large migrant labour force.[2] Despite the vast unskilled labour force employed in

[1] T.C.M., *Annual Reports* A.
[2] It would seem that these risks have increased over time because to the vagaries of weather and harvest has been added the fluctuating level of employment in manufacturing industries and the possibility of political action by other countries to cut off substantial sources of labour.

83

the gold mines, and despite the fact that the real earnings of these workers did not rise over time there was, nevertheless, a steady process of mechanisation in the industry.

As early as 1905 mine managements began to replace hammers with mechanical drills with which two men could produce as much as twelve with hammers.[1] The next major change in technique was the introduction, beginning in the 1930s, of locomotives instead of endless rope haulages for the underground transport of ore. At the same time mechanical scrapers and loaders were introduced.[2] Before the Second World War development ends in a mine were cleared by eight 'lashers' who loaded, and four 'tramming boys' who propelled, hoppers under the supervision of a 'boss-boy'.[3] These thirteen men worked from 4 a.m. until 11 a.m., and in seven hours could normally just finish the job. By the 1960s a development end three times the size could be cleared by three men in one and a half hours using a mechanical loader and a small locomotive.[4] Other highly capital intensive innovations included the specially designed mechanical cactus grab which was largely responsible for the phenomenal increase in the rate of shaft sinking during the 1950s. Taking 1932 as the base year we find that by 1951 the index had increased from 100 to only 119; but by 1960 it had soared to 262 with mines able to sink shafts at the rate of 1,100 feet a month.[5]

Apart from changes in the relative prices of labour and capital, there was another pressure on the industry to develop new methods of mining. This was the need to ensure that all the factors of production already at work in the mines were being fully utilised. A breakdown of the capital invested in gold mines during the early 1960s showed that the two most important parts of the investment were shaft sinking and underground development, and one group estimated that this capital was being used to no more than 60% of its capacity. In order to ensure that neither the shaft nor any other part of the mine was being under-utilised managers had long sought to remove any bottlenecks. One of the mos⁺ serious of these had been at the stope face until, during the Second World War, the method of concentrated mining was worked out whereby fewer stopes were worked more intensively. As early as 1939 the inspector for Brakpan described a new method whereby the holes

[1] Diamond, *African Labour Problems*, p. 83 D.
[2] R. B. Smart, 'Mechanization applied to mining in relation to native labour on Sub Nigel', *Association of Mine Managers* (Johannesburg, 1939) C.
[3] The work of *lashers* (known in British coal mines as *fillers*) has been graphically described by George Orwell in his essay *Down the Mine*. See plate 2. The word is perhaps derived from the Xhosa *ukulayisha* meaning 'to load'.
[4] The old development ends measured 6 ft × 6 ft; the later ones 10 ft × 10½ ft (1·8 × 1·8 metres and 3·0 × 3·2 metres).
[5] Menell, *Mining Finance Houses*, p. 116 D.

were drilled far more closely together in order to blast a larger tonnage of ore over a shorter length of stope face. Further developments were the use of longer drill-bits and, two decades later, the change from drilling at right angles to drilling at an angle of 70° combined with the sequential blasting of the different charges so that they reinforced each other and broke more ground. By reducing the area being mined at any one time, the method made possible a reduction in the amount of supervision, sampling, and the expensive reticulation of air and water. On some mines the bottleneck at the stope face lay not so much in the actual blasting as in the slowness with which the broken ore could be cleaned out. Some relatively minor changes in scraper technique solved this particular problem. Mines experimenting with the concentrated mining technique claimed to have been able to double their rate of ore extraction, but there were sceptics within the industry who pointed out that, while attainable in the short run, such results could not be maintained over longer periods.

One of the more interesting aspects of the mechanisation that occurred in the mines was the fact that although white labour became relatively more expensive than black labour as time went on, the machinery introduced tended to be biased towards saving black labour more than white. The reasons for this paradox, due largely to the rigidity of the colour bar, are explored more fully in Appendix 20. The effect of mechanisation in any enterprise is generally, though not always, to increase the demand for skilled labour.[1] Indeed one of the main barriers to mechanisation on the mines was the shortage of artisans to install and particularly to maintain the machines. In 1954 the Government Mining Engineer reported that not only did the shortage of artisans prevent the full mechanisation of stoping methods, but that on certain mines this mechanisation had to be abandoned because 'as a result of increased mechanisation in the mines the demand for skilled artisans could not be met'.[2] South Africa, as the *S.A. Mining and Engineering Journal* wrote in 1957, is 'plagued' by the fact that mechanisation cannot be employed on as large a scale as desirable because of the shortage of artisans.[3] The process of mechanisation on the gold mines had the effect, as the president of the Association of Mine Managers pointed out in 1969, of increasing the demand for more highly skilled workers.[4]

Some measure of the extent to which mechanisation has taken place may be obtained from the increase in the annual number of tons of ore milled

---

[1] The introduction of the most modern, capital intensive, machinery in a Ciskei textile mill was successful because it was found easier to train the unskilled labour force to use machines than to use hand looms.

[2] G.M.E., *Annual Report* (1954), p. 25. [3] *S.A.M. and E.J.*, 23 August 1957.

[4] *Star*, 21 March 1969.

per person at work on the mines between 1936 and 1969; the figure rose from 145 tons a man to 201 tons, an increase of 39%. But, of course, what proportion of this increase in productivity is attributable to mechanisation and what proportion to other factors such as better management or the growing skill of black workers is impossible to discover.[1]

ON SHORTAGES

The signature tune of South Africa's economic history is surely the wailing of employers over the shortage of labour. We have already seen (p. 2) how the mineral discoveries created great difficulties for farmers. Nor was agriculture the only sector; a constant thread running through the annual reports of the mining industry has been the complaint about the shortage of labour, both black and white. In their analysis of 'dynamic shortages and price rises' Arrow and Capron have pointed out that temporary labour shortages will always occur when a shift in demand leads to an excess of demand over supply which is not immediately balanced by a rise in wages.[2] The lag in wages they point out is due partly to the time taken by employers to realise the existence of a shortage at the current salary level and to adjust the salaries accordingly, and partly to the time needed by potential employees to recognise and act upon the alternatives available. While this concept of 'dynamic shortage' is helpful in that it integrates labour market imperfections into a theoretical model, it is insufficient in itself to explain the reasons for the constantly recurring shortages in the gold mining industry.

By the second half of the 1930s, the expansion of the industry, coupled with the increased labour requirements of other sectors, was beginning to strain the supplies of both white and black labour. Having had all the black labour they wanted for some years past, the gold mines were being increasingly hit by seasonal fluctuations in supply and the consequent shortages that developed in the second half of the calendar year. There were also shortages of white artisans but, as a mines inspector pointed out, 'owing to the shortage of native labour, the lack of skilled miners was not felt as severely as would have been the case if there had been a full complement of natives'.[3] During the early years of the Second World War the situation was reversed, for there were adequate supplies of black labour but shortages of whites, some five thousand of whom had gone off on military service. In 1941 the mines had their full complements of black labour but, despite the

[1] See Appendix 29.
[2] K. J. Arrow and W. M. Capron, 'Dynamic shortages and price rises: the engineer–scientist case', *Q.J.E.* LXXIII (1959) C.
[3] G.M.E., *Annual Report* (1937), p. 239 A.

Chamber's assurance that there was no longer cause for real anxiety in the matter of black labour supply, it was not for another sixteen years that the mines again had enough unskilled labourers to enable them to work at full capacity. During the intervening years the shortage of labour was acute; between 1946 and 1956, it was estimated at between 15% and 23% of requirements.[1] So bad was the shortage in 1951 that the industry approached the governments of British Somaliland, Ruanda Urundi, Reunion, Madagascar, and Mauritius about the possibility of recruiting unskilled labour, although supplies improved before any firm arrangements were made. Meanwhile this shortage of unskilled men helped to mask, though not hide completely, the lack of skilled artisans, miners and officials. In those years when supplies of black labour improved, 'the shortage of Europeans was brought into greater prominence'.[2] After 1958 there was a sharp, unexpected and largely inexplicable, increase in the number of Africans offering themselves for employment and for the next ten years the industry revelled in the luxury of having all the black labour it needed. However the shortage of whites now became acute and by 1966 it was estimated that the industry was short of 2,000 skilled men to do jobs which, by law, could only be done by whites.[3] Then in 1969 the industry had to curtail its output due to a sharp fall in the supply of black labour towards the end of the year.[4] The manner in which the industry responded to the pressures exerted by these shortages, and the reasons why it did not always respond by raising wages, will be analysed in a later chapter (p. 102).

Closely related to the persistent labour shortages was the extreme seasonal fluctuation in the black labour supply. From February until August, labour was generally relatively plentiful but towards the end of each year the numbers tended to drop off to such an extent that the difference between the maximum and minimum monthly employment averages in the industry was 20,000 or more. This fluctuation, it has often been suggested, is directly related to the fact that the rains usually fall in August and ploughing has to be done in the ensuing weeks. Having ploughed, men stay at home for Christmas and wait to enjoy the first maize before returning to the mines to earn the cash necessary to tide them over the year.

The effect of such fluctuation upon efficiency lies not only in the strain which it imposes on the induction facilities of the mines when there is a sudden large inflow of labour, but also in the waste inherent in the stop–go nature of production caused thereby. In 1936 the average monthly number (in thousands) of men distributed by the two recruiting corporations was

---

[1] G.M.E. and T.C.M., *Annual Reports*.   [2] G.M.E., *Annual Report* (1953), p. 26 A.
[3] Republic of South Africa, *Hansard* (1966), col. 444 A.   [4] *Sunday Times*, 12 April 1970.

25·6 with a variance of 1·8; by 1964 the average distribution was 29 and the variance had risen to 5·6. The major source of the sharp increase in fluctuation lay within South Africa and the three former High Commission Territories, but another factor was the increasing inability of the W.N.L.A. to stagger its recruiting from Mozambique and further north so as to iron out the N.R.C. fluctuation. An attempt in 1964 by one group to reduce fluctuations by introducing a rule that all workers had to give thirty days' notice before leaving seemed to be effective. In 1961 the average monthly intake (in thousands) of six mines was 3·9 with a variance of 1·6, whereas by 1965, although the intake had risen to 4·4, the variance had plummeted to 0·1. In 1969 the variance was 0·5 while the monthly intake had fallen to 3·6.

Having considered the supply of, and demand for, men to work in the gold mines we must now turn to consider another dimension of the picture: changes through training and other means in the skill or quality of the labour being demanded and supplied.

CHAPTER 5

HUMAN CAPITAL

Many persons hold the opinion that the metal industries are fortuitous and that the occupation is one of sordid toil, and altogether a kind of business requiring not so much skill as labour. But as for myself, when I reflect carefully upon its special points one by one, it appears to be far otherwise, for a miner must have the greatest skill in his work ...

Georgius Agricola, *De Re Metallica* (1556)

In his pioneering paper on the significance of the quality, as distinct from the mere quantity, of labour working in an economic enterprise, Gary S. Becker defined investment in human capital as the 'activities that influence future real income through the imbedding of resources in people'.[1] His paper, together with the work of other economists, was concerned with the nature and cost of these activities and with determining their influence by means of the general analysis of investment.[2] Of the four different methods which have so far been developed for assessing the economic significance of education Becker's investment approach is the best one for illuminating an important dimension of the labour market in the South African gold mines.[3]

Becker introduced an important distinction between specific and general training. The former is defined as training that has no effect on the productivity of trainees that would be usable in firms other than the one which provides such training; the latter is defined as that which increases the productivity of trainees even if they should subsequently go to work in other firms.[4] Teaching someone how to read one's indecipherable writing is an example of the one; training someone to type exemplifies the other. The distinction enables one to understand why some firms invest in on-the-job training and why others do not. Moreover it helps to clarify the reasons for different attitudes held by workers as to whether they should spend time and money on training themselves. By analysing such expenditure as investment

---

[1] G. S. Becker, 'Investment in human capital: a theoretical analysis', *J.P.E.* LXX (supplement, 1962), 9 C.
[2] J. Mincer, 'The distribution of labor incomes: a survey with special reference to the human capital approach', *Journal of Economic Literature* VIII (1970) C.
[3] W. G. Bowen, *Economic Aspects of Education* (Industrial Relations Section, Princeton, 1964) B.
[4] G. S. Becker, *Human Capital* (National Bureau of Economic Research, New York, 1964), p. 18 B.

rather than consumption one is led to consider part, at least, of wages not as earnings but as a return on investment. The extent to which workers are able to capture these returns will determine to a large degree the sort of training that a firm will provide for its employees: man being what he is, it is unlikely that any individual or firm would invest in training if all the returns were to go elsewhere. Thus in the case of general training, which raises the marginal productivity and hence, under conditions of perfect competition, the wages of a worker even if he should move on to another firm, the original firm would only provide such training if it did not have to pay any of the costs, or if it could by some means prevent the worker from moving to another firm after he had been trained. Or again, trainees might be willing to invest in themselves and bear the costs of training if they could be reasonably certain that they would receive the returns later on in the form of higher wages. Specific training, on the other hand, which provides skills that cannot readily be transferred from one firm to another, may raise the productivity of a worker but not necessarily his wages. Theoretically, a firm which invested in specific training could capture all the returns on its investment but in practice it would be unlikely to do so, for if he was paid the going market wage the worker who had been trained at the firm's expense would lose nothing by moving, whereas the firm would lose the cost of the training. The firm could reduce the risk of losing this investment by sharing part of the return with the worker and paying him a wage higher than the market rate.[1]

Looking at this conclusion from another angle, one sees that the less likely labour is to move on to other firms the more likely is any one firm to invest in training. Thus one would expect firms with monopsony power over labour to spend relatively more on specific investment than firms operating under more competitive conditions. Moreover, the fact that specific investment produces an increase in labour productivity which can be shared between the worker and the firm suggests that the worker would be less likely to quit, and the firm less likely to fire, than would be true in more competitive industries. Similarly, as Becker pointed out, the existence of effective long-term contracts would reduce turnover and make firms more willing to pay for all kinds of training – assuming future wages were set at an appropriate level – since a contract has the effect of turning all training into completely specific training.[2] The gold mines, which have both monopsony power and effective contracts, provide plenty of empirical evidence with which to test these predictions.

---

[1] In a competitive labour market the wage paid would be equal to the marginal revenue product of the worker *before* specific training. *Ibid*. p. 28.

[2] *Ibid*. p. 27.

INVESTMENT IN MINERS

As far back as 1922 the Mining Industry Board, appointed to enquire into the roots of the Rand rebellion, reported that the only criticism of the two Government Miners' Training Schools (G.M.T.S.), founded under a scheme first developed in 1911, was that there were not enough of them:

Under conditions prevailing in South Africa where the white man supervises and the native does the work, it is manifestly impossible to train young miners, as is done elsewhere in the world, by letting them work under the direction of a father or friend. The white lad in this country refuses to do what is termed 'Kaffir Work' alongside of the native, and since he can only learn, in the true sense of the word, by actually doing the work, conditions have to be created under which he need not be associated with the native in doing so. The Government Miners Training Schools seem to have solved this difficulty satisfactorily, but they require to be extended to supply the demand more adequately.[1]

By 1936 there were schools operating in eight mines, and in the following year four new schools were opened. At the same time a scheme for the training of winding engine drivers, who operated the cages or lifts in the mine shafts, was brought under the aegis of the schools.[2] The training course for those in the G.M.T.S. consists of an eighteen-month period of underground work combined with lectures. During the first nine months of the course the young white apprentices, most of whom have passed Standard VI[3] are given lectures on mining regulations, health measures and safety, in preparation for an examination which qualifies them for a provisional blasting certificate. The men are then allowed to work underground, but under the close supervision of instructors. During the second stage of training, lectures are given on explosives, methods of breaking ground, support of workings, pipe-fitting, track-laying, reclamation, handling of broken rock, ventilation, shaft sinking and all the other technicalities of mining. Thus qualified, the man is able to work as a fully fledged miner.

The training is specific to the industry as a whole in that the knowledge and skill obtained would not be much use in other sectors of the economy but, because workers are free to move from mine to mine, it is not specific to any one mine. Following Becker's analysis one would expect that under such conditions individual mines would be unlikely to invest in such training although it would pay the industry as a whole to do so. This is borne out by the facts. It is the industry as a whole, acting through the Chamber of Mines, which contributes one-third of the capital expenditure and three-quarters

---

[1] South Africa, *Report of the Mining Industry Board* (Solomon) (U.G. 39, Cape Town, 1922), para. 123 A.

[2] T.C.M., *Forty Eighth Annual Report* (1937) A.　　[3] Equivalent to eight years of schooling.

of the maintenance cost of the G.M.T.S. The balance is met, not by the individual mines, but by the state which, because of the need for export earnings, also has a direct interest in the efficiency of the industry. Between 1936 and 1965 the net cost per white trainee rose from R196 to R1,768.[1]

Nor was it only for the day's pay men that special training conditions had to be created. A learner officials scheme was set up on the same whites-only basis. Inaugurated by the Chamber of Mines in 1948, this provides a two-year course for young men of matriculation standard.[2] The training includes a period underground doing 'black' work, a year going through the service departments in order to get an overall view of mining, and a period as a miner working with a 'gang' of black men. During the early 1960s the training period was extended to three years, so that trainees could spend their first two years in theoretical work at the Witwatersrand Technical College. It was also the industry as a whole which took the initiative to meet the need for mining engineers. In 1936 it founded a number of scholarships to enable selected apprentices to study at the university; by 1957 there were 166 such bursaries. After 1959, in an attempt to forge closer links between potential engineers and the group for which they would work, bursaries were awarded by the group rather than by the Chamber.

The position with regard to black workers is quite different. We have already seen how the migrant contract labour system not only limits the period of continuous employment to approximately one year but also ensures that the vast majority of workers are unable to move between individual mines during the contract period. Thus one would expect that it would be the individual mines themselves which would bear the costs of training; furthermore one would expect that such training as is given would be severely limited by the shortness of the period over which the mines could hope to capture the returns of such investment. Again the hypothesis is borne out by the facts.

Before the Second World War there was almost no training for the vast majority of the black labour force not destined to become 'boss-boys'; all were encouraged to obtain first aid certificates but upon arrival at the mines the new recruit was sent straight underground with no induction or training.[3] The arrival from tropical areas of men to whom industrial life at that time was completely new posed special problems. By the end of the war, however, the inspector of mines for Krugersdorp reported that these had been overcome by the establishment of surface training schools, each in the form of a

---

[1] The Government Miners' Training Schools, *Annual Reports* (Johannesburg) A.
[2] Equivalent to ten years of schooling.
[3] By 1969 a total of more than 1·5 million black mineworkers had obtained their first aid certificates, *Rand Daily Mail*, 19 May 1969.

model stope, development end and haulage, where men were not only taught what to expect underground but also trained how to perform basic mine operations and how to work safely. There was also teaching for both black and white, in Fanakalo (pidgin Zulu) so that men might be able to understand instructions.[1] After this surface instruction there was a further period in an underground school and 'tropicals' were generally allocated, in the first instance, to the upper levels where heat and other working conditions were less severe. 'Since the introduction of these schools,' wrote an inspector, 'a reduction in minor injuries has taken place and an improvement in the output per native has resulted.'[2] By 1949 the disadvantages of short contracts were recognised by the Government Mining Engineer who pointed out that, while the shortage of labour had intensified efforts to promote efficiency by careful training of new recruits and of 'boss-boys', the shortness of the contract necessitated efforts to minimise the period of training.[3] Despite this, however, he was able to report the following year that the training scheme for blacks had been expanded, and that some mines also had a physical education training programme for men of poor physique, most of whom came from tropical areas. By 1950 there was some form of training for new recruits on all the large gold mines, and after that date the quality of training improved steadily.

Those concerned with training on the mines said that it was almost impossible to estimate the return on the investment although it was 'readily observable' that, for example, a man with three days' training as a 'machine boy' advanced much faster at the stope face than a man who had to learn by trial and error. Indeed, so convinced were many mine managements of the value of training that there was pressure to increase it. The cost of acclimatising and training a single new recruit on one mine in 1959 was R22·40.[4] On one new mine on the far west Rand the average period of training for a black worker in 1965 was four shifts.[5] The greatly expanded training programme initiated by one of the groups in 1962 was accompanied by wage increases and a promise to individual black workers that if they returned within a

---

[1] In a paper to the association of mine managers in 1957 one official reported that poor *Fanakalo* resulted in misunderstandings which led to accidents, assaults and inefficiency. Tests had shown that learner officials who underwent three months' training in *Fanakalo* learnt as much as other men gained in twenty years' experience. W. E. M. Kramers, '*Fanakalo* training for learner officials', *Papers and Discussions of the Association of Mine Managers* (T.C.M., Johannesburg, 1958) C. The phrase 'pasop lo nyawu' used in a training film about 'the care of feet' illustrates the fusion of Afrikaans and Zulu in *Fanakalo*. An even better example is the translation for 'zebra' – 'idonki ngo football jersey'.

[2] G.M.E., *Annual Report* (1945), p. 106 A. [3] *Ibid.* (1949), p. 26 A.

[4] Menell, *Mining Finance Houses*, p. 10 D.

[5] The period of training varied from two shifts for induction, to an aggregate of eighteen shifts for 'boss-boys'.

certain period to the same mine they would be placed in their old jobs as soon as possible, at the higher rate of pay previously achieved. Thus, to capture the maximum possible returns on its training investment the group was trying to lengthen the period of effective service by sharing with the worker concerned some part of the returns.

One fact not satisfactorily explained by the Becker hypothesis was the fifty-year delay in starting training for blacks even although the mines had long since discovered the value of training whites and the effect of elementary training for blacks was readily observable.[1] The simple idea that the black labour force consisted not of an undifferentiated mass of black labour units but of individual, sometimes bewildered, human beings who would respond to training and opportunities for advancement took a long time to sink into the minds of men who lived in the social environment of South Africa.

The analysis of on-the-job training as an investment can be broadened to include formal education by considering who bears the costs and who captures the returns. It is beyond the scope of this study to estimate the precise returns on investment in people, but the above analysis suggests the importance of considering the economic implications of society's educational structure when examining the distribution of earnings. Little work has yet been done on this subject in South Africa but the fact that in 1960 no less than 65% of all black South Africans over the age of 19 had had no education at all compared with 2% of whites; that 85% of whites over the age of nine had passed Standard v compared with 12% of blacks; that 23% of whites over the age of fourteen had passed Standard x compared with 0·2% of blacks; and that the expenditure by the state on each white pupil was nearly twelve times as high as for each black pupil, suggest that part, at least, of the vast gap in earnings between black and white mineworkers was due to differences in their formal education.[2]

Combined with improved methods of on-the-job training, one of the most important developments in the more efficient utilisation of mine labour after 1945 was the introduction of methods of selecting or grading the recruits before training them. Previously the black labour force had been regarded largely as an undifferentiated mass of interchangeable units. It used to be little more than mere chance that determined whether a man should spend his life sweeping with a stable broom or operating a mechanical scraper. In the late 1930s a small beginning was made with the selection of 'intelligent and experienced natives' for training as 'boss-boys'. But, besides these few

---

1 I am indebted to Dr. Richard Jolly for this point.
2 The gap does not, as Mr. J. B. Knight has pointed out, *necessarily* imply that the quality of white education is twelve times better than black. Part of the gap is due to the difference in earnings of equally qualified black and white teachers. See Appendix 21.

men, and apart from some simple rules of thumb the rest of the labour force was undifferentiated;[1] job placement was a hit or miss process although it was recognised that some men were better in some jobs than others. Basotho, for example, considered themselves (and were thought by managements) to be superior shaft sinkers. However in 1947 the Government Mining Engineer reported that one mine was experimenting with tests which would aid in making the most of the labour available. A year later, drawing attention to the fact that 75,000 new recruits who had never worked in the mines before were entering the industry, the Government Mining Engineer pointed out that although aptitude testing was still in its infancy, results had proved encouraging and 'high hopes are entertained that the experiment will prove successful'.[2] So successful was it that by 1955 all the mines in the pioneering group used aptitude tests, which soon spread to other groups. By 1967 it was estimated that 45 mines had tested some two million men.[3] The essence of the tests is to sort the recruits into three categories: potential 'boss-boys'; potential semi-skilled workers; and those who, given their education and scores on intelligence tests, were unlikely to be capable of coping with anything but unskilled jobs.[4]

The research initiated by the Chamber of Mines into the elimination of pneumonia is one of the most notable examples anywhere in the world of private investment in health leading directly to an increase in the supply of labour to a particular industry (see p. 68).

Another health problem was the ever present possibility of men succumbing to heatstroke. Methods of acclimatising men before they started the hard physical work in the fiery conditions underground were first developed as part of the effort to lower the death rate of men from tropical areas. In the 1930s, such men were employed in open-air occupations for a month before being sent underground, but the cost of employing men unproductively for so long was high and the method was replaced by one in which new recruits worked for twenty-six days at the shallower underground levels. After further experiment, the period of acclimatisation was reduced from twenty-six to eight days, of which four were spent on the surface. But, with further mechanisation, it became increasingly difficult to find productive work during this period and so it was combined with training. For eight days the

---

[1] Examples of the rules of thumb are: (i) where possible, 'brothers' are allocated to the same mine, (ii) the Pondo are excellent 'machine-boys'.
[2] G.M.E., *Annual Report* (1948), p. 28 A.
[3] *Rand Daily Mail*, 4 August 1967. The development of aptitude testing was largely due to the work of Dr. Simon Biesheuval.
[4] Of new recruits tested in 1968, 2·7% were found to be 'highly intelligent' and fit for supervisory work; 34·2% suitable as construction workers; 43·3% suitable as drivers of various types of machinery; and 18·8% suitable as general labourers. *Star*, 21 March 1969.

H

new recruits spent four hours a day learning about mining and the other four hours becoming acclimatised by the singularly tortuous method of stepping on and off a bench 24 times every minute in a 'hot-box' full of steam at a temperature of approximately 90°F.[1] There is no process of acclimatisation for white workers. The stated reason is that whites know that they should stop work when they feel their temperatures rising and also that they are more able to ease off as they do not work in gangs under direct supervision. Moreover blacks are more prone to heatstroke than whites because they have to exert far more physical energy during the course of their work as whites are supervisors not manual labourers.

The importance which the industry attaches to highly scientific methods of feeding is a measure of the food's value as an investment rather than a mere wage. As an inspector of mines pointed out in 1946, new recruits were often in poor physical condition because of undernourishment and disease and they needed 'a considerable period of feeding and manual labour before they became efficient workers.'[2] Moreover fatigue, due partly to the lack of food before starting work, was thought to be the cause of most accidents in the latter half of the shift.[3] Physical strength is not an attribute required only by unskilled workers. Nevertheless there is little doubt that, in the gold mining industry, the unskilled and semi-skilled work done by blacks required far greater stamina than the work done by most whites. In view of this fact it is probably no accident that the average age of black miners is considerably lower than that of whites: the average (median) ages of the two groups in 1960 were 27 and 35 respectively.[4]

LABOUR MANAGEMENT

One of the most important determinants of the productivity of labour in any economic enterprise is the ability with which management uses that labour. A belief widely held in South Africa is that the relatively low productivity of black mineworkers is due to their lack of skill. The evidence from the gold mines suggests, however, that this is not the only cause. The ineptitude, throughout much of the period under consideration, with which mine managers used their black labour compared with their far greater sophistication in managing the white labour force must surely have been a major reason for the fact that, as the Chamber of Mines claimed in 1943, 'the native labourer underground as an individual was no more efficient than he was 30

---

[1] *Star*, 21 March 1969.   [2] G.M.E., *Annual Report* (1946), p. 105 A.
[3] R. R. Mitchell, 'A pre-shift feeding room', *Papers and Proceedings of the Association of Mine Managers* (T.C.M., Johannesburg, 1956–7), p. 691 C. An attempt, in the O.F.S., to make breakfast compulsory proved so unpopular that it had to be abandoned.
[4] See Appendix 20.

years ago'.[1] In a devastating passage drawing attention to the fact that at one stage less than 70% of the few men who had actually been trained could perform the standard jobs that they were supposed to have learnt, a mine officer in 1949 described the qualifications of those whites chosen to train black workers:

In the past, the chief qualifications of an instructor shift boss in charge of the boss boy and new boys training school were 'years of experience at shift-bossing', 'failing health', 'good man', or 'he is now entitled to an easier job'. In extreme cases a niche had to be found for a man who failed to make the grade at producing. Management took it for granted that the qualifications were adequate and seldom paused to question the difference between a good production man and an able instructor, nor was his suitability questioned or results checked. Invariably the pupils were blamed and not the teachers when results were unsatisfactory.[2]

Gradually, however, the industry became aware that it needed to devote more thought to the better utilisation of its black labour force which, as a future president of the Chamber pointed out in 1949, formed such a high proportion of total working costs.

There are two essential aspects of labour management. The one concerns the problem of allocating the labour in an optimum manner; the other is the task of ensuring that the labour, once allocated to particular jobs, works at its fullest potential. Both aspects were considerably developed during the years that followed the Second World War, but there was in some instances a wide gap between the theoretical knowledge gained and the practice. With regard to allocation we have already seen (p. 80) how the colour bar prevents managers from using their available labour in the most economically efficient way. Nevertheless, within the framework of the law, there was some attempt to use it more efficiently. The development of selection procedures (see p. 94) was a major step in this direction.

The extent to which the potential of workers on a particular job is realised depends, amongst other things, on three interacting factors: their experience in that job, the incentives provided for harder and better work, and the degree to which workers are made to feel part of the enterprise. One measure of experience is the rate of turnover which may be defined as the arithmetical mean of the total number of people entering and leaving the gold mines, divided by the average number in service during any given year, expressed as a percentage.[3] It was estimated in 1948 that, for whites, movement in and out of the industry as a whole accounted for approximately one-third of total

---

[1] Cited by Diamond, *African Labour Problems*, p. 144 D. Cf. remarks of an inspector of mines on p. 93.
[2] H. J. Nieuwenhuizen, 'Training mine Native labour', *Papers and Proceedings of the Association of Mine Managers* (T.C.M., Johannesburg, 1948–9) C.
[3] See Appendix 23.

turnover; the other two-thirds was made up of individual movements between mines.[1] For blacks, on the other hand, who can only move between mines if they are South Africans, the external turnover is a much higher proportion of the total. In 1936 the total turnover of blacks for the year was 97% and of whites it was 48%;[2] twenty years later the figures had changed only slightly to 107% and 42% respectively. However the shortage of skilled labour exerted a pressure on the industry to make white workers feel more integrated into the running of the mine. One of the reasons for the fact that so many men left the industry after only a few weeks or months in service was that they tended to feel anonymous in a vast impersonal machine. This led, albeit slowly, to an increasing awareness by employers of the economic value of personnel management, which was able to reduce, in a spectacular manner, the rate of white turnover from 42% in 1965 to 29% three years later.[3] One group which introduced a personnel department in the 1950s reduced its separation rate in six mines from 55% in 1956 to 16% in 1962.[4] By 1964, due probably to the boom which began at that time, the rate had risen again to 21%, still well below half its former level. While this fall in turnover coincided with a slight recession in manufacturing it seems that it can be traced very largely to the work of the personnel department with its three-pronged approach of: better selection; better labour relations, described by a personnel officer as 'No more *skiet en donder*';[5] and a process of induction whereby new workers were welcomed to the mine, shown around, and made to feel wanted and at home by the management. The fact that most men who left the industry did not stay more than three months underlined the importance of good selection and induction.

With regard to blacks the general picture of labour management is not nearly so encouraging. The migrant labour system makes it virtually impossible for the industry to reduce turnover of black workers much below 100% per annum. Although many mineworkers come back more than once, the time between contracts is so long the experience of recruits who have previously worked on the mines can seldom be fully used. The costs of turnover are high: it was estimated in 1941 that for every 20% of turnover the cost to an industry was 1% of the total wage bill.[6] Thus, as a rough

[1] South Africa, *Conditions of Employment*, table 30.
[2] G.M.E. and W.N.L.A., *Annual Reports*.   [3] *Ibid.*
[4] The *separation rate* is defined as the number of people who leave the mines in any one year as a percentage of the total number in service.
[5] Not readily translatable. Perhaps a combination of 'no more blood and thunder' with 'no more shooting and beating up' captures the sense best.
[6] J. S. Ford, 'Scientific management with particular application to a Witwatersrand gold mine', *Papers and Proceedings of the Association of Mine Managers* (T.C.M., Johannesburg, 1942–5), p. 923 C. The figures were taken from an American survey.

approximation, we may say that the cost of black turnover on the mines was between three and four million rand in 1969. The lack of black trade unions, combined with the industry's attitude that black workers are not ripe for full consultation with employers, means that there is virtually no direct communication between top management and the vast majority of mineworkers. At a much lower level the white compound managers are kept in some sort of touch with the feelings of workers by means of regular discussion with *indunas* and *izibondo*,[1] but a wide gulf remains. This may account, to some extent, for the fact that until the 1960s black workers were generally regarded as a mass of labour units rather than as individual human beings. However a new system of labour management, first developed by Union Minière du Haut Katanga, and subsequently adopted on the Zambian Copperbelt, was brought from there to South Africa. What was new about the scheme to improve the utilisation of black labour was, firstly, the attempt to develop incentive schemes by rationalising the wage structure (see p. 55) in order to ensure that it encouraged workers to increase their own productivity and, secondly, the introduction of black personnel assistants, known as P.A.'s, to implement the assumption underlying the scheme: that greater productivity would only be achieved by treating each black worker as an individual with human aspirations.

The P.A.'s, men who have generally completed secondary school, help new workers to adjust to their jobs, make performance appraisals on which to base promotion, ensure that each labour gang has its full complement of men every day, and investigate grievances by blacks and whites against each other. They work under the general supervision of a departmental personnel officer (D.P.O.) who replaced the native controller. Previously this latter official had, in the eyes of management, been of singularly low status and calibre although, in the eyes of black workers, he was one of the most powerful men on a mine, as he had arbitrarily decided who should do particular jobs. When the D.P.O. scheme was first introduced there was one P.A. for each mine overseer's section in which there were approximately 600 men. After a year the number of P.A.'s was doubled, thus enabling them to get to know their men individually and to assess their performance in the light of regular visits underground and discussions with both black and white workers. The system of counselling made possible the solution of personal problems as well as the settling of grievances.

In the context of the South African gold mines, the appointment of these African personnel assistants was a revolutionary departure from the accepted white ideas of the sort of work a black man should and could do. However,

[1] See p. 58.

thanks to careful preparatory work by managements in explaining to their white miners the objects of the new system, it was successfully introduced on a number of mines and was said to enjoy a wide measure of support from the white miners to whom it was a source of added income. For the remuneration of the white contract miner depended very largely on the number of tons of rock which he broke each month; this in turn depended upon the efficiency of his gang of black workers. The D.P.O. system increased this efficiency both by ensuring that each gang had its full complement of men every day and by means of the new wage structure which provided effective rewards for hard work, skill, and initiative. Furthermore, the scheme provided white miners with a better disciplinary weapon than assault (which was often used before), in that promotion within a gang depended to a considerable extent on what he told the P.A. upon whom he depended for a regular supply of high quality labour. For example, one of the most vociferous of the 'rebel' miners (see p. 116), who was strongly opposed to any relaxation of the colour bar, had made the management particularly anxious about the introduction of the D.P.O. system in his area. But, after its introduction, the miner was observed regularly sharing his lunch sandwiches underground with his P.A. and discussing with him, at great length, the particular problems of his gang. It is difficult to assess the precise effects of the D.P.O. system on productivity as it was introduced in combination with increased mechanisation, in the form of better scrapers and heavier winches, but there is little doubt that it marked a breakthrough, one that was long overdue, in the management of labour on the gold mines of the group concerned.[1] Those working the system were convinced that its effect on productivity was considerable.

By 1969 the general picture of labour in the gold mines was one of a body of men in whom the industry had imbedded considerable resources, by way of training programmes and health precautions, and for whom better management was an important determinant of increased productivity. The interaction of the various forces of supply and demand together with the factors outlined in the above chapter are matters to which we must now turn.

[1] The above description is based on the scheme introduced by one of the mining groups during the 1960s. Other groups were experimenting with similar schemes.

CHAPTER 6

INTERACTION OF FORCES[1]

We get a better clue to actual behaviour if we think of wages as being determined by an interplay between social and economic factors, instead of being based on economic factors – and crude economic factors at that – alone.

J. R. Hicks, *Economic Foundations of Wage Policy*

The facts about the labour market of the gold mines need some explaining. Why, for example, is there any gap between the average earnings of white and black workers? Why is the gap so much greater than in secondary industry? Why has it widened so markedly since the Second World War? Furthermore why, in the face of this widening gap, has the ratio of black to white workers remained so constant?[2] Given the acute shortages of unskilled labour over much of the period under consideration, why have the real incomes of black mineworkers remained static? And why did the collusion which has existed in the industry throughout most of its history and which (see pp. 4–5) was maintained in the face of increasing competition from secondary industry, begin, albeit tentatively, to break down in 1962 when the industry for the first time in years at last had adequate supplies of un- skilled labour at the existing wage rate? Other questions that spring to mind are: why has the gold mining industry chosen to go far afield to recruit its unskilled labour rather than hire it at the gate as has happened both in other sectors of the South African economy and on the copper mines of Zambia? And what role, if any, have the strong white trade unions played in raising the real incomes of their members? Has the absence of a powerful black trade union movement improved (as has been argued) the lot of unskilled workers in the country as a whole by making possible more employment than there would otherwise have been?[3] How has the existence of a rigid colour bar affected the wage structure? Has the monopsony power of the Chamber of Mines enabled it to exploit black workers?

[1] Non-economists are encouraged to persevere. Despite the four diagrams, which could not be relegated to the appendixes, the chapter is not as ominous as, perhaps, it looks. Wherever it has been impossible to avoid using a technical term there is a footnote to explain its meaning.
[2] See Appendix 24.
[3] W. H. Hutt, *The Economics of the Colour Bar* (Deutsch, London, 1964), p. 108 B.

Labour in the South African gold mines

COLLUSION

Let us start with the question of collusion. It is possible to show that, in those economies where the total labour force is being employed by only a few big firms, it may be in the interests of individual firms to collude with others in holding down wages even although this implies a shortage of labour.[1] The reason for this, as Berg has demonstrated, lies in the fear of retaliation. Suppose that a large individual firm could get the labour it needed if it raised its wages provided none of the other firms followed suit: it is quite possible that it would end up making lower profits than it was before it raised wages if the other firms raised their wages as well.[2] However, where there is collusion firms may tend to pay hidden earnings in the form of better working conditions and other perquisites, in the hope of attracting labour from other firms without causing them to retaliate. Whether or not management could make workers aware of better total earnings in order to attract them, without the other firms noticing the discrepancy and striking back, is a moot point but certainly in the mining industry individual managements have worked on this assumption. It could be argued that payments under the counter result in a longer time lag between an increase in one firm and a response by others.

But the argument for collusion seems to be valid only in those circumstances where a few firms are competing for a limited amount of homogeneous labour. Such was the case in the early days of the mining industry when the policy of collusion against black labour was developed. But by the 1930s conditions had changed considerably; the manufacturing sector was expanding rapidly. Such circumstances, in a more perfect market, would have led to a breakdown of collusion. The imperfections that enabled the gold mines to maintain their policy of collusion lay in legislation that enabled them to isolate their labour sources from the competing sector. As we have seen (pp. 71, 81), the barriers to geographical mobility discriminate not only between black and white but also between one sector and another. The pass laws operate in favour of the mining and agricultural sectors at the expense of manufacturing; passport control favours the mines. As there are no such barriers for whites in any sector it seems likely that one of the major reasons for the difference in the racial wage gap between the gold mines and secondary industry is the legislation which has had the effect of restricting the supply of unskilled labour to manufacturing and so causing black wages to be higher in that sector than in mining.

[1] E. J. Berg, *Recruitment of a Labor Force in Sub-Saharan Africa* (Ph.D. thesis, Harvard, 1960), p. 392 D. Cf. Van der Horst, *Native Labour*, pp. 201–3, for an alternative explanation of the labour shortage.
[2] See Appendix 25.

That influx control is an important factor in influencing the relative supplies of unskilled labour to the mining and manufacturing sectors was tacitly admitted by the *Mining Journal* in 1959 when among the reasons for the sharp increase in the black labour supply it included 'the government policy of repatriating unemployed Natives in the towns, either inside or outside the Union...Some quarters may regard this last as a police state action, but the growth of a large unemployed population in the urban areas, constitutes a serious social problem, as shown in the increase in incidence of serious crime...Once repatriated, it is possible for the Natives to apply for work on the mines.'[1]

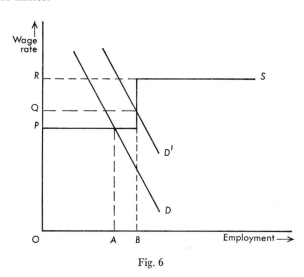

Fig. 6

The difference that developed after 1936 in the level of unskilled earnings in the two sectors reinforced the policy of collusion. Once such a differential has come into being those paying wages on the lower level have an added incentive to collude either when the supplies of labour isolated for the sole use of the gold mines diminish (e.g. because of changed restrictions) or when their demand increases to exceed the available supplies of isolated labour. Suppose that, in fig. 6, the black wage rate in the mining industry is *OP* and in the manufacturing sector is *OR*. For a demand *D* the mines are able to obtain *OA* units of labour. But suppose now that their demand rises to *D'*. A little more labour (*AB*) can be obtained from the isolated sources but any more will only come by drawing it away from secondary industry.

The mines will collude to hold wages at *OP*, for a rise to *OQ* would not increase their supply. It would seem that this 'kink' in the supply curve of

[1] See also p. 81.

black labour to the mines which developed after the 1930s as a result of the creation of different barriers to geographical mobility, explains the desire of the mines to maintain collusion in the face of increasing wages in other sectors. One might postulate that the industry would also do all in its power to prevent its supply of isolated labour OB, from diminishing either by being drawn into other sectors or by being prevented by law from coming to the mines.

So long as the demand curve for mine labour intersects in the kink there will be collusion. But what happens if, either because of an increase in demand or a contraction of supply, OB, the demand intersects the supply curve beyond the kink?

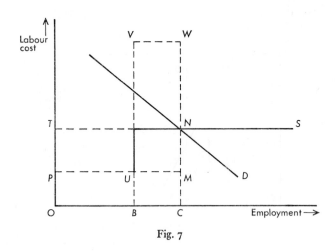

Fig. 7

The mines could raise their wage rate from OP to OT, compete with manufacturing industry, and employ OC units of labour (see fig. 7). Alternatively they could seek, via recruiting, to increase the supply of labour, available at wage OP, from OB to OC and maintain their collusion. Clearly, if recruiting were costless it would invariably be chosen, but an assessment between the two alternatives has to make allowance for the cost of recruiting. To show this diagrammatically we may think of the industry as weighing up the alternative costs of increasing its labour supply from OB to OC. A wage increase would involve an additional expenditure equal to the area $PMNT$. The advantage of recruiting is that it enables a form of perfectly discriminating monopsony whereby the employer is able to pay more (in the form of transport subsidies etc.) for his additional workers without having to increase his payments to those already employed. Nevertheless the annual recruitment cost per person ($= UV$) may be so high as to outweigh such advantages. In fig. 7 employment would be expanded from OB to OC by means of recruiting so long as the area $UVWM$ was less than the area $PMNT$. For whites, recruitment has always been a much less viable alternative due not only to the very large *per capita* costs of recruiting men from as far away as Europe, but also to the fact that there is no kink to cause a large extra cost of increasing the labour supply.

This far we have assumed that there is only one recruiting versus wage decision, but in practice there are several separate sources, each with its own particular recruiting cost, from which black mine labour can be drawn.

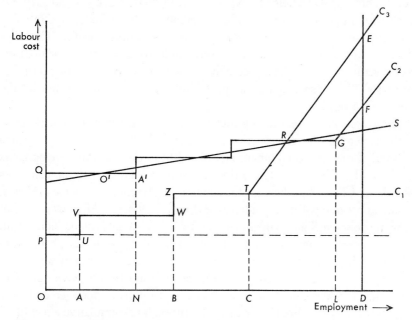

NOTE: $OA = O'A'$.

Fig. 8

Suppose that in the short run, the amount of black labour required by the industry was fixed at OD (see fig. 8). Let OP be the wage rate on the mines. OA units of labour are available at that wage without being recruited. A further AB units of labour could be recruited (at a cost of UV per head) from inside South Africa and other neighbouring countries where the N.R.C. operates. For a total recruiting cost of $UV + WZ$ per head a further BC units of labour could be obtained by the W.N.L.A. from Mozambique and CD units more from the tropical areas. S is the supply of labour available to the mines from secondary industry. Now suppose that a substantial risk factor (due to the possibility of sudden boycott) was added to the employment of 'tropicals'.

This risk is one which increases with the number of 'tropicals' employed, thus the supply of labour to the mines changes from PTC_1 to PTC_3. The industry might continue to recruit 'tropicals' as before, or it might decide that it is cheaper to replace 'tropicals' with labour drawn from the manufacturing sector. By putting up the wage of all mine workers from OP to OQ an extra OO' units of local labour could be attracted. This would be worthwhile if the area $PQRT$ were less than the area $EFGR$. The industry would raise wages and continue to recruit, but the number of 'tropicals' would fall from CD to LD.

The above analysis helps to explain why, in 1962, when the industry was faced with an adequate supply of black labour at the current wage rate one of the groups appealed to the Technical Advisory Committee of the Chamber of Mines to suspend the maximum permissible average. Shortly before this, events had occurred whose net effect was to raise the cost of recruiting 'tropicals' in just such a way as postulated in the above diagram by the movement from TC_1 to TC_3.

The years 1960–1 were significant for South Africa. Apart from marking its birth as a republic it was the period in which South Africans suddenly began to realise that they could no longer be isolated from the political developments north of the Limpopo. The Prime Minister of Great Britain made his 'Winds of Change' speech in the House of Assembly, nineteen African countries became politically independent, and sixty-seven Africans were shot by white police at Sharpeville in an action which outraged the outside world. External pressure against the policy of apartheid began to rise, a pressure not eased by South Africa's withdrawal from the Commonwealth. One manifestation of this pressure was the cancellation by the government of Tanzania of its agreement with the W.N.L.A. to allow 10,000 men each year to go to work on the South African gold mines. The cumulative effect of all these events on the gold mining industry was to increase the risk of employing men from foreign countries.

It was suddenly realised that the mining industry in which 60% of the black labour force was from beyond the country's borders was somewhat vulnerable to external political pressure. Thus, in a short space of time, a significant risk was added to the normal cost of recruiting foreign labour. The precise value attached to this risk varied from mine to mine depending on the relative importance of foreign, especially 'tropical', labour in its production.

The result of the request to put up wages, made by the group which probably had the highest proportion of 'tropical' labour, sparked off a vigorous, not to say acrimonious, debate within the industry. All were agreed that there was some risk in employing foreigners but not all were equally able to pay the hard cash necessary to reduce the proportion. In this sense the risk may be seen as analogous to credit which poorer mines needed much more than those making large profits. Inevitably, if the group which bore the biggest risk was also the one most able to afford minimising it, it would have taken the initiative in attempting to do so while other groups would have played down the risk factor in order to prevent a rise in wages they felt unable to afford. Following the Anglo American Corporation's request, a compromise arrangement was made whereby the maximum permissible average wage was retained for all except the most highly paid 15% of the total black labour force. By the mid 1960s, it was claimed by some that the maximum permissible average had been entirely abolished while others within the industry said that it remained as a sword of Damocles over the heads of any mines which bid up wages too high. Whatever the precise truth, it is clear that, for the first time since the monopsonistic collusion became properly organised, the winds of competition were being felt. However with the subsequent reduction in the risk factor due it would seem to the successful development of South Africa's new 'outward' policy, the pressure on increasing the supplies of South African workers by raising wages to a competitive level was considerably eased and the gains of the early 1960s were not consolidated by further wage increases for black workers in the years that followed (see chapter 3).

The above analysis of collusion is based on the assumption that each mine has identical cost curves and profit margins, but, as we have just seen, it was the difference in profit margins which caused one group of mines to break the collusion. Immediately the question arises as to why it did not do this before. In the gold mining industry the costs of labour shortage are considerable. Black labour is a major determinant of output (see p. 43) and a shortage is likely to cause not only a temporary reduction in output but an overall loss to the mine, because the inflationary trend has the effect of transposing some of the payable ore reserves not mined on one day into the unpayable range of the next – unless the price of gold is rising as fast as the costs of production. In a situation where the terms of trade have moved against gold the time factor is a crucial variable in determining the total profits of a mine during its working life.[1]

The main reason why the breakaway did not come earlier than it did lay in the nature of the industry's organisation into a few financial groups which control the individual mines (see p. 26). In each of these groups there are both rich and marginal mines. Ultimately the ability of the group to raise

[1] Over the period 1936–69 the index of retail prices rose by 195% whilst the average price received per fine ounce of gold rose by 86%.

capital for investment (which is the primary justification for its existence) is determined by the profitability of the ventures in which it has already invested capital. Under these circumstances the group faced with the choice either of raising the profitability of its rich mines by raising wages and hence eliminating any shortage, but at the same time causing its marginal mines to close down, or of keeping wages constant and its marginal mine in business, but thereby losing some profits on its wealthy mine, is likely to choose to

TABLE 9. *Distribution of mines, according to profitability between mining houses, 1936 and 1961*

Group	No. of producing mines 1936 1961	Rich 1936 1961	Average 1936 1961	Poor 1936 1961	No. of poor mines more than 30 years old 1936 1961
Anglo American	4 12	– 3	3 3	1 6	– 5
Anglo-Transvaal	1 4	– –	– 1	1 3	– 1
Rand Mines/Central	11 8	– 1	4 1	7 6	7 6
General Mining	2 3	– –	1 2	1 1	1 –
Consolidated Gold Fields	5 11	1 1	2 2	2 8	2 5
Union Corporation	2 7	– –	2 5	– 2	– 2
Johannesburg Consolidated Investment	7 2	– –	2 –	5 2	3 –

NOTE: Mines are graded according to their wealth, measured by the working profit per ton milled, as follows:

	Working profit/tons milled (current cents) *1936*	*1961*
Poor	0–9·9	0–19·9
Average	10–29·9	20–59·9
Rich	⩾30	⩾60

SOURCES: T.C.M. and W.N.L.A. *Annual Reports*, 1936 and 1961.

keep its marginal mine in operation simply because of the fact that once a mine is closed down it is difficult, if not impossible, to re-open it. In a situation where price, exogenously determined, *might* rise, all mines will keep going as long as possible in the hopes of such a development. Table 9, showing the distribution, between different groups, of poor, average, and rich mines, helps one to understand why it is that the pressure for higher wages should have come from the Anglo American Corporation when it did.

By 1961 not only were the majority of Anglo American's poor mines old, but the three rich ones were all in the O.F.S. where the proportion of non-

South African black labour was particularly high – up to 85% in some cases. Under these circumstances one can see why the group decided at that time that, as a whole, it would gain more than it would lose by breaking the collusion. In fact the group got the best of both worlds, for as long as labour supplies remained adequate there was nothing to prevent it from paying the industry rate in its marginal mines while paying a higher rate on the richer mines in order to increase the proportion of South African labour.[1]

But the risk of political action suddenly affecting the amount of labour available is not the only one of which the mining industry has had to take account; there have been other risks whose effect on wages has been in the opposite direction, tending to dampen any upward movements. These risks lie in the unpredictability of abrupt changes in the exogenous variables affecting the black labour supply. Mine managers believe (see p. 75) that in years of drought and poor crops the supply of labour at a given wage rate is far higher than in years of rain and plenty. Thus it is understandable, given the normal ratchet effect which makes a downward movement in money wages almost impossible, for an industry to be reluctant to increase wages to meet a shortage if it is at all likely that conditions will soon change so that the labour supply will be sufficient to meet demand even at the old wage. There is an analogy here with primary commodities whose supplies are also known to fluctuate widely. If the price of the commodity once determined could not be lowered, it would probably be fixed at the lowest level at which it was thought that long-run supply would equal the long-run demand, and it would not be raised for what were thought to be short-run falls in supply. Carrying the analogy a stage further it is not unhelpful to think of the maximum permissible average as similar to the price of a primary product fixed by an international commodity agreement. As with commodity schemes the real difficulty lies in adjusting the price to the long-run trends about which the fluctuations take place. In fact there appears to be no empirical evidence (see p. 82) to support the hypothesis that either the price of wool or the maize crop affect, substantially, the supply of labour to the mines. Nevertheless the sharp increase in the supply of labour to the mines after 1958, while at first partly due to a downturn in the secondary sector, still remains to be satisfactorily explained, as does the subsequent reduction in supply towards the end of 1969. Whatever the reasons, the black labour supply under a migrant system remained subject to sudden changes. The role of uncertainty concerning those external factors over which the mining industry has no control, but which directly affect the supply of unskilled

[1] As an exercise in detective work, readers might like to work out from the table which of the major finance houses were strongly opposed to the proposed wage increase.

labour, is an important factor which has to be taken into consideration when a choice is made between raising wages or reducing the shortage in some other manner such as recruiting or raising the productivity of the labour force. For even where the rational choice seemed to be to put up wages it could be argued that raising the productivity of the labour already employed was less risky than increasing the wage rate in the hopes of getting more men.

Although the few mining groups hire a large amount of white labour the possibility of collusion is severely restricted, but not entirely eliminated, by the fact that whites are free to move between one sector and another. In addition their trade unions provide a powerful counterbalance to the monopsony of the Chamber. However the sheer size of the gold mining industry, and the fact that complete sector mobility is prevented by job specialisation, provides an incentive for the mines to collude (and thus an incentive to break the collusion by means of 'hidden' earnings). At the same time the unions, by pressing continually for increases in minimum rates applicable throughout the industry, tend to remove the conditions under which collusion can take place.[1]

The fact that the gold mining industry has not been able to isolate its white labour market from the rest of the economy has meant that the general level of wages could not be kept below that in manufacturing industry. Indeed in practice wages for whites in mining have been somewhat higher than for whites of similar qualifications in manufacturing industry. There seem to be three interlocking reasons why this should be so. Firstly, working conditions underground are more disagreeable than those in factories on the surface; thus there must be some wage difference to allow for this. Secondly, the potential loss to the industry of an experienced and trained miner moving to manufacturing industry gives him a bargaining point to get part of the returns from the specific investment in him by the gold mines (see p. 91). Thirdly, there is the effect of the colour bar. So far our analysis of the wage structure has been based on the assumption that skilled and unskilled are totally non-competing groups with no connection between each other. It is now time to consider the interaction of the two.

COLOUR BAR

The colour bar as built up in the South African gold mining industry contains two related, but distinct, elements. The first of these affects the supply of, the second the demand for, both skilled and unskilled labour. The one

[1] By narrowing the divergence between the two supply curves S_1 and S_2 in the diagram of Appendix 25.

element defines precisely which particular jobs may or may not be performed by a given racial group: it reserves jobs. Thus, for example, the easily defined job of blasting may legally only be done by whites.[1] The other aspect of the colour bar is that which effectively fixes the maximum ratio of the number of blacks to the number of whites employed in the industry. It has been shown that the effect of the colour bar was to fix this ratio, over a long period, at 8:1.[2]

The effect of reservation is to prevent blacks moving into the skilled labour pool, which is thus kept artificially small, thereby causing skilled wages to be higher than they would otherwise be; the effect of the ratio is to create a joint demand where the demand for blacks depends on the supply of whites, and vice versa. In fig. 9 we explore some of the implications, on relative earnings, of these two constraints: let us define B_8W as that unit of labour which is made up of one white and eight blacks. The demand for these B_8W units is their marginal revenue product which, in the case of gold where price is fixed, varies directly with their marginal physical product.[3] This rises as either the productivity of white labour or of black labour (or of both) increases. On the supply side, because of the rigidity of the colour bar, the curves for skilled and unskilled are determined independently of each other. But the supply of B_8W is a combination of the two.

In fig. 9 S_B, S_W, and S_{B_8W} are the supply curves of unskilled blacks (in units of 8 men), skilled whites, and B_8W units. MC'_B, and MC'_{B_8W} are the respective marginal charge curves which show the additional cost at any level of employment of hiring one more unit.[4] D_{B_8W} is the demand curve for B_8W, that is the marginal revenue product of units of one white and eight blacks taken together. The point P, at the intersection of the supply and the demand schedules for B_8W units, shows the number (ON) of such units that are employed and at what wage rate (NP). Drawing a line vertically down from P, the points of intersection, Q and R, show the effective or 'derived'

---

[1] For historical reasons, whites, in this case, include St. Helenans and Mauritians.

[2] See Appendix 26.

[3] The *marginal revenue product* of a factor of production (in this case a B_8W unit) is defined as the addition to total revenue derived from the sale of the product of that factor. The *marginal physical product* of a factor of production is the addition to total output made by that factor. In algebraic terms

$$MRP_n = TR_n - TR_{n-1}$$
$$MPP_n = TO_n - TO_{n-1}$$

Under perfect competition (where the price of a product does not fall as more of it is put onto the market) $MRP = Price \times MPP$. See R. G. Lipsey, *An Introduction to Positive Economics* (Weidenfeld & Nicolson, London, 2nd edn., 1966), pp. 417 ff. B.

[4] The MC curve for the relatively inelastic S'_B is higher than the average supply curve, because under conditions of monopsony the employer knows that if he hires more men he will drive up the wage rate not only of the extra men he wishes to hire but of his other employees as well. We assume that the mines have no monopsony power in the white labour market. Lipsey, *Positive Economics*. p. 455 B.

I   III

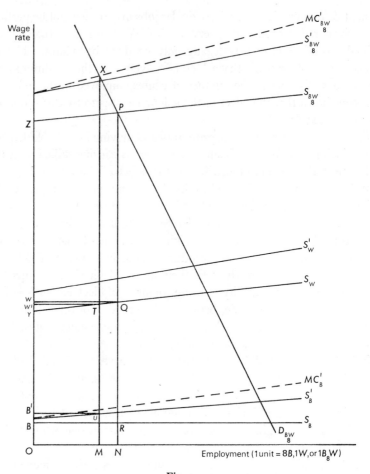

Fig. 9

demand for whites and blacks and their wage rates Ow and OB. The ratio of ON whites to ON blacks is $1:8$ as required by the colour bar. Now suppose that, for some reason (say the development of secondary industry), the supply curve of blacks ceases to be perfectly elastic and moves its position from SB to $S'B$. This would shift the supply of B_8W units from SB_8W to $S'B_8W$; and the effective demands for black and white workers would be given by the intersections, T and U, of the vertical line through X, which is the new point of intersection of the demand and marginal charge schedules of B_8W units.[1] Employment of both blacks and whites will fall from ON to OM; but, while

---

[1] X is the point because if the industry employed less than OM units the extra revenue derived from employing one more unit would be greater than the extra cost of hiring it. Similarly profits would be decreased if employment was increased beyond OM.

the wage rates of blacks will rise from O_B to $O_{B'}$, the wage rate for whites will *fall* from O_W to $O_{W'}$.[1] Alternatively, if by some means the supply of blacks could be effectively increased from S'_B to S_B, then employment of both groups would increase, the wage rate for blacks would fall, but that for whites would rise.

This diagram helps to illustrate the economic pressures behind the political forces operating in the labour market. White workers, organised in trade unions, want to increase their wage rate without bringing any unemployment upon themselves. This they can do if, somehow, they can shift the employers' demand for them out to the right. This is achieved by shifting the supply curve for B_8W down to the right by means of increasing the supply of blacks. The ratio element of the colour bar ensures that the industry does not alter its techniques so as to use the more unskilled workers, while the reservation element prevents management from training blacks as skilled workers and so shifting the S_W curve which represents the supply of skilled workers irrespective of colour down to the right. Given the colour bar, management is indifferent whether the shift from S'_{B_8W} to S_{B_8W} is achieved by means of shifting S'_B to S_B, or S'_W to S_W. Thus, given its demand for labour, management will do what it can to increase the supply of B_8W units at the given wage, by acting to shift either S'_B or S'_W. It will push against whichever of these two curves is most likely to yield. Theoretically it could shift the S'_W curve by insisting on employing blacks as skilled workers, while it could alter the S'_B curve by pressing for greater influx and passport control in its favour. The interests of white workers also lie in shifting the supply curve of B_8W units from S'_{B_8W} to S_{B_8W} – *provided* that this can be done without altering their own supply curve. White workers, by virtue of their trade union strike potential and political voting power, are in a far stronger position to resist employers' attempts to alter their supply curve than blacks.

However, as the economy expands and the supply of both skilled and unskilled labour to the mining industry becomes more inelastic the ability of management to hold down black wages diminishes.[2] At the same time, however, the upward shift to the left of the S_W curve, due to the acute artificial scarcity of skilled workers, increases the interests of management in holding down the S_W curve by means of employing blacks as skilled workers. In other words, during the years before the Second World War, the pressures on the colour bar were not as great as they have now become; for not only was the supply of whites reasonably adequate to meet the existing demand for

---

[1] Assuming no 'ratchet' effect.
[2] Elasticity is a measure of the responsiveness of the quantity demanded or supplied to a change in some variable: in this case, the wage rate. The more elastic the supply, the more will the quantity change in response to a given change in wages.

skilled workers, but also it was possible, via recruiting, to exert a downward pressure on black labour costs. Under these conditions an alliance between white workers and management was possible. But during the fifties and sixties, both tendencies were reversed. With the rise of secondary industry the increasing demand, over time, for skilled workers could not be met by the supply of whites only; whilst the expansion of the economy, increased risk of employing foreigners, and, towards the end of the period, the development of competitive recruiting organisations from the farms, railways and factories of the Western Cape, made it more difficult for the mines to hold wages down.[1] With the widening of the gap between white and black earnings (expressed graphically as an increasing distance between the Sw and Sb curves) the interests of management and black labour have come closer and closer together in favouring the abolition of the colour bar. For not only would this lower the costs to the industry, but it would raise the wage of those blacks who could go straight into skilled jobs as well as raising the wages of the unskilled by reducing the number available to do these unskilled jobs. A further pressure against the colour bar has been the steady inflation which has raised the costs of production in an industry where it has not been possible to pass on these costs to consumers by raising the price of the final product.[2]

Over the years there has been a quiet, but none the less real, struggle between the white trade unions seeking to maintain a rigid colour bar and mine managements who seek to prevent labour costs from rising by breaching the colour bar and thus increasing the supply of skilled labour. Two weapons lie within the hands of the trade unionists: the law and the strike. The mere memory of the 1922 Rand rebellion is a potent influence in persuading employers not to tamper with the colour bar and the trade unions ensure that the memory is kept fresh by periodic strikes. Added to the power of potential strike action is the force of law. Hardly a year passed without the Government Mining Engineer charging white miners with contravening regulations by 'inciting' blacks who were not holders of blasting certificates to charge drill holes in a mine.[3] The fines which in 1936 were approximately R25 for each miner had by 1967 risen to R60.[4] But the employers have not been completely powerless. The weapon that lies within their hands is the acute shortage of suitably skilled whites to fill all the jobs which are by law or tradition closed to blacks. At first the pressure could be eased by relaxing the skill requirements or by employing women in clerical jobs on the surface. However these minor changes were not sufficient,[5] and something else had

---

[1] See table 7, p. 66.
[2] See p. 36.
[3] G.M.E., *Annual Report* (1936), p. 68 A.
[4] *Rand Daily Mail*, 25 January 1967.
[5] Special exemptions were made from time to time by the Government Mining Engineer after it had been ascertained that no suitable, unemployed, qualified men were available.

to be done. In practice the managements of individual mines seemed to have been able to convince their white workers that to allow some blacks to do white jobs would in no wise endanger their own position nor lead to the undercutting of wages. But this conditional breach of the colour bar has taken place under the ever watchful eye of the trade unions. In 1958, for example, the M.U.J.C. complained that 'mines were employing non-Europeans on work previously and traditionally performed by Europeans'. The matter was carefully investigated by the Chamber of Mines which assured the M.U.J.C. somewhat ambiguously that 'no attempt had been made, as a matter of policy, to replace Europeans by non-Europeans'.[1]

But the pressure of the skilled-labour shortage continued to mount and in 1964 the first official attempt to ease the conflict of interest between white workers and white management occurred. Twelve mines belonging to different groups obtained permission, with the full backing of the white unions, to conduct an experiment whereby the regulation demanding early examination was temporarily relaxed. Under this regulation, no black men were allowed into a working place at the beginning of a shift until it had been declared safe by a white miner. In practice this resulted in the loss of large numbers of man-hours while the gang of black workers waited at the foot of the shaft for anything up to an hour.[2] In terms of the experiment, however, a 'competent non-scheduled person' (i.e. a 'boss-boy') was permitted to inspect the working place. The experiment worked satisfactorily for some months: production went up, both black and white wages increased, and the accident rate fell. Management was satisfied; white workers, now on monthly salaries and earning more money for less effort, were pleased; and some blacks, with wider opportunities and greater earning potential, were better off. All seemed well until some 'rebel' miners, working on mines not involved in the experiment, raised the old battle cry of unfair competition and the danger of being replaced by black men. Under this powerful political pressure from the right, the government, which had originally sanctioned the experiment, appointed a commission to investigate it.[3] The commission, while finding that the scheme had not, economically speaking, been a failure, advised that because of its wider implications it should be abandoned. The government concurred and in 1965 a tiny crack in the colour bar was sealed.

But not for long. The economic pressures continued to build up. In February 1966 the Minister of Mines admitted in the House of Assembly

[1] T.C.M., *Sixty Ninth Annual Report* (1958), p. 17 A.
[2] This practice was investigated – and condemned – by an official commission as far back as 1914. South Africa, *Natives Grievances Inquiry*, para. 58 A.
[3] Suid-Afrika *Verslag van die Kommissie van Ondersoek Insake Proefnemings op Sekere Myne* (Viljoen) (Roneoed, Pretoria, 1965) A.

that the industry was short of approximately 2,000 white mineworkers.[1] A few months later the Chamber of Mines and the Federation of Mining Unions began negotiating a new scheme on a 'productivity bargaining' basis.[2] While negotiations were going on there was a great deal of unrest amongst the white miners who were suspicious not only that the employers were trying once again to attack the colour bar, but also that their own leaders would not stand firm against the arguments of the Chamber. 1966 saw a wave of wildcat strikes by 'rebel' miners who were determined that their leaders be men who would not bow before the pressures. In November the 'rebels' gained control of the Mine Workers Union and appointed an interim secretary who was sworn in with the oath that he would resist with all his strength 'the onslaught of Kaffir, Moor and Indian on the White working community'.[3] At the same time they demanded that the Chamber increase salaries to a level approximately double what they were. Negotiations continued and in December, the Chamber announced that it would offer monthly salaries to day's pay men provided that this was linked with increased productivity. The Mine Workers Union rejected the idea of increased productivity which they maintained could only be achieved by allowing blacks to advance, and argued that the increased salaries should come from profits and taxation. In January 1967 one of the leaders of the M.W.U. told striking mineworkers, 'Your jobs in the gold mining industry are in danger. Certain types of work are being taken over by the Kaffir, and you are gradually being pushed out of the industry.'[4] Still the negotiations continued and in April agreement was finally reached.[5]

The agreement which took effect from the beginning of June 1967 was a triumph for the trade unions, for the key to the whole scheme was the fact that the lion's share of any increase in productivity due to the elimination of some restrictive practices would go to white workers. Moreover the expected increase in productivity was anticipated by an immediate rise in incomes of the 22,000 members of the mining unions, who were put on to a monthly salary basis with improved pension, accident, and sick pay benefits, all of which raised the total white wage bill by no less than 11%.[6] The main concessions made by the trade unions were firstly that black workers would officially be allowed to handle explosives (although not to charge up), that they would be allowed to drive locomotives hauling whites underground provided they did not exceed a speed of 10 miles per hour (anything faster had to be driven by whites) and, the most important concession of all, that black workers would no longer have to wait at the beginning of every shift for the

[1] South Africa, *Hansard* (1966), col. 444.
[2] *Star*, 26 July 1966.
[3] *Rand Daily Mail*, 25 November 1966.
[4] *Rand Daily Mail*, 4 January 1967.
[5] *Star*, 24 April 1967.
[6] *Ibid*. See also p. 55.

working area to be examined by a white miner. This last concession, however, was in a form significantly different from what it had been in the earlier experiment in 1965. In terms of the 1967 agreement blacks were not upgraded as 'competent non-scheduled persons' to do the white jobs of examining the working place; what happened was that instead of being in charge of one gang of black workers as before the white miner was allowed to command two or three. And the white miner was given the power to instruct one of the 'boss-boys' under him to take a gang of men to an area which had not been blasted since the last examination, provided he (the white) visited it within two hours and also examined it at some time during the shift. It was a neat arrangement. The colour bar was rigidly maintained, white workers were assured by the Chamber of Mines that none of them would be retrenched, and the increased output due to black miners doing more work was used to increase white salaries.[1]

Even this, however, was not enough. Wages for white miners were high, but working conditions compared with other sectors were tough. Fewer and fewer young whites were willing to follow their fathers into the bowels of the earth. And so by the end of the 1960s, when the white miners already in the industry were able to use their unique bargaining position to obtain far higher wages than similarly qualified men were earning in other sectors, there was increasing talk of turning underground jobs into work for black men only. No less a person than a former chairman of the Board of Trade and Industries, Dr. A. J. Norval, addressing the annual meeting of the Institute for Bankers at the end of 1968, stated baldly that if the life of the gold mining industry was to be prolonged everything possible would have to be done to mechanise the mines and to substitute black workers for white. Replacing 70% of the white mine labour force with blacks would, he estimated at that time, have resulted in savings of R30 million a year.[2] The statement was, naturally, greeted with considerable wrath by the trade unions, and the government immediately dissociated itself from Dr. Norval. However it is likely that his views represented some section, at least, of National Party thinking. The chairman of the Federale Mynbou General Mining Group, himself a brother of a cabinet minister, was one of those who during the 1966 crisis had pressed hard for the use of black mine workers in higher jobs.[3] In the public and other sectors of our economy, he pointed out in his presidential address, the status and material well-being of the white worker is being advanced and strengthened by the allocation to blacks of

[1] In the coal mines (where the black–white employment ratio is considerably higher than for gold mines) a similar agreement was reached. But in this case black miners were allowed to take charge of explosives. *Rand Daily Mail*, 31 March 1967.
[2] *Star*, 22 November 1968.   [3] *Star*, 21 June 1966.

tasks of a routine nature formerly done by white men. 'It is an anomaly', he went on to complain, 'that mining, which needs more than any other sector to improve its labour productivity, should be denied the right to allocate tasks of this kind to Bantu so as to free white men for responsible and productive work at a time when the industry and the country are short of skilled labour.'[1]

In the rapidly expanding economy the shortage of white workers seems likely to get worse rather than better; meanwhile the uneasy co-existence between the Chamber and the white trade unions continues.[2] It is probable that, unless the price of gold rises sufficiently to enable the industry to absorb the continued pressure for white wage increases, considerable bending of the colour bar, at least underground, will have to take place in the not too distant future. It is important to realise that the dispute within the mining industry is not whether there should be a colour bar or not but whether it should be more flexible, as it is in most other sectors of the economy, or whether it should be rigid as some white mineworkers, fearing the thin end of the wedge, maintain it must be.

This brings us to one of the most fascinating of all questions that faces any student of the South African economy. Is it possible that the existence of the colour bar is actually against the interests of white workers? For quite apart from the fact that the existence of the colour bar may make mining more dangerous and unhealthy than it would otherwise be,[3] it can be argued that by relaxing the colour bar and thus lowering costs the subsequent expansion of the industry would create more jobs, both skilled and unskilled, than before. Looking at the argument another way, one can show how imposition of a colour bar, which is theoretically exactly the same as a tax on labour, would reduce employment of both blacks and whites.[4] Whether or not the conditions in the gold mining industry are such that the substitution of blacks in white jobs following a relaxation of the colour bar would be outweighed by the expansion of the industry and the consequent demand for new jobs, cannot be answered without a much more detailed examination of individual mines than has been undertaken in this study. But the possibility exists. And it is instructive, though not conclusive, to note that on the

---

[1] *Mining Survey*, September 1969.

[2] An attempt by the mines to nibble at the conventional, as opposed to the legal, colour bar was made in 1969 when Africans were used to assist with air sampling and surveying. The Association of Underground Officials did not mind, but the Mine Workers' Union objected vociferously. *Rand Daily Mail*, 15 April 1969; *Star*, 22 May 1969.

[3] One senior official pointed out, for example, that the collecting of dust samples was a measure directly aimed at improving the health of miners and yet, although no whites were available to do the job, the M.W.U. sought to prevent blacks from being employed in such jobs. *Star*, 25 July 1969.

[4] See Appendix 27.

Zambian copperbelt, which saw the breakdown of a mining colour bar from the time of the Second World War, total employment in the copper mines increased between 1941 and 1964 from 30,000 to 46,000, whilst the ratio of blacks to whites in service fell from well over 8:1 to approximately 5:1.[1] On Rhokana mine, between the time of Independence in December 1964 and February 1966 the employment of whites increased from 1,800 to 1,880, despite the fact that the breakdown of the colour bar caused the ratio to move against them from 4·4:1 to 5·6:1.[2] One cannot however attach too much weight to this evidence which relates to a situation very different from the conditions pertaining in the gold mines further south, and which should be modified to take account of other changes (e.g. technical progress or the growth of mines from the development to the production stage) that might have occurred at the same time as the colour bar broke down.

It is interesting to consider the opinions, which vary widely, of people in the gold mining industry who were asked what effect they thought the abolition of the colour bar would have in the short run. An underground manager, who had previously worked on the Copperbelt, estimated that if the industry were given a free hand in reorganising its labour force, 15% of the white underground workers would lose their jobs immediately. Some but by no means all of these men could, he thought, be retrained and absorbed higher up. Another senior official in the industry said that there were in his view sufficient black miners with the necessary experience and ability to obtain without any further training all the blasting certificates that the industry needs to issue. On the other hand, the manager of one of the mines involved in the abortive labour experiment of 1965 said that he did not think that the removal of the colour bar would affect working costs significantly.

Despite the paucity of information concerning the number of 'white' jobs which black miners could do, with or without further training, the evidence does suggest that the colour bar adds to the production of gold a significant cost which restricts output and total employment and which, if it were removed, might lead to an increase in the employment of skilled whites. And as we have seen (p. 114), the rise of white wages relative to black has, irrespective of any changes in the political climate, generated increasing pressure against the barriers to occupational mobility. But why, in the gold mines, is the colour bar so remarkably resistant to the pressures which have tended to bend and break it elsewhere? To answer this question we must analyse the second peculiar feature of gold mining in South Africa: the system of migratory labour.

[1] Northern Rhodesia Chamber of Mines Annual Yearbooks (1956–63) A, Copperbelt of Zambia, *Mining Industry Yearbook* (1964) A, and Zambian Ministry of Finance, *Economic Report* (1966) A.
[2] Figures supplied by the mine's officials.

CHAPTER 7

THE ECONOMICS OF MIGRANT LABOUR

The migratory labour system can be seen as both a symptom and a cause of most of the economic, social and political problems which beset our community; and this perpetual mass movement of people is a dramatic illustration of our failure over the past century to create a unified and coherent economy.

D. Hobart Houghton, *The South African Economy*

The system of migrant labour oscillating backwards and forwards between different areas is by no means unique to South Africa. It exists in other parts of the continent as well as in the industrialised countries of Western Europe and the United States of America.[1] However the reasons for its prolonged existence in South Africa appear to be rather different from those elsewhere and we need to examine carefully whether its root causes are, as is so often alleged, primarily political or whether the system which has been so central to the mining industry's labour market for so long has an economic foundation supporting it.

PUSH–PULL

According to Clyde Mitchell, oscillating migration may be seen as the result of two opposing influences:

From the point of view of the rural areas, the economic drives as a rule operate centrifugally to force men, and sometimes women, outwards to a distant labour centre where they are able to earn cash wages to use in order to satisfy their various wants. The social system, operating particularly through the network of social relationships, tends to act centripetally to hold a man within its hold and to resist the influences pulling him away.[2]

This concept of two sets of opposing forces resulting in a continual movement between the village and the outside economy is helpful and goes a long way towards providing a general model of oscillating migrant labour. How-

---

[1] Cf. R. Descloitres, *The Foreign Worker* (O.E.C.D., Paris, 1967), H. M. Hagmann, *Les Travailleurs Etrangers* (Payot, Lausanne, 1966) B, and President's Commission on Migratory Labor, *Migratory Labor in American Agriculture* (U.S. Govt. Printing Office, Washington, 1951) A.

[2] J. C. Mitchell, 'The causes of labour migration', *Proceedings of the Sixth Inter-African Labour Conference* (C.C.T.A., Abidjan, 1961) C.

ever there are two important respects in which it is inadequate. It assumes that the economic forces operate only centrifugally while the social ones all act centripetally, and it is an explanation based entirely on the supply side.[1] It takes no account of the demand for labour and the effect of this on the migrant system. There seem to be three main types of demand which, assuming suitable conditions in the country of origin, encourage migration. Firstly there is the steady demand of a fully employed expanding economy for settled labour. Secondly there is the seasonal demand which rises very high for part of the year and then falls sharply; for example ice-cream factory workers or labourers who harvest the cocoa, coffee, and other cash crops of Ghana, Uganda, and elsewhere. Thirdly, and this is perhaps confined to 'developing' countries, there is the demand which, while steady, nevertheless finds it more economical to use a labour force whose individual members oscillate between rural and urban areas where by so doing 'wages can be kept below the effective urban subsistence level because of the assumption that the worker gets additional support from his claims upon the products of his native village'[2]

From the point of view of the migrant this additional support implies that there are centripetal economic forces pulling him back to the land. But the nature of these forces varies. In Uganda, for example, the communal system of land tenure makes it impossible for a man to liquefy his assets and therefore men who go to town retain links with their farms.[3] In West Africa, on the other hand, it seems that the crucial restraint upon the movement of families is not the type of land tenure but rather the fact that the demand for labour on the coast comes at a time when peasant farmers in the north are relatively idle, as Berg pointed out:

Several features of the West African economic environment made temporary migration a particularly suitable instrument for the growth of the African agricultural export sector, which is the foundation of these economies. In the savannah zones, the relatively densely populated areas, men are underemployed during the dry season. In the forest and coastal zones, where conditions are favourable to the growth of export crops, suitable land is relatively abundant and people are relatively scarce. At the same time, climatic zones in West Africa are so ordered that the slack season in the savannah zones is the busy season along the southern coast. Thus there is a seasonal dovetailing; the period of inactivity in the savannah regions corresponds to the time of peak agricultural demands in the cocoa and coffee regions of the forest zone. Short-term movement from savannah to forest was thus a

---

[1] As it is difficult to remember the difference it may be helpful to note that 'centrifugal' (from *fugere* = to flee) means 'tending to fly from the centre'. 'Centripetal forces', on the other hand, tend towards the centre.

[2] M. J. Herskovits and M. Hernitz (eds.), *Economic Transition in Africa* (Routledge and Kegan Paul, London, 1964), p. 293 B.

[3] W. Elkan, *Migrants and Proletarians* (O.U.P., London, 1960), p. 136 B.

natural adaptation, particularly because the kinds of work required in the cocoa and coffee region, harvest labour and the clearing of new plantations, lent themselves to seasonal or casual performance. Without the inflow of migrants, inelasticities of labour supply would unquestionably have restrained the expansion of the export sector.[1]

Migrants can thus maximise their earnings by working in both coastal and savannah zones during the course of each year.

Oscillation also offers some security against the risks of sickness, unemployment, and old age. Mitchell argues that this security (which derives from the network of social relationships in which the migrant is enmeshed) is not merely economic but also psychological. Quoting from the Dow Report, Mitchell points out that 'even if we could equate the alternative securities (in urban and tribal area) in actuarial terms, which of course is impossible, the comparison would not necessarily exercise its proper influence on the African mind, for the one security appears to him a certainty whereas the other is both novel and conditional'.[2] But this surely emphasises the economic force underlying the migrant's decision to return to the village. For the 'African mind' in choosing not to move permanently to town is taking account of the considerable risk factor inherent in such movement. One can argue that the migrant makes too high an estimate of the risk, but this is a very different matter from deducing that the pull back to the village is social rather than economic. Mitchell maintains that 'economic factors are not *sufficient* conditions for the *circulation* [oscillation] for they do not in themselves explain why migrants return to their tribal areas'.[3] I would argue, however, that although the precise natures of the economic forces acting centripetally vary from place to place, social factors alone, important as they are, are not sufficient to continue over a long period of time to pull migrants back to their villages. Analysis of migrant systems, as they have existed in other parts of Africa, suggest that while the Mitchell model goes a long way towards generalising reasons for the widespread existence of an oscillating system, it must be modified. Not only are the centripetal forces on the supply side primarily economic, but the concept of opposing forces, pushing and pulling, must be extended to the demand side, for demand may not only pull men to work but may also push them away again. The illuminating diagram which Mitchell has constructed can be modified to illustrate the pressures that produce oscillating migration by putting more emphasis on the economic forces and by adding the pressures that employers exert on the demand side (see fig. 10).[4]

[1] H. Kuper (ed.), *Urbanization and Migration in West Africa* (Berkeley, 1965), p. 164 B.
[2] Mitchell, *Sixth Inter-African Labour Conference*, p. 275 C.
[3] J. A. Jackson (ed.), *Migration* (C.U.P., Cambridge, 1969), p. 178 B.   [4] Cf. *ibid.*, p. 179.

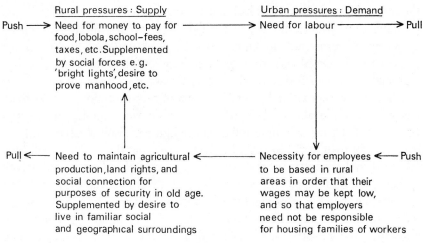

Fig. 10

The strength of the system will depend on the extent to which the pull of demand coincides with the push of supply, and the demand push with that of supply pull. The system becomes more likely to collapse as any one of these four push or pull forces weakens. Where over time they do weaken, the system can only be propped up by legislative action preventing the families of workers settling in the area where the breadwinners are earning their living.

CHANGING PATTERNS

Before analysing whether or not the migrant system in the gold mines needs its legislative prop or not, it would be instructive to consider briefly those patterns of migration which have changed from oscillation to permanence. One focus of employment which saw such a transformation was the sisal industry on the coast of Tanzania. In 1944 the Tanganyika Sisal Growers' Association established its own labour bureau, Silabu, which began by recruiting workers not only locally but also in Mozambique and Ruanda-Urundi. However, in the late 1950s Silabu ceased recruiting outside Tanzania, and in 1965 it closed down altogether. There were, according to Guillebaud, several reasons for this.[1] Many workers, whose families were also transported free of charge when they were recruited, settled locally instead of accepting repatriation on completion of their contract.[2] Thus by

[1] C. W. Guillebaud, *An Economic Survey of the Sisal Industry of Tanganyika* (James Nisbet and Co., London, 3rd edn., 1966), p. 87 B.
[2] H. R. G. Hurst, 'A survey of the development of facilities for migrant labour in Tanganyika during the period 1926–1959', *Bulletin of the Inter-African Labour Institute* VI (1959) C.

the 1960s the sisal plantations had pools of experienced workers upon which to draw. Furthermore, there was a major wage increase in 1960 which by agreement with the trade union concerned was accompanied by an increase in the cutter's normal task, from 70 to 90 bundles (of 30 leaves each) a day. Although each man had to work harder, the wage increase led also to the substitution of capital for labour by means of mechanisation, and to more efficient use of the labour employed. Absenteeism, for example, was reduced by means of stricter discipline and a change in the method of payment, from over 30% in 1959 to 7% in 1964. Production rose but the demand for labour fell: in 1959 the industry produced 202,000 tons of sisal and employed 133,000 workers, but by 1964 an output of 223,000 tons was achieved by only 83,000 workers; an increase in productivity of 77% from 1·5 to 2·7 tons per man.[1] The consequence of all this was that, far from having to recruit labour from a distance, the industry found itself with a surplus of labour settled around the plantations.

Moving south to the copper mines of Zambia and the Congo, one finds that there was a deliberate and successful policy of replacing an oscillating pattern with stabilised labour. In each of the two countries the mines were developed for some years with oscillating migrant labour but first Union Minière du Haut Katanga in 1927, and in 1940, the two main mining corporations of the Copperbelt changed their labour policies. There were, according to Berg, three reasons why the U.M.H.K. policy altered when it did.[2] Firstly, from its beginnings in 1911 until the mid-1920s, the company, despite acute labour shortages, had always managed to recruit enough men to keep going. But with the development of the neighbouring Copperbelt at this time the shortage became greater as both fields were competing for the same labour. The Katanga mines had been developed in an area where there was almost no settled population and so men had been drawn from across the border in what was then Northern Rhodesia. The development of the Copperbelt raised the recruiting costs of Union Minière which now had to go further afield. Secondly, by the late 1920s U.M.H.K. was wanting to use black men as skilled workers. This involved training costs which could only be worthwhile if the trained men stayed on the mines long enough to give the mines an adequate return on this investment in human capital. Thirdly U.M.H.K. was working very high quality grade ore in open pits and making large profits, and so had the financial capacity to undertake a policy which involved a very heavy initial expenditure with returns accruing over a long period.

On the Copperbelt the mines, which had begun life by employing oscil-

---

[1] Guillebaud, *Sisal Industry*, p. 88 B.   [2] Berg, *Recruitment of a Labor Force*, p. 372 D.

lating migrant workers, were confirmed in their belief that this was the best policy by the slump which reduced the copper price from £72 per ton in February 1930 to £27 in 1931 and forced them to retrench their labour force from 30,000 men in 1930 to 7,000 in 1932.[1] If the demand for labour was going to fluctuate so violently it was clearly better from the management's point of view to employ migrants who, when laid off, could be sent back to the rural areas without having to be compensated with unemployment insurance.[2] However, by 1939 demand for copper had picked up again, employment had risen to 26,000 and the industry had become increasingly aware of two cogent reasons in favour of adopting a policy of stabilisation. The first of these was the increasing demand for more highly skilled black workers who had to be trained. The second was the belief that a stable labour force would be easier to control and less prone to industrial unrest.[3] Before 1938 the men from different 'tribes' were mixed residentially.

When the policy of creating a permanent fully industrialised labour force began in 1940, most black workers were hired and housed on the assumption that they were either single or had left their families in some rural area; but by the end of 1952 60% of the total accommodation provided was for married African employees, while by 1966 the estimates of the number of men working on the mines as single men varied between 10% and 15%. The reasons given by officials for the increasing success of the policy of stabilisation were first, that the standard of housing had improved; second, the Government was catching up on the provision of adequate schooling in the urban areas; and third, the 'generous pension scheme' which made workers think twice before leaving. The importance attached to schooling is confirmed by the evidence from the Congo where the rapid growth in the number of children in urban areas in the 1950s was attributed to the fact that, 'many children have been sent to relatives living in towns to attend school'.[4] Walter Elkan has suggested that, 'the success of stabilisation policies in the Belgian Congo may...be attributable as much to...compulsory severance from the land as to the positive inducement of employers'.[5] However, the evidence from the Copperbelt during the first half of the 1960s indicates that the attractive power of the total remuneration offered by the industry

---

[1] Zambia, *Report of the Board of Inquiry Appointed to Inquire into the Advancement of Africans in the Copper Mining Industry in Northern Rhodesia* (Forster) (Government Printer, Lusaka, 1954).
[2] It is certainly arguable that mine workers with links to the land were in a better position to face the slump than the slum dwellers of Glasgow who had nothing to fall back on. See W. Watson, *Tribal Cohesion in a Money Economy* (Manchester University Press, Manchester, 1958), p. 8 B.
[3] There is some difference of opinion on this point. In South Africa the mining authorities seem to believe that migrant labour is easier to control.
[4] H. J. C. Daubresse, *Native Labour in the Belgian Congo* (M.Sc.Econ. thesis, L.S.E., 1960), p. 21 D.
[5] Elkan, *Migrants and Proletarians*, p. 137 D.

Labour in the South African gold mines

was sufficient to draw not only workers but also their families to town on a permanent basis.[1] Given the fact that the policy of stabilisation began on the Copperbelt some 13 years after it was adopted by U.M.H.K., the speed with which workers settled seems to have been about the same in the two areas. By 1957 the average length of service of black employees on the Katanga mines was 11 years. On the Copperbelt the average which in 1956 was 4½ years had, by 1964, increased to 7.[2]

One measure of the success of the policy of stabilisation of black workers on the copper mines is the decrease in the monthly rate of turnover (see table 10).

TABLE 10. *Monthly rate of labour turnover for the mining industry of Zambia, 1952–69*

Year	Black	White
1952	5·98	n.a.
1953	4·64	1·8
1956	1·94	1·17
1959	2·5	1·4
1962	1·4	1·3
1964	0·7	2·1
1969	0·5	2·2

SOURCE: Annual Reports of the Department of Labour, *Mining Yearbook of Zambia*, 1969.

NOTES: 1. Turnover $= \dfrac{\text{Monthly average of departures}}{\text{Average daily labour force}} \times 100$.

     2. The table refers to mines on the Copperbelt and in Broken Hill. 1969 is for the Copperbelt only.

Whatever may have been their view previously, by 1966 those managing the copper industry were overwhelmingly in favour of stabilised as opposed to migrant labour. The main argument put forward again and again in its favour was that without stable labour the higher level of training would have been impossible, and yet the training was absolutely essential if the industry was to have sufficient men of skill to keep it going. Officials seemed to agree that under a migrant system it would not have been possible to employ blacks at a level much above the category of men who marked, drilled and blasted their own holes but who did not act in any supervisory capacity. Those in charge of the impressive training programmes on different mines were convinced that it was an investment which would yield dividends

[1] Berg, *Recruitment of a Labor Force*, p. 368 D.
[2] Northern Rhodesia Chamber of Mines, *Yearbooks* 1956–63 A, Copperbelt of Zambia Mining Industry, *Yearbook*, 1964 A.

to the industry. The outlay was considerable: over the year 1964/65 Nchanga mine trained a total of 5,754 persons for a cost of R836,000, i.e. R146 per trainee. In 1964 the total expenditure by the industry on training, excluding adult education training programmes, was R3 million, an average of R72 per employee in service.[1] This compares with the cost of approximately R6 per black trainee per annum on the gold mines. Part of the difference was due to the disparity of wage levels. In 1968 the average Zambian mineworker earned R1,300 compared with the R189 earned by black workers on the gold mines.[2]

Figures are not available for the amount of training in earlier years but it seems that although there was a certain amount of training, particularly of whites, during the 1950s, it was not until the coming of Independence at the end of 1964 that training became so important a part of the companies' policy. Indeed, one official of a mining company went so far as to say that the industry had been pushed by the political changes to extend its training programme considerably, and it was not until after they had changed that they fully appreciated the value of the training.

THE GOLD MINES

Turning now to the labour force of the gold mining industry our task is to try to assess whether, unlike Central Africa, there are still strong economic 'push–pull' forces maintaining the system, or whether it is propped up entirely by influx control and other legislation. According to the W.N.L.A. in 1959, 'the mining industry has always been dependent on migrant labour and this system of employment suits both the Industry and the Native Labourers themselves. The opportunity to work for short periods on the Gold Mines and then to return home enables the tribal Native, essentially an agriculturalist, to preserve his traditional way of life and, at the same time, provide himself with the wherewithal to withstand the vicissitudes of farming, which are common the world over but more particularly in Africa.'[3]

Anthropological field studies in the areas from which the mining industry

---

[1] Figures supplied by mining officials in Zambia.
[2] The figures are not strictly comparable for, quite apart from differences both in the cost of living and in the significance of wages in kind in the two countries, they take no account of the fact that many of the Zambian mineworkers are doing jobs that in the South African mines are reserved for whites only. It is also worth noting that the Zambian mineworker in 1968 was earning more than twice as much as his counterpart in other, non-agricultural, sectors of the economy. The earnings of peasant farmers were only one-ninth of those on the mines. I.L.O., *Report to the Government of Zambia on Incomes, Wages and Prices in Zambia* (Turner) (Cabinet Office, Lusaka, 1969), p. 9 A.
[3] W.N.L.A., 'Organization of migrant labour in the South African mining industry', *Bulletin of the Inter-African Labour Institute*, VI (1959) C.

draws its black workers indicate that the export of labour enables the rural community to feed a larger population, or maintain a higher standard of living than it would otherwise be able to do. In 1942 Dr. Margaret Read wrote of Malawi: 'It is evident throughout the villages under investigation that standards of living are changing rapidly, and that emigration on the whole is making them rise rather than fall.'[1] This seems to have continued to be true in Malawi, for in 1961 van Velsen concluded that 'compared with other tribal areas the Tonga are relatively prosperous; this prosperity is largely due to their export of labour'.[2] Admittedly the Tonga of Malawi never signed on with the W.N.L.A. to work on the gold mines, but it seems that no less than half the men working abroad managed to get into South Africa illegally where they often worked in the mines on a short-term basis. In Barotseland in 1941 according to Gluckman, 'many Lozi and other Barotse have to go out to work at White country for their money income. Lack of export crops and commodities and high rates of transport...make this essential.'[3] Migration apparently brought a net gain to the community despite the fact that in the indigenous Lozi economy there was work, much of it 'urgent' for men and women in every month of the year. In Botswana the evidence from Schapera also points to economic necessity as having been the underlying cause of migration.[4] Indeed the *Report of an Economic Survey Mission* published in 1960 supported this finding not only for Botswana but for Lesotho and Swaziland as well.[5]

With regard to Mozambique the situation is not quite so straightforward. There has been considerable controversy for many years as to whether the 100,000 men recruited annually in the country by the W.N.L.A. come forward primarily because economic opportunities are better on the gold mines or primarily because the Portuguese labour policy forces them to come. On the one hand it is held that:

There can be no doubt that there is an intimate connection between Mozambique's internal labor policy and the movement to the mines. The African male in southern Mozambique is caught in a great vise. In effect, the Portuguese labor policy decrees that those who cannot find employment within the carefully regulated labor market of Mozambique cities, must face the alternative of emigrating to the mines or of being conscripted as *shibalos*. When the hunt for *shibalos* is intensified in a particular district, the recruiting posts of the W.N.L.A., which are strategically

[1] M. Read, 'Migrant labour in Africa and its effects on tribal life', *International Labour Review* XLV (1942) C.
[2] A. Southall (ed.), *Social Change in Modern Africa* (O.U.P., London, 1961), p. 230 B.
[3] M. Gluckman, *Economy of the Central Barotse Plain* (Rhodes Livingstone Paper No. 7, 1941), p. 113 B.
[4] I. Schapera, *Migrant Labour and Tribal Life* (O.U.P., London, 1947), pp. 121 ff. B.
[5] Basutoland, Bechuanaland Protectorate and Swaziland, *Report of an Economic Survey Mission* (Morse) (H.M.S.O., London, 1960), pp. 52, 227, 447 A.

placed throughout southern Mozambique, are suddenly deluged with Africans anxious to sign mine contracts.[1]

On the other hand it is maintained that the effects of forced labour in increasing the migratory current 'were negligible when compared with economic factors'.[2] It seems to be generally agreed that: 'The cornerstone of Portuguese native policy continues to be the African's obligation to labor'.[3] According to James Duffy the law governing the African worker in Angola and Mozambique is still 'philosophically... of a piece with previous African labor legislation, for although it attempts to correct those sections of earlier labor laws which led to the unchecked use of the African as m̃ao de obra, the *Código de 1928* permits almost equal abuse, particularly in the matter of labor recruitment'.[4] However Duffy also points out that 'in no sense has the recruitment of workers in Mozambique by the W.N.L.A. been the degrading spectacle that was the contract labor scandal in Angola'. However: 'There is little doubt...that pressures were often put on the chief, if not by the agents, then by Portuguese officials, to procure workers, although there has been less indication in recent years (1959) that the W.N.L.A. has had to rely on anything more than its promises and the testimonies of men returning from the mines – with their boots and blankets and phonographs.'[5]

Summing up the situation in Mozambique it seems fair to say, until there is further evidence one way or the other, that although the labour laws almost certainly work to the advantage of the W.N.L.A. their repeal, given the difference in the relative stages of economic development of the two countries, would be unlikely to affect perceptibly the flow of migrants out of Mozambique into South Africa.[6] In 1955 it was estimated that a man could earn twice as much by going to work on the gold mines as he could if he stayed at home to work in any of the agricultural, industrial, or transport jobs offered by the provincial government or by private employers within Mozambique.[7] A. Rita-Ferreira is probably nearest the truth when he suggests, pointing to the ex-Protectorates for comparison, that migration from

---

[1] M. Harris, *Portugal's African 'Wards'* (American Committee on Africa, New York, 1958), p. 28 B.

[2] A. Rita-Ferreira, 'Comments on *Labour Emigration among the Mocambique Thonga by M. Harris' Africa* XXX (1960), 75 C.

[3] J. Duffy, *Portuguese Africa* (H.U.P., Cambridge, Mass., 1959), especially ch. 6 and 12 B.

[4] *Ibid.* p. 319.   [5] *Ibid.* pp. 173 and 171.

[6] I.L.O., *Report of the Commission Appointed under Article 26 of the Constitution of the International Labour Organization to Examine the Complaint Filed by the Government of Ghana Concerning the Observance by the Government of Portugal of the Abolition of Forced Labour Convention, 1957 (No. 105)* (Official Bulletin, 1962) A.

[7] M. Harris, 'Labour emigration among the Mocambique Thonga: cultural and political factors', *Africa* XXIX (1959).

129

Mozambique is not so much due to deplorable labour conditions there as to the economic factors which push men to the gold mines from all over Southern Africa.[1] The export of labour seems to have resulted in a net gain to Mozambique. 'Much of the vigour and excellence of the aboriginal agricultural effort actually depended upon the presence of men. None the less women were quite capable of carrying on alone; with the help of good rainfalls they could meet the basic requirements of the household while the men were away working for Europeans. Thus the withdrawal of a high percentage of the men from the Thonga households has never seriously threatened the ability of the population to survive and reproduce.'[2]

Inside South Africa itself there is no doubt whatever that it is economic necessity which drives men from the reserves to seek work in town. Summarising the findings of a detailed social and economic survey of the Keiskammahoek district carried out over the years 1947–51, Houghton wrote: 'Productivity is generally so low that the population is wholly unable to support itself from activities within the district. It is dependent upon imports to the area for all its clothing and manufactured articles, and a very large part of its food. Apart from a small quantity of wool, it is only *labour* that can be exported to pay for the imports. Remittances from emigrant workers in the industrial centres support the economy of the reserve to the extent of almost 50% of its total cash income. Without the earnings of the emigrants the population of the district would starve.'[3]

Despite the general agreement on the economic benefits to be obtained from migration some of the field studies also stress the economic loss to the village economy of the system of migrant labour. In Barotseland, 'the general effect of labour migration and drift is to render it more difficult for Lozi-landers to make ends meet...Home production falls greatly.'[4] Similarly, in Botswana, 'Owing to labour migration, many people are no longer available at home to attend the routine tasks of tribal life, and as a result both animal husbandry and agriculture have suffered.'[5] In South Africa the absence of men for the greater part of the year was in 1930, 'invariably reflected in the cultural operations of the land and the resultant low yields. Even while the responsible male times his visit home to coincide with the ploughing and seeding season, agriculture suffers. It allows of no preparatory cultivation nor does it enable him to take advantage of favourable rainfalls. It necessitates leaving to the women and to juniors the major part of the work. There can

---

[1] Rita-Ferreira, *Africa* (1960), p. 149.
[2] Harris, *Africa* (1959), p. 57. The Thonga of Mocambique should not be confused with the Tonga of Malawi.
[3] D. Hobart Houghton, *Life in the Ciskei* (S.A.I.R.R., Johannesburg, 1955), p. 36 B.
[4] Gluckman, *Economy of the Barotse*, p. 117 B.   [5] Schapera, *Migrant Labour*, p. 164, B.

be no organised system of working. The standard of agriculture, therefore, is low and there can be no development.'[1] Twenty years later the situation remained unchanged. 'This very exodus', wrote Houghton in 1952, 'is itself a potent cause of the perpetuation of the poverty at home, for the absence of so many in the prime of life inhibits economic progress and certainly accounts in no small measure for the low agricultural productivity of the District. In many cases land is not ploughed for the simple reason that there is no one to do the ploughing.'[2]

There are times when observers imply a seemingly contradictory state of affairs. Some see it as both economically beneficial and detrimental to the community. To reconcile the apparent inconsistencies it is necessary to be very clear as to what is meant by the statement that migration leads to a deterioration of village agriculture and hence is itself a cause of poverty. All the evidence suggests that the men who migrate do so because 'remuneration is higher and opportunities of employment greater than in the Reserves'.[3] In other words, men choose to become part-time miners rather than remain as full-time farmers because by so doing they can earn more. Although this decision often results in a deterioration of home, primarily agricultural, production, the fact remains that the total income of the community (including both those who stay at home and the migrants) is greater than it would have been if there was no migration. But the important point is that the process may be accompanied by changes in the pattern of consumption. For example in some areas less food is consumed in order to buy more clothes and furniture. Furthermore, although the migration leads to a greater gross community product it may, and in some cases almost certainly does, have a secondary effect of redistributing this income in such a way that some of those left behind are actually worse off than they would have been if there had been no migration. For if everybody stayed at home the food which the able-bodied men produced would be used not only to feed themselves, their wives and children but would also be given to the old and crippled. However where migration exists, not only may the worker spend a relatively higher proportion of his earnings on himself than he would in the country, but such money as he does send home may be used to feed and clothe a tighter family circle than previously. What little evidence there is suggests that the extent to which income redistribution occurred as a result of migration varied from place to place.

[1] *Ibid.* p. 166. Citing Germond, evidence to *Native Economic Commission 1930–32*, p. 213.
[2] D. Hobart Houghton and E. M. Walton, *The Economy of a Native Reserve* (Shuter and Shooter, Pietermaritzberg, 1952), pp. 112–13 B.
[3] Mitchell, *Proceedings of the Sixth Inter-African Labour Conference*, p. 267 C, citing Houghton and Walton B.

Labour in the South African gold mines

Amongst the Bemba, who as late as 1939 were still working in the gold mines, there was in the traditional society definite training and strong sanctions enforcing the sharing of food and the provision for dependants.[1] However under later conditions where the young men went off as migrants, the elders were powerless to exact their full due of service. In fact, many young husbands 'though they consider themselves entirely responsible for clothing their wives and children. . . do not feel bound to feed them until later in life.'[2] As a result of these changes, given the traditional method of food production amongst the Bemba which involved a lot of very heavy work such as pollarding trees for wood and making fences to protect the millet from raids by pig and buck, wives whose husbands were away could be 'reduced to desperation' by constant raids which left them with nothing to eat.[3] In other areas, e.g. Mozambique, it is implicitly suggested that the distribution of income is not affected by the migrant system.[4] Within South Africa there is no evidence one way or the other that any of the people who remain behind in the reserves are actually poorer than they would be if the able-bodied men stayed at home to eke what little more they could from the soil, but implicit in much of the writing on the *economic* disadvantages of migrant labour is the assumption that some such redistribution of income does in fact take place. It is a hypothesis which was held to be true in Zambia in 1940.[5] In South Africa it remains to be tested with empirical data.

So much for the economic forces driving men from areas all over Southern Africa to seek work on the gold mines. What of the conditions, still on the supply side, which pulled these men back to their rural communities? In Barotseland in 1941 there were sound economic reasons why men maintained their links with the rural base. Wages paid to migrants were, on the whole, not high enough for saving and so, 'most workers have to contemplate a return in old age, and in unemployment, to the rural areas'.[6] So long as there seemed little social security at the labour centres it was in a migrant's interest to maintain relationships with his relatives at home for 'land abandoned in Loziland is not easily replaced'. It would seem that this pull remained equally strong over the years for, writing in 1959, Professor Gluckman was still able to say that, 'in a way, those who stay at home hold the land as security for support in money from those who go out to work. And those who go out to work pass money to those who remain, in payment for this security.'[7]

[1] A. I. Richards, *Land, Labour and Diet in Northern Rhodesia* (O.U.P., London, 1939), pp. 199, 397 B.
[2] *Ibid.* p. 133.   [3] *Ibid.* p. 298.   [4] Harris, *Africa* (1959), pp. 56–7 C.
[5] G. B. Wilson, *The Economics of Detribalization in Northern Rhodesia* (Rhodes Livingstone Papers Nos. 5–6, 1941–2), pp. 62, 80 B.
[6] Gluckman, *Economy of Barotse*, p. 110 B.   [7] Southall (ed.), *Social Change*, p. 78 B.

This is true not only of Barotseland but also of Malawi, for as van Velsen pointed out with regard to the community which he studied, 'when Tonga migrants eventually retire to their village, they do not fall back upon the security of a tribal society which *happens* to have continued during their absence; the migrants themselves, during their absence, have been contributing actively and consciously to its continuance because they know that they may have to rely on it when they are no longer usefully employed in their urban habitat... the fundamental fact is that the majority of Tonga working abroad look to the economic and social system of their tribal area for their ultimate security... The labour migrant sees his contributions of cash and goods to the rural economy as a kind of insurance premium: "How can we expect our *abali* (kin, friends) to help us later when we are old, if we do not help them now?".'[1]

This emphasis on the necessity for maintaining links with the rural base suggests that it may be mistaken to regard the need to plough as the primary force that pulls black miners regularly back to their homes in the Ciskei and other parts of Southern Africa. Could it not be that the real need is to maintain the rural links thereby paying one's insurance premium against illness and old age? If men have to maintain these links by going home it is likely that they would choose to go at a time when their presence there is most needed. Thus we would postulate that the seasonal demand for able-bodied men in the reserves is not the primary factor pulling them back, for they could still earn more by staying at work in the mines; but given the fact that they have to come back to maintain their old-age unemployment security, the agricultural and festival seasons determine the time at which they come.[2] However the need to ensure security for himself and his family when he can no longer work is not the only economic factor pulling a mineworker back to the rural base. Even if there were no legal restrictions a man's family would not necessarily accompany him to town for it would cost him much more to maintain them there than in the rural areas where there is often no rent to pay and where the family, by tilling the land, is able to contribute something to the total family income. Indeed wages are so low that a black mineworker could not support his family in town where the cost of living is higher and where the family could do little to support itself. For many areas from which mine labour is drawn, e.g. Malawi or Mozambique, it seems to be true that a migrant's family grows sufficient food to feed itself but in other areas, particularly in South Africa and Lesotho and to a lesser extent Botswana, basic

[1] *Ibid.* pp. 223, 227.
[2] In Swaziland, for example, the *Incwala* (first fruits) festival at the summer solstice is an important event for which men try to be home. H. Kuper, *An African Aristocracy* (O.U.P., London, 1947), pp. 197 ff. B.

Labour in the South African gold mines

foodstuffs are bought with money sent by the men who are away working.[1] There have long been many families living in the South African reserves who have no land or whose size of land-holding is totally inadequate to provide sufficient food for subsistence.[2]

In an attempt to deal with the problem of poverty in the reserves a government commission recommended in 1955 that the land should be redivided into 'economic units', that is units which under existing methods and prices would yield a full-time farmer and his family a minimum gross income of R120 per year.[3] It was estimated that under the mixed farming conditions of the Transkei a peasant would need 5 morgen of arable land and 10 cattle-units to enable him to remain as a full-time farmer. But the land was too densely populated to permit such redivision. In one village I investigated early in 1963 it was found that there were 360 families living on land sufficient for only 102 economic units. This village seems to have been representative of the Transkei and Ciskei as a whole, for the Tomlinson Commission estimated that the land could, *if fully developed agriculturally*, provide a full-time living for 43% of the 1951 population, provided the other 57% moved off the land.[4] The pattern that in fact has evolved was that all families continue to live in the reserves because the law forbids them to move permanently to the industrial centres. Even in those areas where government agriculturalists are trying to improve the methods of farming they find it necessary, as in the case of the village investigated, to allot half – and even quarter – economic units so that each family is not left completely destitute. Moreover, there is no doubt that the families of many migrant workers have no arable land and that they have to rely entirely on remittances sent from the towns.[5]

Thus amongst the men working on the gold mines there are some like the Tonga who come from areas which exert strong economic forces pulling them back, while on the other extreme there are those, e.g. landless Xhosa, for whom the economic pull is non-existent. In other words it seems that the conditions considered by a migrant when deciding whether to go permanently or temporarily to town vary enormously from place to place, and changed considerably over time. For some the rural base provides adequate social security, opportunity for the family to grow food, and free land. For others rent has to be paid for a housing plot, there is no arable land on which to grow food and social security is little better than in the urban areas. Such

[1] Southall (ed.), *Social Change*, p. 230 B. Harris, *Africa* (1959), p. 57 C.
[2] See Appendix 28.
[3] South Africa, *Summary of the Report of the Commission for the Socio-Economic Development of the Bantu Areas within the Union of South Africa* (Tomlinson) (U.G. 61, Pretoria, 1955), p. 113 A.
[4] *Ibid.* p. 116. [5] See Appendix 28.

people would only choose to oscillate if they were prevented from moving permanently (e.g. by 'pass' legislation or the unavailability of land or housing in the urban areas) or – a short term factor – if they had definite preferences that, for example, their children should be brought up in the country.[1] It should be noted that a government aware of such preferences can act to encourage its own choice of the desirable type of migration by adjusting certain conditions. In view of the stress laid by black South African parents on their children's education it is no accident, given the government's preferences, that schooling for black children is notoriously inadequate in the urban areas.

One important deduction from these facts is that the movement of Africans from neighbouring countries to the gold mines does not necessarily mean, as is often asserted, that black South Africans are better off.[2] Rural income is almost certainly far higher in Malawi than in the Ciskei; moreoever the wages remitted home can probably buy more in Malawi or Mozambique.

Turning now to the demand side, there are a number of factors that must be taken into account when assessing whether it is in the economic interests of the gold mining industry to maintain the oscillating pattern. Amongst the benefits which employers believe they derive from the migrant pattern are: lower wages, less leave and absenteeism, better control, less risk of the men getting silicosis, and greater output in jobs involving hard physical work.

Lower wages can be paid in so far as the rural base provides supplementary income for the oscillating worker. This, as we have seen, consists chiefly of food produced by the family, free land, and more certain social security. Although it seems true to say that for black South Africans there has been a decline (over the years) in the income to be derived from the reserves this has not led to a corresponding rise in wages paid by the mining industry. This is because the mines have been able to draw increasingly on labour pools in areas where the rural base still provides a significant income. In 1961 a major group estimated that to provide a black mineworker's family with adequate food, housing and fuel in the urban area would cost another R180 per annum.[3] Furthermore, community services, including medical facilities for families, were estimated to cost R20. The average cost of recruiting was of the order of R30 per worker per annum. Thus by employing migrant rather than stabilised labour, the group, which may be taken as representative

[1] As early as 1914 there was a 'growing wish', amongst African mineworkers, to settle in town. See p. 6.
[2] Cf. Max Beloff, *The Times*, 22 September 1966.
[3] Cost of rations = R70 p.a.; amortisation over 20 years of R1,000 required for each housing unit = R86 p.a.; fuel supply = R24 p.a. On this basis the families of many South African mineworkers would probably be considerably better fed, housed and fuelled than they are at present.

of the industry as a whole, saved a total of R170 per worker per annum. Furthermore, the costs of wastage under a stabilised system would be higher: leave facilities (wages and housing of additional workers) would cost R40 per employee per annum. Besides leave, another reason for higher wastage was that black workers, like their white brothers, might find it easier to absent themselves on grounds of such illness as the common cold.

On the medical side it is sometimes maintained that a positive benefit of the migrant system is the fact that for hard physical work the peak performance is reached after four to six months and then declines. If blacks spent all their working lives in the mines, so it is implied, they would burn out. This is improbable and even if it was possible, one must note that this factor has not, as far as I am aware, been put forward as a reason for establishing a pattern of oscillating migration in the mining industries of other countries.[1] In fact, given the poverty of the reserves the evidence points to the opposite conclusion, namely that the health of mineworkers deteriorates when they leave the mines for any length of time. Moreover even if there are gains in physical productivity from such enforced 'rests' they may well be offset by losses, on the psychological side, due to living in an unnatural community which excludes all women. Emotional health, as Becker points out, is increasingly considered an important determinant of earnings in all parts of the world.[2] It is also sometimes held that the shortness of the black working life in the gold mines reduces the risk of silicosis. Presumably this is equally true of white miners who generally choose to settle with their families at the place of work. A senior medical officer in the industry assured me that the increased risk of silicosis was not so great as to constitute a valid argument for the migrant system.

One very important benefit to the industry of the oscillating system, given the socio-political framework within which it operates, is the tighter control of labour, and hence minimisation of industrial unrest which it makes possible in the short term.[3] Comparison between the two strikes of 1922 (white) and 1946 (black) illustrates the importance of this factor and of the role it must have played in the industry's own calculations. We have already seen (p. 125) that the links with the rural base because of the oscillating migration

---

[1] Dealing with this argument in a memorandum to the Fagan Commission (U.G. 28, Pretoria, 1948) the Secretary of Health said, 'I know of no evidence, statistical or otherwise, in support of this assertion. If the health and feeding services on the mines are effective, they should be as effective over a long period as over a short one. I believe they are... There is in fact some evidence to show that the argument regarding the value of the "rest period" goes the other way. Labourers returning for a second contract, who were fit when discharged from the previous contracts, are often found to be in need of a period of "conditioning" – feeding – before commencing heavy work' (p. 40).

[2] Becker, *Human Capital*, p. 33 B.

[3] Cf. Copperbelt; see p. 125.

then prevalent cushioned the effect of the depression on the Copperbelt in the 1930s. This experience is still being used within the gold mining industry to justify oscillating migration on the grounds that in the new mining towns of the O.F.S. and far west Rand, acute social problems will be created when the mines become exhausted. It is certainly possible that the end of the mines will see the emergence of some ghost towns, though much can happen before the gold is mined out. But there is no reason to believe that the possible up-rooting of a stabilised community would be any more socially destructive than the continuance of the oscillating pattern.

While there are a number of clear gains to the industry resulting from the migrant system, it also entails considerable losses. These include the costs of recruitment (R30 per head per annum) engagement and termination (R1·35 per head per annum), aptitude testing (between 45 cents and 55 cents per head) and direct training costs (between R1·00 and R1·60 per trainee per shift).[1] But perhaps the most important cost to the industry lies, as experiences on the Copperbelt suggest, in the fact that the average length of a contract varies between nine and sixteen months, and that the total period of service of the average black mineworker is not only broken by long intervals away but in total is probably less than half as long as the total service, equal in 1971 to 14 years, of the average white mineworker. The limited time horizon prevents the industry from ever developing the full skill potential of the majority of its labour force because it severely restricts the period in which the industry would otherwise have been able to reap the returns of greater specific investment in it.

However, so long as the colour bar exists to prevent blacks from moving into more skilled jobs, so long will the cost of the limited time horizon be obscured. This loss can only be redeemed by relaxation of the colour bar, together with the adoption of a policy of stabilisation which minimises labour turnover.

A final, longer term, factor to be considered in assessing the costs and benefits of the oscillating pattern is its effect on society as a whole. On the one hand it is maintained that in an 'underdeveloped' economy the migrant system provides a bridge between the old and the new, that it helps to preserve traditional values, and that it softens the harsh consequences which accompany industrial revolution. It is true that without the compulsion of law many men who today work on the mines would almost certainly still choose to leave their families in their home countries or in the reserves. Within the framework of the system the organisation of recruiting, with protection from unscrupulous touts, free transport, medical care, and facilities

---

[1] Figures in parentheses are the estimates of a major group in 1961.

for sending money home, is a model of its kind. But there is another side to the picture, and there are many miners who would prefer to go to work each morning from a home rather than from a place where there is no room for wife or children. By breaking for long periods of time the fundamental unit of human community, the compulsory system in fact destroys the fibres that hold society together[1]. Certainly the migrant pattern, like an army barracks, encourages the growth of prostitution and homosexuality, and poses grave difficulties for the bringing up of children. Investigation of these effects lies outside the field of economics but no cost–benefit analysis of the migrant labour system can ignore them. No one has stated this more clearly than Dr. Anthony Barker, superintendent for more than twenty years of a large hospital in Zululand:

Economic or even social analysis of migratory labour will fail to reveal the full picture of its cost in terms of human misery. To learn this you must listen to the lonely wife, the anxious mother, the insecure child . . . It is at family level that the most pain is felt, and we cannot forget that the African cultural heritage enshrines a broader, more noble concept of family than that of the West. The extended family has proved a marvellous security for those for whom, otherwise, there was no security at all. The extended family is a net wide enough to gather the child who falls from the feeble control of neglectful parents; it receives the widow, tolerates the batty, gives status to grannies. Migratory labour destroys this, by taking away for long months together, the father, the brother, the lover and the friend. Each must go, and no one fools themselves that these men can live decent lives in a sexual vacuum. The resultant promiscuity is but one aspect of a mood of irresponsibility. For your migrant is concerned with nobody but himself; his own survival is the only survival that he can influence by any act that he performs. He may be well fed; doubtless he is. He may be well cared for; doubtless he is. He may have the companionship of others like himself. Yet the food he eats cannot fill the bellies of his children, nor the blanket he sleeps under warm any but himself. His care, his love, his family loyalty cannot reach out to his wife, nor caress his children, nor extend to the grandmother who brought him up . . . Deprived of their natural guides, children of migrants grow through an insecure, uncertain childhood to an adult life whose sole pre-occupation may be to escape the system. There must be a

---

1 This assertion is based on conversations, over many years, with men from the Ciskei whose need for money to support their families has forced them to become migrant workers. The views of an unknown man, met by chance on a quiet Ciskei road in June 1970, illustrate a number of points. He was back home from the mines (where he had started working in 1964) for a period between his third and fourth contracts; but, so he informed me, he would much rather go to work in Cape Town.

Why? – Because one could earn more money there.
Why didn't he go to Cape Town? – The laws made it difficult.
If he was allowed to go to town with his wife and children would he take them? – Yes.
But didn't he have cattle? – Yes.
What would he do about those? – Sell them.
And land? – He had no land.
How did his family live when he was away? – Only on the money he sent back from the mines.

harvest of aggression, with the weeds of violence growing rank within it. The dreadful society is the community of the careless, those who, treated like boys, behave like boys; of those who, having had no responsibility laid upon them, owe none to any man. In that chill climate will there be any place for trust? Any hope for human intercourse at all?[1]

Summing up it seems clear that, given the colour bar, the short-term economic interests of those who control the industry lie in maintaining the system. The costs are little more than those of recruitment, engagement, and training and they total probably less than R40 per head per annum. The benefits include a direct saving in labour costs of R240 per worker per annum, and very tight control against the possibility of industrial unrest. However, if the colour bar were to be removed, the picture would change entirely. No industry can afford to have a 100% annual turnover of its skilled labour force. Furthermore, taking a longer-term view, one can argue, on the basis of historical evidence elsewhere, that maintenance of the migrant system will in the end prove very costly to the society. When analysing the disproportion of the sexes in the urban and rural areas of Zambia at the beginning of the Second World War Godfrey Wilson pointed out that the contradiction inherent in such a situation would have to be resolved either by 'urban stabilisation, rural development, a rising standard of living, and a relaxation of racial tension' or by 'a general acceptance of totalitarian forms of government, and...an equilibrium of slavery...with the present free movements of population suppressed.'[2] Thirty years later in South Africa it seems that the whites have chosen to move towards the equilibrium of slavery.

[1] A. Barker, 'Community of the careless', *South African Outlook* (April 1970), 55 C.
[2] Wilson, *Economics of Detribalization* (1942), p. 82 B.

CHAPTER 8

IMPLICATIONS

It may be necessary to stress the importance of the need for objective analysis. The question is not in the first place whether the given phenomena are *desirable* . . . but whether they are *economically understandable*. Only after having answered the purely 'scientific' question could we, as economists, rationally pursue the matter in terms of political economy, i.e. what should be done about economically undesirable tendencies. In South Africa we are so tragically impatient to settle the last question that we seldom attempt to address our minds unreservedly to answering the first. Yet it should be possible to do so without the perpetual fear that differences in political philosophy might cause misunderstandings.

> J. A. Lombard, *The Determination of Racial Income Differentials in South Africa*

Poverty in the midst of plenty has become an increasing scandal in the eyes of men and women everywhere. So has the widening gap between rich and poor. In South Africa these differences are exacerbated by the fact that they are closely correlated with colour. Thus it is not surprising that there are profound disagreements within the society not only about the facts but also about the reasons for the facts being what they are. The academic is sometimes tempted to steer clear of such areas for fear that his objectivity should become contaminated by too close an involvement with his subject. Yet surely it is precisely where political differences are strongest that the social scientist has an obligation to uncover the facts, to try to see how they fit together and then, in the light of his understanding, to analyse the consequences of policies that people may wish to pursue in order to change the facts.

In this book we have focused our attention on one sector of one relatively small economy. Such a micro-study is severely limited in the extent to which it can be generalised. Yet the history of the gold mining industry in South Africa does provide insights into the world-wide problem of the economic relations between rich and poor. Among these insights is a realisation of the importance of the distribution of power in moulding the forces which shape even a micro-economic structure and determine the range of choices within it. Another is an awareness of the danger of attempting to deal with one situation by adopting proposals that were, in fact, worked out to solve a similar problem in a different situation.

THE WAGE DEBATE[1]

In the lively wage debate among South African economists during the 1960s much of the discussion was implicitly based on conditions in the manufacturing sector and some writers weakened their arguments by making their proposals for the whole economy. The labour markets of the major sectors are of course connected, but as Hobart Houghton has pointed out, there are important differences between them.[2] Bearing this in mind, let us use our understanding of the gold mines to examine various proposals for reducing the black–white earnings gap, and for eliminating poverty.

The problem of raising the standard of living in South Africa falls into two parts: steps to increase the gross national product, and measures to alter the distribution of earnings between rich and poor.

While it is true that the problem of eliminating poverty is essentially a long-run one which will only be solved by increasing the size of the national cake, one of the first lessons to be drawn from the history of the gold mines is that the forces which determine distribution are of fundamental importance. Despite the enormous development of the gold mines during the first eighty years of their existence the real wages of black miners did not increase at all; indeed, over the period 1889 to 1969, they seem actually to have fallen. Meanwhile real earnings of whites increased by at least two-thirds. And this despite the fact that the black–white employment ratio did not change significantly. The importance of distribution may be gauged by the fact that had black mineworkers had sufficient bargaining power to ensure that their wages increased at the same rate as those paid to whites it would have been possible over the period 1936–69 for black wages to have increased in real terms by 40% instead of falling as they in fact did. In other words, with a different distribution of power it would have been quite possible for the mining industry in 1969 to have been paying the average black mineworkers an annual wage of R282 instead of the R199 it actually paid. This could have

---

1 S. P. Viljoen, 'Higher productivity and higher wages of Native labour in South Africa', *S.A.J.E.* xxix (1961), 35–44 c. L. B. Katzen, 'The case for minimum wage legislation in South Africa', *S.A.J.E.* xxix (1961), 195–212 c. W. F. J. Steenkamp, 'Comment', *S.A.J.E.* xxix (1961), 213–17; and 'Bantu wages in South Africa', *S.A.J.E.* xxx (1962) c. O. P. F. Horwood, 'Is minimum wage legislation the answer for South Africa?' *S.A.J.E.* xxx (1962) c. J. A. Lombard, *The Determination of Racial Income Differentials in South Africa* (Institute for Social Research, Durban, 1962) B. J. B. Knight, 'A theory of income distribution in South Africa', *Bulletin of the Oxford Institute of Economics and Statistics* xxvi (1964) B. See also Ian Hume, 'Notes on South African wage movements', *S.A.J.E.* xxxviii, September 1970 c.
2 Hobart Houghton, *The South African Economy* (1st edn.), p. 151.

been achieved with exactly the same number of workers, both black and white, as were actually employed, and with real white wages also rising by two fifths over the period. In current terms white wages would have increased from R786 to R3,244 instead of to R4,006. And it is worth noting that this R3,244 would itself have been no less than the R3,216 that was in fact paid to whites three years previously, in 1966.[1] All of which goes to show the fallacy of applying the results of static analysis to a dynamic situation. For whilst it is easy to show that a sudden large increase in black wages in 1969 would have either forced a number of mines to close down or resulted in a drastic reduction in the level of employment it is quite wrong to suggest that this proves the impossibility of raising wages without either putting the mines out of business or a large number of men out of work. For in a dynamic situation a number of small changes spread over a period of time can add up to a great deal.

The ability of the white trade unions to appropriate the productivity gains from extra work by black miners (see pp. 55, 116) raises the question whether or not the latter are exploited in the technical sense of the term. Exploitation is said by economists to occur if a factor of production, e.g. labour, receives a reward less than the value of its marginal revenue product.[2] Under competitive conditions, exploitation as thus defined cannot occur because it will be profitable for an individual firm to employ labour up to the point where the addition to total revenue derived from the sale of the product produced by the last man hired is just equal to the wage it has to pay him. A number of economists have argued that such exploitation is not a significant feature of the South African economy.[3] According to W. F. J. Steenkamp there are only two possible types of exploitation, both of which are fast disappearing. Both relate to the monopsonistic power of the employers whose workers form a large proportion of the labour force. Analysis of the gold mines suggests, however, a third possible form: exploitation of black workers not by their employers but by their fellow white workers. This possibility arises from the fact that the ratio aspect of the colour bar prevents blacks from being employed in as large numbers as they would otherwise be was there no colour bar. Their employment is limited by the available supplies of white labour. Fig. 11 may help to clarify the argument.

Suppose that S and D represent the supply and the demand for black labour in the gold mines. The industry would then choose to employ OA

[1] See p. 46.
[2] See p. 111, n. 3. For a theoretical treatment of exploitation, see A. M. Cartter, *Theory of Wages and Employment* (Irwin, Homewood, Illinois, 1959), pp. 65–70 B.
[3] Horwood, *S.A.J.E.* (1962) C. W. F. J. Steenkamp, 'In quest of norms for minimum wage fixing in terms of the Wage Act [1925]', *S.A.J.E.* XXXI (1963) C. See also Kenneth E. Boulding, 'Interview', *Argus* (1970) C.

men at a wage rate of OC. However, suppose that, because of the constraint that black workers could not outnumber whites by more than 8 to 1, the industry could only employ OB blacks (equal, let us say, to ON in fig. 8, p. 112). The wage rate would still be OC (assuming a perfectly elastic supply curve for black labour) which would be less then the marginal revenue product at that level of employment by an amount FE, which is a measure of the exploitation. Although, given the power of the white trade unions, it is unlikely that B_8W units are exploited in the sense of their receiving a total payment which, after allowing for returns on specific investment, is less than their combined marginal revenue product, it seems reasonable to suggest that black workers are in fact exploited. It seems implausible that over the

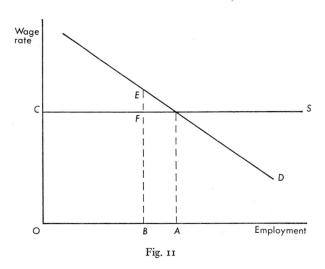

Fig. 11

years 1936 to 1965 when the productivity of all workers had risen by 59%, the failure of black incomes to rise in real terms was due to the fact that the apparent increase in their productivity was entirely due to more efficient white labour and the use of more capital.[1]

It seems more probable that the superior bargaining strength of the white workers enabled them to appropriate to themselves most of the share of that increase in B_8W productivity that was due to labour of whatever colour. In supporting this conclusion it is worth recalling the words of the president of the Chamber of Mines in his annual report of 1966:

Productivity in the mining industry has improved markedly over the years, mainly as a result of improved technique and increased mechanization. This has made it possible for employers more easily to meet the demands for wage rises resulting

[1] See Appendix 29.

from the competition for the limited skilled labour available. In consequence increases in pay granted in the last decade have been at a rate approximately double that of the increase of the cost of living index. However, advances in productivity as a result purely of technical progress can no longer effectively cushion increases in the wage bill. It is, therefore, imperative that labour itself should become more productive.[1]

The president was referring to whites. It was soon after this that the industry entered into the productivity agreement which resulted in whites getting more pay as a result of greater work by blacks. The very fact that a colour bar is imposed implies that there is exploitation, for the purpose of such a barrier is to prevent employers from employing as many men as they wish at the existing wage rate.

However, analysis of exploitation in the narrow technical sense of the term is inadequate for it begs a more important question. Even if it were to be shown that black mineworkers are not being paid less than their marginal revenue product it could be argued that they are being exploited in the sense that the whole supply curve for labour is manipulated by the political and economic powers within the economy for the benefit of the privileged. The powerful cannot avoid the charge of exploitation merely by showing that workers are not paid less than their marginal revenue product. So long as one group of workers does not have the opportunities for education and training that others have, so long as one group of workers is denied the power to withstand pressures from other power blocks within the economy, so long as one group of workers is denied the opportunity to use any skills that they may develop, so long will it be true to say that that group of workers is being used by others for their own ends. And that is exploitation.

But could the wages of black mineworkers be increased without, in practice, creating unemployment? In arguing the case for minimum wage legislation Leo Katzen maintained that, because of the inefficiency with which unskilled labour is so often used, the payment of higher wages to the unskilled would not lead to the substitution of capital for labour. Management would be more likely, he argued, to try to get greater output from the existing labour force before replacing it with expensive machinery.[2] In the case of the gold mines, however, the argument is wrong. For the very fact that labour is inefficiently used enabled managements to reduce the level of employment when they were under pressure to increase wages. After detailed investigation at the beginning of the 1960s, one group found that each of its mines could, through better organisation, reduce the total number of black workers in service by no less than 12% with almost no outlay on additional

[1] T.C.M., *Seventy-seventh Annual Report* (1966), p. 11 A.   [2] Katzen, *S.A.J.E.*, p. 205 C.

144

equipment. And a further 8%, it was estimated, could be fairly easily saved by a certain amount of capital expenditure. The basic premise of the steps taken after 1962 by the Anglo American Corporation when it started to raise black wages was that the total wage bill must not thereby be increased.[1] In other words for every 10% increase in black wages there was a 10% reduction in employment. In an industry where labour oscillates between town and country and where it has no trade union or political power, it is possible to lay off workers without difficulty. Labour is not, as elsewhere, a quasi-fixed factor of production.[2] Thus in a situation where labour is inefficiently managed the effect of raising wages is, contrary to Katzen's argument, to reduce the level of employment and thus, effectively, to increase the capital–labour ratio.

However there is another argument in favour of minimum wage legislation. Even if employment in some firms should fall as a result of the legislation the effect of a general increase in wages throughout the economy would, it is suggested, be to increase aggregate demand and so raise the total level of employment. The possibility of inflation being caused by such a step would, argues Katzen, probably be offset by three factors: increased productivity, the availability of idle capacity, and the willingness of firms to accept lower profits rather than increased prices.[3] These factors apply specifically to the manufacturing sector but there is one question that analysis of the gold mines suggests. Is not the extent of idle capacity severely limited? Despite the probable under-utilisation of both capital and unskilled black labour, the shortage of skilled labour is crippling. Expansion without inflation would only be possible if the two idle factors of production could be combined without using any more skilled white labour. But, given the political difficulties, particularly in the gold mines, this is unlikely. The possibility of increasing the supply of skilled labour is severely limited by the existence of a rigid colour bar combined with a discriminatory educational system. Whilst the protagonists of minimum wage legislation do not for a moment suggest that their proposal would alone solve the problem, some do seem to think that it would immediately help the poor. In some situations it undoubtedly would; however in the gold mines, under the existing conditions, there seems little doubt that although it would raise the wages of those who kept their jobs it would do so at the expense not of profits, but of those workers who would be laid off. This does not mean that nothing can be done about black wages on the mines but rather that minimum wage legislation alone is insufficient.

[1] See p. 55.
[2] W. Y. Oi, 'Labor as a quasi-fixed factor of production', *J.P.E.* LXX (1962) c.
[3] Katzen, *S.A.J.E.*, p. 208 c.

Labour in the South African gold mines

The apparent paradox between arguing, on the one hand, that black wages could have been increased over the period 1936–69 without affecting either employment or the total wage bill, and arguing that raising wages by means of minimum wage legislation would automatically create unemployment of black mineworkers is resolved by recognising that the steps that would have been necessary to achieve the goal of higher black wages for the same number of workers would have had to encompass more than the pressure of legislation. If it is to achieve its goal, minimum wage legislation must be part of a package deal. For example, had the African mineworkers won their strike in 1946 they would have been in a position not only to exert pressure on the wage rate but also to ensure, as the white unions did, that none of their members were laid off as a result. In other words black unions would have been in a position to force the industry to divide the gains from the increased productivity over the years differently from the way in which they were actually apportioned.

Some South African economists, while favouring the principle of raising black wages, argue that it would be a mistake to do so because marginal mines whose export earnings are so important to the economy would be put out of production by such wage increases. This is true, but the implications of the argument are that the cost of export earnings should be borne by those blacks in non-marginal mines whose wages are kept down. An alternative policy would be either to raise the wages of all black mineworkers and then, by fiscal means, help the marginal mines to meet the cost of this increase, or to ensure that those mines which could afford to do so put up their wages whilst marginal mines continued to use such labour as was available at the existing wage rate. The choice between these different alternatives is one involving value-judgments and depends upon the relative power of different interest groups within the economy.

But steps merely to increase the existing wage rate of employees, however well thought out, are not enough. Where, as Steenkamp has pointed out, the problem is essentially a long-term one, it is necessary that the *causes* of black wages being low, both absolutely and relatively to those of whites, be eliminated. One proposal in this direction is that priority should be given to the development of the Bantustans in order to increase the wage which industry would have to pay to attract labour away from these areas.[1] But it is by no means clear that this is the most effective method of raising the black standard of living, for the analysis on which this proposal is based does not take account of the oscillating factor in the black labour market.[2] Sir Arnold Plant has argued that:

[1] Horwood, *S.A.J.E.* (1962) c.   [2] See p. 74.

the possession of land in a reserve increases rather than reduces the bargaining power of the natives setting a lower limit to the terms which an employer can offer, not excluding the monopsonist labour department of the Chamber of Mines, despite the skill displayed by recruiting staff. A good harvest does *not* enable the mining companies to cut wages. On the contrary. It is therefore consequently quite erroneous to argue that the inadequacy of the wages of urbanised natives is explained by a general readiness of those from the reserves to accept less than the full cost of subsistence.[1]

Houghton finds this argument 'irrefutable' but remains puzzled by the fact that there seems to be strong empirical evidence to suggest that the urban earnings of many migrant workers are insufficient for the support of a family in the reserves.[2] Does the answer to the puzzle not lie in Plant's failure to distinguish between those migrants who go do work in order to raise their income to the subsistence level, and those who go to raise it higher? There is a crucial difference between the man who migrates to earn food for his family and the man who goes in order to buy a bicycle. Provided rural earnings are at, or above, subsistence level, potential migrants are able to hold out for higher wages, although there is no reason why their supply price should not be well below the cash equivalent of their rural earnings. But those migrants whose income from the land is nil or far below what is necessary for subsistence have no bargaining power. The only constraint on the long-run average urban wage is that it should be sufficient to bridge the gap between rural earnings and the subsistence level; the smaller the gap is between the subsistence level and the rural earnings, the lower the urban wage may be. In other words, *provided* rural earnings remain below the subsistence level, economic development of the reserves would, by reducing the gap, ease rather than increase the pressure on the urban wage level. Competitive pressure to raise wages will only be increased by removing the artificial barriers to mobility and by expansion of those sectors, e.g. manufacturing, which have the most potential for growth in terms of output and employment. Of these sectors, as table 11 shows, agriculture is one of the least important.

In manufacturing, construction, the railways, and the civil service employment increased at a faster rate than the economically active population, while in both agriculture and gold mining the rate was slower. Indeed, during the 1960s employment in the gold mines began to decline and in agriculture it seemed that employment had reached its peak and that in the future, due to increasing mechanisation, employment of black farm workers was likely to

[1] A. Plant, 'An African survey', *Economica* VI (1939) C.
[2] D. Hobart Houghton, 'Land reform in the Bantu areas and its effect upon urban labour', *S.A.J.E.* XXIX (1961), 172 C.

TABLE 11. *Average annual growth rates of employment in different sectors*

	%
Agriculture[a] (1946–60)	0·7
Gold mining[b] (1936–61)	1·2
South African railways and harbours[c] (1936–57)	4·0
Construction[d] (1936/7–61/2)	4·4
Civil service[e] (1939–64)	4·6
Manufacturing[f] (1936/7–61/2)	4·7
Total economically active population[g] (1946–60)	2·2

SOURCES: [a] *S.Y.B.*, 1964, H-6.
[b] T.C.M., 1964, p. 73.
[c] *Union Statistics*, G-15, and *S.Y.B.*, 1964, H-36.
[d] *Union Statistics*, L-29, and *S.Y.B.*, 1964, M-55.
[e] *State of South Africa Yearbook*, 1965.
[f] Major Industry Groups Nos. 1–21; *Union Statistics*, L-3; *S.Y.B.*, 1964, M-7.
[g] *S.Y.B.*, 1964, H-6 (figures for 1936 not available; 1946 included only those aged 15 years or older).

decline as it had been doing for whites ever since the 1930s.[1] Whilst the pattern of employment in small-scale subsistence farming in the Bantustans is considerably different from that on the white-owned farms, the fact remains that the possibility of increasing the level of employment in the agricultural sector as a whole remains remote.

SOME PROPOSALS

In the United States there is a good deal of evidence to suggest that the causes of the differences in earnings between blacks and whites lie deep within the social structure of the society. In analysing the situation the economist finds that he is forced to take into account factors that lie outside the textbook scope of his subject. For example, G. W. Scully in an analysis of wage differentials found in 1969 that 'The North–South wage differential as it now exists is primarily noneconomic in character; arising out of the political and social milieu which has generated differential endowments of human capital and a white–nonwhite differential which is not particularly amenable to elimination by the normal operation of the labor market. This wage differential is likely to continue until basic decisions are made in the political and social arena which will eliminate these two factors in our society.'[2] And in an earlier analysis another American economist had affirmed that 'there is a strong indication...that, in the final analysis, changes within individual fields are primarily determined by what are usually called non-

[1] Wilson and Thompson (eds.), *Oxford History*, II, 142 B.
[2] G. W. Scully, 'Interstate wage differentials: a cross section analysis', *A.E.R.* LIX (1969), 771 C.

economic variables. These would include the impact of social changes, such as the decrease in racial prejudice and discrimination that would open up for Negroes opportunities for jobs, housing, education and union membership.'[1] This conclusion seems to be equally true of the South African gold mines. If the gap between black and white earnings in the industry is to narrow, and if the real level of unskilled earnings is to rise (without being accompanied by a significant increase in unemployment) then there are at least five steps that must be taken.

1. The limitation on black wages imposed by the maximum permissible average must be removed. 2. The colour bar, both as a conventional ratio requirement and in the legal form of job reservation, must be abolished. 3. The legal barriers against the development of a stabilised urban labour force must be withdrawn. 4. The trade union legislation must be widened so as to include black mineworkers. 5. The educational structure of the country must be altered so that it does not discriminate against those who are not white.

The existence, in however modified a form, of a monopsonistic constraint upon the wages that employers may pay their workers has the effect, as the Buckle Commission pointed out at the beginning of the First World War, of penalising efficiency.[2] It is true that within the restrictions, managements have in recent years begun to develop incentive schemes for their black workers. But the fact remains that so long as there is a low ceiling upon the overall rate of wages that can be paid to any group of workers, so long will the development of a rational wage structure which effectively stimulates increased labour productivity be shackled.

The migrant labour system, as it operates on the gold mines, curtails the amount of experience and skill which 99% of the black labour force can gain, and it limits the amount of specific training that the industry invests in them. However, these losses are hidden so long as the colour bar prevents blacks from doing skilled jobs. Migrant labour and the colour bar operate as a joint restriction holding back an otherwise attainable increase in the productivity of black workers.[3] But gains from the relaxation of these barriers would come only if they were both slackened together. However the removal of either restriction would generate pressure for the abolition of the other. It is no accident that both in Zambia and the Congo, the decision to stabilise the labour force by encouraging families to settle near the copper mines was

[1] D. L. Hiestand, *Economic Growth and Employment Opportunities for Minorities* (Columbia University Press, New York, 1964), p. 118 B.

[2] South Africa, *Native Grievances Inquiry*, ch. 4, cited by *Witwatersrand Mine Natives' Wages Commission*, para. 81 A. See also Van der Horst, *Native Labour*, p. 209 B.

[3] See p. 139.

soon followed by the systematic removal of the various colour barriers within the industry.[1]

The argument for the unionisation of black mineworkers is based not only on the need for a countervailing power to eliminate any monopsony profits still retained by management, but also as a necessary first step in reducing the relative power of white mineworkers. Whilst in some circumstances it may be valid to argue that the unionisation of wage earners harms the poor by enabling the former to establish themselves as an elite at the expense either of the unemployed, or of the development of other sectors of the economy, application of such an argument to black workers on the South African gold mines is far more dubious.[2] For, given the existence of the white trade unions, neither the government nor the Chamber of Mines, even if they wished it, have the power to raise black wages at the expense of white increases. Only trade unions embracing unskilled workers with the right to strike would have the power to raise real wages by appropriating some, at least, of the increase in productivity. H. A. Turner's hypothesis with regard to England during the first half of this century, that 'the narrowing of the differential [was] due to the development in that period, of trade unionism itself',[3] would surely have been true for South Africa as well, if the African Mineworkers' Union had not been crushed in 1946 and subsequently prevented from re-emerging.

But perhaps the most cogent argument in favour of unionisation is the danger of complete and violent breakdown in communication between management and black workers. Whatever the immediate problems that would arise as a result of unionising black workers it is essential that a labour movement be recognised and encouraged. As Kenneth Boulding has observed, the greatest significance of trade unionism lies in the fact that it 'is an excellent insurance against internal disorder... The thing the labor movement [in America] gives us is this sociological sense of identification of the worker with something that is an integral part of his society which otherwise he may not have. And that is a tremendous safeguard against revolution.'[4] Blunt words: but the history of the white trade union movement in South Africa itself bears out their truth. What about the majority of South African workers? Are we condemned to repeat the lessons of history?

[1] See pp. 119, 124.
[2] Cf. Zambia: R. E. Baldwin, *Economic Development and Export Growth: a Study of Northern Rhodesia, 1920–1960* (University of California Press, Berkeley, 1966) pp. 106–8 B; and Tanzania: I. Davies, *African Trade Unions* (Penguin, Harmondsworth, 1966), pp. 163–4 B.
[3] H. A. Turner, 'Trade unions, differentials and the levelling of wages', *Manchester School of Economic and Social Studies* vol. 20, (1952) C.
[4] D. McCord Wright (ed.), *The Impact of the Union* (Kelley and Millman, Inc., New York, 1956), pp. 345 B.

In eighty years of mining the men who run the gold industry have, despite their other notable achievements, failed utterly to provide what the Montreux Conference on Development called 'a meaningful collaboration between centres of wealth and power and the areas of poverty and weakness' within the industry.[1] For the majority of mineworkers there are still no means whereby they can participate effectively in the decisions which affect their lives. Of course the gold mines are not the only industry, nor is South Africa the only country, where there has been this failure, but there can be few industries and few countries where the power between rich and poor is more unevenly distributed. In this connection it is worth calling to attention the conclusion to which Philip Mason comes after his exhaustive study of the *Patterns of Dominance* in the world.[2] He finds that:

Everywhere in recorded history the mass of mankind has let itself be duped into submission to the social order with all its injustices, as something unalterable – and today this age-old willingness to be saddled and bridled by a ruling group is everywhere coming to an end.[3]

We ignore such a warning at our peril. The existence of trade unions would, I submit, ease the process of historical change which if it continues to be bottled up can surely do nothing but explode.

The fifth step concerns the structure of education in South Africa. Over the long run, as T. W. Schultz has pointed out: 'Differences in the amounts invested in human capital in workers may be the single most important factor accounting for differences in wages.'[4] But while it is a powerful determinant of differences, education, as economists in the United States and elsewhere have shown, is also a major factor in raising the standard of living.[5] No proposals for raising real incomes in South Africa can ignore the economic implications of education policy. Little work has so far been done on this subject, and it is a matter requiring urgent attention. However the scraps of evidence available, combined with the analyses done in other countries, suggest strongly that the past and present structure of education in South Africa is one which not only inhibits growth but which serves also to exacerbate the racial differences in earnings.[6] Complete remodelling of the educational framework is a fundamental prerequisite both for economic

---

[1] World Council of Churches, *Fetters of Injustice* (Report of the World Consultation on Ecumenical Assistance for Development Projects), W.C.C., Geneva (1970), p. 103 B.
[2] P. Mason, *Patterns of Dominance* (O.U.P., London, 1970) B.
[3] Summary by V. G. Kiernan, *The Listener*, 16 April 1970.
[4] T. W. Schultz, *The Economic Value of Education* (Columbia University Press, New York, 1963), p. 53 B.
[5] Bowen, *Economic Aspects of Education*, pp. 1–38 B.   [6] See p. 94.

growth and, even more, for movement towards the elimination of racial discrimination in the distribution of wealth in the country.

There are two further proposals that have been made by various people concerned to raise black wages. One is that the mines should be nationalised; the other is that the flow of non-South African labour from Malawi, Mozambique and elsewhere should be halted. A detailed examination of the pros and cons of nationalisation, as it might affect the gold mines, lies outside the scope of this book. But there is one important point that emerges from our analysis. It is this: in the circumstances in which nationalisation became a practical possibility it might be that other means would be more effective in achieving the goals desired.[1] The proposal is based on the assumption that nationalisation would be the best way for a government supported by the majority of the people living in South Africa, to achieve the goal of higher wages for black mineworkers. But would it? Nationalisation would give a government the power to alter the allocation of revenue between profits and wages. However such a government would have the power even if it did not nationalise the mines to counter the strength of exclusively white trade unions. And any government would be able, as the present government is able, to tax profits in order to finance other projects. Like minimum wage legislation, nationalisation, as R. H. Tawney pointed out, is not an end, but a means to an end, and it must be analysed as such.[2] It *might* be that in the circumstances in which it could be implemented, a policy of nationalisation would on balance be the most effective means of raising living standards of the poor, but without a detailed analysis of the actual circumstances it is not possible to come to a conclusion either way.

The other proposal, namely that workers from neighbouring countries should not be allowed to enter South Africa, is even more complex. There is no doubt that any government elected by a majority of South Africans would be under heavy political pressure to keep out competitive workers, as numerous African governments have done since independence, and just as the American government was forced, despite powerful support from big business, to prohibit the Mexican *braceros* coming across to work on the fruit farms of California. Fanti fishermen forcibly repatriated to Ghana, Kenyans expelled from Uganda, Foulahs to Guinea, Dahomeyans forced to return to their country from several French-speaking countries, and Ghana's

[1] We are not considering that form of nationalisation proposed by exclusively white groups (e.g. the Herstige Nationale Party) which, we assume, is aimed more at increasing the power of white workers relative to management, than at raising black earnings.
[2] R. H. Tawney, *The Acquisitive Society* (Fontana, London, 1961) B. Cf. D. Jay, *Socialism in the New Society* (Longmans, London, 1960), for the argument that in order to redistribute incomes society has less clumsy instruments than industry-by-industry nationalisation.

sudden order in 1969 expelling thousands of workers from Upper Volta, Nigeria and elsewhere, all bear witness to the fact that 'politicians cannot ignore the feelings of their voters, and immigrants seldom have votes'.[1] Of course the expulsion of non-South Africans from the gold mines would lead to an increase in the wages of unskilled labour; as we have shown the mining industry would have to double the wages of their black workers if they hoped to compete with the manufacturing sector for labour. And, if they had not already done so, the mines would thereby be forced to shift the colour bar and stabilise their migrant labour force so as to increase productivity. But against this must be set the fact that in a situation where political and economic boundaries do not coincide those who control the economy may have certain obligations to people who live on the other side of some political line. In the case of the gold mines, whose development has been so enormously dependent on labour from other countries, it would seem that the modern 'tribalist' concept of one's responsibility to others extending no further than the national boundary is particularly inappropriate.[2] More especially is this true when one considers that for several of the countries (e.g. Lesotho and Mozambique) the economic ties with the gold mines have extended over so many years and have included such a significant proportion of their manpower resources that they have moulded the whole structure of their economies in a manner that cannot be changed within a few years. Furthermore it can be argued that these countries (together with the Bantu-stans) have, for eighty years, supported the development of South Africa's towns by virtue of the fact that the pattern of oscillating migration has enabled urban employers to pay wages less than the minimum necessary to maintain a worker and his family in town. Once again it is beyond the scope of this book to weigh up all the pros and cons of such a policy but it is important to appreciate that its implementation, while undoubtedly effective in raising the level of unskilled wages on the mines, would, apart from its possibly harmful effects to the South African economy, entail substantial social costs along the lines outlined above.[3] If this is so then perhaps the five proposals already made contain all that should be done. A society of twenty million people is after all very small in today's world and it should be possible in an economy as dynamic as the South African one to raise the standard of living of the poor without doing it at the expense of those other poor who

---

[1] *Africa Research Bulletin* (December 1969), p. 1535.
[2] B. Ward, 'We modern tribalists', *South African Outlook* (August 1968) C.
[3] See C. Helman 'The Agro-Economic Development of the Lowland Region' (M.A. thesis, Cape Town, 1971) for discussion of the importance to Lesotho of employment in the gold mines. In 1971 the average daily wage in Lesotho was 20 cents which was exactly half the minimum starting cash wage on the mines. See also p. 129.

have shared the burden of developing the country, but who do not happen to have been born in the right place.

CONCLUSION

This brings us back to the question which was asked at the beginning of the book.[1] In the light of our analysis it does seem that had the balance of power in the mining industry been different from what it was; for example, had the government enforced a cost of living allowance for black workers as was recommended in 1943, or had the African Mineworkers Union in 1946 acquired the power that the white trade unions acquired after the battles of 1913 and 1922, then the distribution of earnings within the industry would have been different from what it is. And it would have been possible to have had a thriving gold mining industry with a labour force that was more rationally used, better trained, and more highly paid. Quite what this would have meant at a macro-level is more difficult to analyse but it seems plausible to argue that any restrictions on the rate of growth, by virtue of the fact that savings might have been lower had income distribution been more equitable, could have been more than offset by the boost to development which a more rational use of the economy's manpower resources would have made possible. Such expansion would probably have gone a long way towards eliminating any reduction in the level of employment due to higher wages.

What then of the future? In the short run, at least, it does not seem likely that any fundamental changes in the power structure of the mining industry will occur. Does this mean that the pattern of the past eighty years will continue for the next eighty? Not necessarily, for there is within the industry one important force for change: the pressure of inflation. The cost of the colour bar, although impossible to calculate exactly, is high. Dr. Norval, former chairman of the Board of Trade and Industries, calculated in 1968 that a 70% replacement of white workers by Africans would result in a saving to the gold mining industry of some R30 million annually (approximately 6% of working costs). The rise in white earnings since that date will have increased the cost still further. During this time, however, the premium received from the sale of gold on the free market has enabled the industry to meet the increased cost of wages and equipment. But should the price of gold not rise substantially in the future – and this is a factor which lies outside the control of the producers of gold – then there will be very heavy pressure on the industry to slow down the rising costs which threaten to force yet more mines either to run at a loss (with government subsidy) or to

[1] See p. 16, line 6.

close down. And the one way in which costs could be reduced substantially would be by shifting the colour bar. Given the memory of 1922 and the balance of power within the economy it is highly unlikely that the Chamber of Mines would ever advocate complete abolition of the colour bar, but what is possible is that the industry will continue to press for the colour bar to shift from its present position to a new one which would enable blacks to do more of the underground work at lower wages than whites are paid. This would provide the necessary resources for the industry to upgrade the whites whose jobs have turned black into other tasks involving less sweat and more ink. In other words, if the price of at least some of the gold produced by the industry fails to rise during the 1970s and if there is no fundamental change in the methods of mining, then we can expect that under the pressure of rising costs the Chamber of Mines will find some means of making the colour bar more flexible. This will not alter the fundamental structure of the economy, nor will it be any proof that economic development can itself generate sufficient pressure to reduce the relative power which whites exercise in their control of the society. What it will do, as we have shown (p. 118), is to bring the mines into line with other sectors of the economy (e.g. manufacturing and railways) where the very real colour bar which prevents black men from becoming managers or senior officials is none the less sufficiently flexible to allow the economy to grow while ensuring that the vast majority of whites retain their position on the upper reaches of the pyramid. But the price which the Chamber of Mines may have to pay its white mineworkers for such a change will be high. The unions, as they have proved during the 1960s, are in a strong bargaining position.

Our task, as an American economist has pointed out, is not so much to redress the past as to anticipate the future.[1] Although the future grows out of the past, much of it is, created by the present. And if economists have any function, it is, surely, to increase society's understanding of what has happened in order that man may not act blindly when building his future. This work has been done in the hope that it serves to shed some light on one small aspect of the South African scene and that it will help, with the work of other social scientists, to inform the debate about future policy on which our well-being depends. For, as Keynes showed so clearly with regard to unemployment, until we understand there is little that can be done to improve the situation. The cure may demand political action: the diagnosis requires economic analysis.

[1] Hiestand, *Economic Growth and Employment Opportunities for Minorities*, p. 119 B.

APPENDIXES

APPENDIX I. CAPITAL COSTS OF DEVELOPING A GOLD MINE, 1969

	Total (R million)	Proportion (%)
Shaft sinking	25·0	41·7
Reduction plant	9·0	15·0
Underground development	7·0	11·7
Compressed air	1·8	2·9
Electricity	2·5	4·2
Ventilation	0·8	1·3
Water pumping	1·0	1·7
Other underground equipment	2·0	3·3
Surface buildings	1·8	2·9
Surface transport and services	0·3	0·4
Houses, hostels and staff amenities	8·5[a]	14·2
General expenses	0·5	0·8
Total	60·0	100·0

[a] In 1954 the total cost of houses, hostels and staff amenities on a new mine was estimated to be R6·om. of which R3·5m. (58%) was for white housing and club facilities and R2·5m. (42%) was for black housing, recreational and hospital facilities. Source: Anglo American Corporation, *The O.F.S. Goldfield*, Johannesburg, 1947.

SOURCE: Chamber of Mines, *Gold in South Africa*, P.R.D. Series No. 135, Johannesburg, 1969, p. 13.

APPENDIX 2. SIZE OF GOLD MINES

	1936	1969
Number of mines[a]	33	45
Black labour force[b]		
Average[c]	8,636	7,435
Largest	25,154	13,980
Smallest	1,130	1,001
Tons milled (000s)		
Average	1,432	1,784
Largest	4,612	3,434
Smallest	201	160
Gold production (thousands of fine ounces)		
Average	327	684
Largest	1,022	2,102
Smallest	34	20

[a] Excluding new mines not yet producing, and old mines in the process of closing down during the year.
[b] Employment of black labourers at 31 December.
[c] Arithmetic mean.
SOURCES: T.C.M. Annual Reports and W.N.L.A. Annual Reports.

APPENDIX 3. EMPLOYMENT ON GOLD MINES[a]

Date	White[b]	Black[c]	Index (1936 = 100) White	Index (1936 = 100) Black	Ratio Black:White	Remarks
1910	23,621	183,793	67	62	7·8:1	
1911	24,746	190,137	70	64	7·7:1	Mines and Works Act
1912	23,867	192,767	67	65	8·1:1	
1913	23,179	184,812	66	62	8·0:1	White miners' strike
1914	21,164	169,385	60	57	8·0:1	Black labour unrest
1915	22,080	195,426	62	66	8·9:1	
1916	22,329	203,666	63	69	9·1:1	
1917	22,475	183,304	64	62	8·2:1	
1918	22,764	179,628	64	60	7·9:1	*Status Quo* Agreement
1919	23,179	171,326	66	58	7·4:1	
1920	22,198	176,057	63	59	7·9:1	Black miners' strike
1921	21,036	172,694	59	58	8·2:1	
1922	14,207	161,351	40	54	11·4:1	Rand rebellion
1923	17,727	177,855	50	60	10·0:1	
1924	18,457	178,395	52	60	9·7:1	
1925	19,263	174,539	54	59	9·1:1	
1926	19,713	181,577	56	61	9·2:1	
1927	20,765	186,407	59	63	9·0:1	
1928	21,701	196,660	61	66	9·1:1	
1929	21,949	193,221	62	65	8·8:1	
1930	22,112	202,118	63	68	9·1:1	
1931	22,654	210,238	64	71	9·3:1	

Appendixes

			Index (1936 = 100)			
Date	White^b	Black^c	White	Black	Ratio Black : White	Remarks
1932	23,448	217,774	66	73	9·3:1	Sharp increase in gold price
1933	25,218	229,696	71	77	9·1:1	
1934	28,334	249,200	80	84	8·8:1	
1935	31,898	273,218	90	92	8·6:1	
1936	35,393	297,441	100	100	8·5:1	
1937	38,327	303,087	108	102	8·0:1	
1938	40,793	316,862	115	107	7·9:1	
1939	43,183	321,400	122	108	7·5:1	
1940	42,852	351,826	121	188	8·3:1	Increase in black labour supply
1941	41,424	368,417	117	124	9·0:1	
1942	40,555	357,573	115	120	8·9:1	
1943	38,508	306,285	109	103	8·0:1	
1944	37,166	297,591	105	100	8·1:1	
1945	36,328	307,291	103	103	8·5:1	
1946	39,642	304,782	112	103	7·7:1	Black miners' strike
1947	38,829	295,867	110	100	7·7:1	
1948	39,019	279,218	110	94	7·3:1	
1949	39,527	294,180	112	99	7·5:1	Sharp increase in gold price
1950	43,109	305,165	122	103	7·2:1	
1951	44,291	298,754	125	100	6·9:1	Acute shortage of black labour
1952	45,105	298,980	127	101	6·8:1	
1953	46,355	290,962	131	98	6·4:1	
1954	47,967	314,399	136	106	6·7:1	
1955	49,266	327,475	139	110	6·7:1	
1956	49,469	336,215	140	113	6·8:1	
1957	47,903	335,098	135	113	7·0:1	
1958	47,303	339,867	134	114	7·2:1	
1959	48,600	380,473	137	128	7·7:1	Large influx of black labour
1960	49,688	387,577	140	130	7·7:1	
1961	49,144	399,009	139	134	8·1:1	
1962	48,639	392,733	137	132	8·1:1	
1963	47,352	381,440	134	128	8·1:1	
1964	45,774	380,949	129	128	8·3:1	First official attempt to ease colour bar (since 1922)
1965	44,181	375,329	125	126	8·5:1	
1966	43,439	370,469	123	125	8·5:1	
1967	42,296	361,893	120	122	8·6:1	
1968	40,491	368,135	114	124	9·1:1	
1969	39,660	364,151	112	122	9·2:1	

^a Members of the Chamber of Mines.
^b Figures for 1940–5 exclude some 5,000 men on full-time national service.
^c These figures include small numbers of Coloured and Indian workers. In 1936, 0·6% of the total labour force was Coloured and 0·05% was Indian. In 1968 the figures were 0·09% and 0·007% respectively.

SOURCES: T.C.M. Annual Reports and G.M.E. Annual Reports.

APPENDIX 4. REVENUE, COSTS AND PROFIT, 1911–69

	1911	1916	1921	1926	1931	1936	1941	1946	1951	1956	1961	1966	1969
A. *Revenue*													
Ore milled (millions of tons)[a]	24·9	29·5	23·9	30·5	33·2	50·0	70·4	59·3	61·6	70·2	75·6	81·7	80·7
Index[a]	50	59	48	61	66	100	141	119	123	140	151	163	161
Grade (pennyweight/ton milled)[a]	6·6	6·3	6·7	6·5	6·4	4·6	4·1	4·0	3·8	4·6	6·1	7·8	7·7
Index[a]	143	137	146	141	139	100	89	87	83	100	133	170	167
Gold output (millions of fine ounces)[a]	8·2	9·3	8·1	10·0	10·9	11·3	14·4	11·9	11·5	15·9	22·9	30·9	31·3
Index[a]	73	82	72	88	96	100	127	105	102	141	203	273	277
Price (rand/fine ounce)	8·50	8·50	10·68	8·50	8·50	14·03	16·80	17·25	24·83	24·97	25·06	25·14	26·13
Index[a] (in real terms)[b]	73	63	54	54	57	100	104	86	98	82	73	65	63
Total revenue[c] (R million)	70·1	79·0	86·8	84·6	92·4	159·0	242·0	205·7	285·9	397·0	574·9	776·2	817·3
Index[a] (in real terms)[b]	53	52	39	47	55	100	133	91	99	114	149	178	174
Revenue p.t.m. (R/ton milled)	2·8	2·7	3·5	2·8	2·8	3·2	3·5	3·5	4·7	5·7	8·2	10·1	10·1
Index[a] (in real terms)[b]	105	88	78	78	82	100	95	77	81	82	106	115	107

M

APPENDIX 4. REVENUE, COSTS AND PROFIT, 1911–69 (cont.)

	1911	1916	1921	1926	1931	1936	1941	1946	1951	1956	1961	1966	1969
B. Working costs													
White cash earnings[d] (R million)	17·1	16·1	21·3	15·3	17·4	28·6	40·4	46·0	73·2	102·8	122·6	140·8	158·9
Proportion of revenue (a) (%)	24·2	20·4	24·5	18·1	18·8	18·0	16·7	22·4	25·6	25·9	21·3	18·1	19·4
Black cash earnings[d] (R million)	11·5	12·4	11·8	12·9	14·6	21·2	27·0	27·8	34·0	45·4	58·8	67·9	72·3
Proportion of revenue (b) (%)	16·4	15·7	13·6	15·2	15·8	13·3	11·1	13·5	11·9	11·4	10·2	8·7	8·8
Stores consumed[e] (R million)	23·3	24·5	28·8	27·9	31·7	54·2	70·0	75·2	132·2	213·4	268·2	296·8	332·1
Proportion of revenue (c) (%)	33·2	31·0	33·1	33·0	34·3	34·1	28·9	36·6	46·2	53·8	46·6	38·2	39·9
C. Gross profits[f]													
Taxation (R millions)	2·4	2·9	5·2	6·3	6·8	18·8	47·0	34·0	45·4	34·0	71·4	135·1	122·2
Proportion of revenue (d) (%)	3·4	3·7	6·0	7·4	7·4	11·8	19·4	16·5	15·9	8·6	12·4	17·4	15·0
Dividends (R million)	16·1	14·5	14·5	16·0	16·1	34·5	n.a.	27·2	48·7	61·2	102·4	134·5	156·6
Proportion of revenue (e) (%)	23·0	18·4	16·7	18·9	17·4	21·7	n.a.	13·2	17·0	15·4	17·8	17·3	19·2
Total proportion[g] (a+b+c+d+e) (%)	100·4	89·2	93·9	92·6	93·7	98·9	n.a.	102·2	116·6	115·1	108·3	99·7	102·3

[a] 1936 = 100.
[b] Deflated using retail price index; 1938 as base year.
[c] From gold only.
[d] For breakdown of cash earnings see Appendix 7.
[e] For breakdown of stores consumed see p. 41; and also T.C.M. Annual Reports.
[f] Revenue less working costs.
[g] Amongst the reasons why the figures do not add up to 100% are:
  (i) Most figures are for the year ending 31 December, but taxation is for the year ending 31 March.
  (ii) No account is taken of miscellaneous costs.
  (iii) Profits retained for ploughing back into the mines are not reflected in the figures.
  (iv) The absence of standardised accounting procedure in the industry.
Despite these difficulties the figures provide a reasonably accurate picture of the change in relative position of the different components. See diagram on p. 35.

SOURCES: T.C.M. Annual Reports and G.M.E. Annual Reports.

APPENDIX 5. MULTIPLE REGRESSION ANALYSIS OF GOLD MINING, 1936 AND 1966

Equation number	Date	Equation	Partial correlation between dependent variable and:					Multiple correlation co-efficient	R^2
			E	G	K	Q	V		
1a	1936	P = −13·1−·0001E+5·8G−·0002K+·001Q−·03V [·23] [20·0]* [·43] [·66] [·78]	·10	·97	−·02	·02	−·23	·97	·94
1b	1966	P = ·83+·0002E+·12G+·0003K−·005Q−·07V [·77] [2·10]† [3·04]* [·38] [3·25]*	·42	·30	·53	·39	−·46	·52	·27
2a	1936	C = 13·2+·0001E+1·1G+·0001K−·001Q+·03V [·26] [4·01]* [40] [·66] [·81]	·04	·65	·21	−·19	·01	·53	·28
2b	1966	C = 64+·0006E+·02G+·0001K−·003Q−·03V [5·59]* [1·30] [1·85]° [6·0]* [4·49]*	·22	·27	·25	·00	−·39	·62	·38
3a	1936	Q = 325+·24E−·65G−·16K−2·9V [18·1]* [2·63]† [8·62]* [·83]	·85	−·03	·27		·05	·90	·81
3b	1966	Q = 225+·20E−6·9G+·006K−2·8V [13·5]* [1·23] [·53] [1·15]	·93	−·00	·47		−·29	·87	·76
4a	1936	log Q = 0·83+1·56 log E−·45 log G−·67 log K [7·40]* [1·59] [3·97]*	·68	·04	·18			·66	·44
4b	1966	log Q = −2·15+1·06 log E−·09 log G+·03 log K [25·0]* [1·63]° [·49]	·98	·24	·52			·97	·94
5a	1936	R = −10·3+2·5C−·21V [4·69]* [1·48]					−·20	·42	·18
5b	1966	R = 1·2+1·7C−·08V [4·03]* [2·86]*					−·53	·50	·25

c = Working Costs (rand per ton milled)
E = Employment of black labour (at 31 December)
G = Grade of ore (pennyweights p.t.m.)
K = Capital invested (£000s)

P = Profitability (R. p.t.m.)
Q = Ore milled (thousands of tons)
R = Revenue (R. p.t.m.)
v = Vintage of mine (years)

Appendixes

NOTES: 1. 31 mines were analysed for 1936 and 46 mines for 1966.
2. Figures in brackets [ ] are t values.
3. Multiple correlation co-efficients corrected according to figures in Ezekiel and Fox, *Methods of Correlation and Regression Analysis* (3rd edition, 1959), pp. 294–7 B.
4. Regression co-efficients significant to the: $°$ = 90% ⎫
   $†$ = 95% ⎬ level
   $*$ = 99% ⎭

SOURCES: C, G, P, Q, R and V: T.C.M. Annual Reports, 1936 and 1966.
E: W.N.L.A. Annual Reports, 1936–66.
K: Frankel, *Investment and the Return to Equity Capital* (1967), p. 88, column 4 B.

How to read the equations

One does not have to be a statistician to glean some useful information from statistical tables. Multiple regression analysis is a method of assessing the relationship between variables. Consider equation 1a which comes in the form $Y = a + bx_1 + cx_2 + dx_3 + ex_4 + fx_5$ (where Y is the dependent variable; x_1, x_2, x_3, x_4, x_5 are independent variables; a is the intercept; b, c, d, e, and f are the regression coefficients).

The R^2 ($+·94$) tells us that 94% of the variance (between different gold mines in 1936) of profitability could be accounted for by differences in the level of employment; grade of ore, capital invested, amount of ore milled, and their age or vintage.

The co-efficients of partial correlation measure the relative importance of each of the several variables. (The square of the co-efficient is the proportion of variance, left unexplained by the other variables, that is due to differences in the variable concerned. Suppose, for example, that 20% of the variance in profitability was found to be due to differences in E, G, K and Q. If the partial correlation co-efficient (r) between P and V were $-·23$ ($∴r^2 = ·05$) then it would mean that 5% of the 80% unexplained by E, G, K and Q alone, was now accounted for.)

The t values, in brackets, are an estimate of reliability of the regression co-efficients and measure the ratio of the co-efficient to its standard error. Where $t \geq 2·8$ the co-efficient is said to be significant at the 99% level. In other words the probability that the regression co-efficient could have been obtained by chance if its true value was zero was only one in a hundred.

The sign of the regression co-efficients (and of the partial correlation co-efficients) shows whether the variable concerned is positively or negatively correlated with the dependent variable. Thus we see (from equation 1b) that in 1966 the profitability of a mine decreased with its age or vintage but increased with the grade of ore mined.

Those wishing to probe more deeply into the mysteries of multiple regression analysis are referred to Ezekiel and Fox, *Methods of Correlation and Regression Analysis* (John Wiley and Sons, New York, 3rd edition, 1959) B. For the purposes of the above table, pp. 24, 194, 295 and 396 are especially useful.

APPENDIX 6. COLOURED, INDIAN AND CONVICT EARNINGS

'Black' employees on the gold mines include a number of convicts as well as some 'other Coloured persons', i.e. 'Coloureds' *not* including Indians. Figures are not available to make exact corrections to determine precise earnings each year for blacks alone but, as the following calculations make clear, the inclusion of convicts and O.C.P. does not significantly affect the accuracy of the average figures given in table 5 (p. 46).

In 1936 there were 1,132 convicts on the large gold mines of the country earning a total of R40,954, i.e. R41·47 per man per annum. At the same time the large gold mines employed 1,070 'other Coloured persons'. No figures are available for the wages paid to these men but if we assume that, as in other parts of the country, their earnings are roughly the same as those for Indians (an assumption supported by the fact that when returning white ex-servicemen received a gratuity of R60 for each year on military service, the gratuity for 'Asians' and 'Coloureds' was calculated at the rate of R24 per annum), then the total wage bill paid to O.C.P. in the large gold mines would have been R2,140 × R196·28 = R210,020. Thus the total wage bill for blacks excluding both convicts and O.C.P. in 1936 was approximately R(21,142,062 − 46,954 − 210,020) = R20,885,088 and the total number in service was (309,909 − 1,132 − 1,070) = 307,681.

Therefore average wage/black = R67·9, cf. uncorrected R68·2. Similar calculations for 1949, when the number of convicts was 1,075 earning a total of R67,972 and the number of O.C.P. in service was 443, give a corrected annual wage per black of R93·6, cf. the uncorrected figure of R93·9. After 1954 the use of convicts fell sharply: by 1960 there were very few convicts on the mines (total wage bill R1,410) and by 1968 the number of 'other Coloured persons' in service was less than 0·1% of the total labour force (source: G.M.E. Annual Reports).

Although the position of Indians half way between blacks and whites in the wage structure is itself a peculiar phenomenon we shall not make any attempt to analyse the reasons for this. We shall ignore 'Indian' (and 'Coloured') earnings partly because they form an insignificant proportion of the labour force, partly because almost no information is available as to the jobs these men occupy in the gold mines, and partly because it seems evident that the wages of 'Coloureds' and 'Indians' are determined not so much by conditions of supply and demand in the mines as by those forces operating in the manufacturing industries of Natal and the Cape where these two groups form an essential part of the labour market. In other words, to understand the position of 'Coloureds' and 'Indians' relative to blacks and whites in the wage structure it would be necessary to examine the structure of earnings in non-mining industry. Although many of the factors operating in the gold mining and manufacturing sectors are the same, others are significantly different. The analysis of the labour market in secondary industry lies outside the scope of the present study.

Appendixes

APPENDIX 7. BREAKDOWN OF WHITE SALARIES AND WAGES (INCLUDING ALLOWANCES) 1936–65

		Of which:			As proportion of total		
		Leave pay	C.o.l.a.	Bonus	Leave pay	C.o.l.a.	Bonus
Year	Total (Rm.)	(Rm.)	(Rm.)	(Rm.)	(%)	(%)	(%)
1936	26·3	2·5	–	0·2	9·5	0	0·8
1941	37·0	3·4	0·5	0·3	9·2	1·4	0·9
1946	45·3	3·6	6·8	0·5	8·0	15·1	1·0
1951	64·5	5·8	14·3	0·9	9·1	22·1	1·3
1956	83·7	9·1	9·8	1·9	10·8	11·8	2·2
1961	97·2	9·7	13·3	3·5	9·9	13·6	3·6
1965	107·5	12·5	0·5	n.a.	11·6	0·5	n.a.

NOTES: 1. All white employees, including administrative, technical and clerical staffs on the large gold mines of the Transvaal. Figures for the O.F.S. are excluded.
2. After 1965 the Government Mining Engineer ceased to provide a breakdown of the total.
3. In 1955 and 1964 part of the cost of living allowance was consolidated into basic wages, hence the apparent sharp fall in the allowance at that time.
4. In 1946 other components of the total were: medical benefit 4·9%; savings fund 3·3%; active service allowance 2·5%. The latter fell away after the war whilst the two former were consolidated, after 1949, into basic pay.

SOURCES: G.M.E. Annual Reports, 1936–65.

APPENDIX 8. DISTRIBUTION OF CASH EARNINGS 1936 AND 1943

White officials, 1936		White day's pay men, 1936		Blacks, 1943	
Rates of pay (R/month)	Proportion of total (%)	Rates of pay cents/shift	Proportion of total (%)	Rates of pay (cents/shift)	Proportion of black labour force (%)
0– 30	4·9	50–100	5·2	17·5	1·6
30– 40	3·2	100–150	5·6	17·6–19	10·1
40– 50	15·7	150–200	12·8	20	41·8
50– 60	24·1	200–250	53·5	21–22·5	23·2
60– 70	2·3	250–300	15·0	23–25	10·7
70– 80	9·0	300–400	7·0	26–27·5	4·7
80– 90	1·6	400–500	0·0	28–30	2·4
90–100	25·8	500–600	0·8	31–40	2·9
100–120	2·9			41–60	2·2
120–140	2·7			76	0·4
140–160	3·9				
160–180	1·2				
180–200	0·6				
220–240	1·1				
300–320	0·1				
440–460	0·6				

Median = R64·8/month (i.e. 265 cents/shift) Total white officials = 6,990	Median = 224 cents/shift Total day's pay men = 21,646	Median = 20 cents/shift Total blacks = 299,777

SOURCES: G.M.E. Annual Report, 1936.
South Africa, *Report of the Witwatersrand Mine Natives' Wages Commission* (U.G. 21, Pretoria, 1944)

APPENDIX 9. SKILL DISTRIBUTION OF BLACK LABOUR FORCE
(Three gold mines, 1965)

Category	Grade	Distribution (%)	Rate of pay (cents)
Unskilled	1a	—	25
	1	} 20·0	40– 45
	2	18·0	52– 57
	3	19·8	61– 66
Semi-skilled	4a	} 18·9	71– 76
	4b		
	5	10·7	81– 86
Supervisory	C	3·6	81– 86
	B	3·2	103–113
	A	} 3·7	128–143
	AI		148–167

NOTES: 1. All three gold mines belong to one group.
2. Rates of pay are on the highest (D) scale introduced in 1965 by one of the groups.
3. There was also a grade 6 (for ambulance and lorry drivers) which, like grade 1a, included surface workers only.

Appendixes

APPENDIX 10. NEW RATES OF PAY IN ONE GROUP 1962-65

Scale	Date introduced	Stope workers (cents/shift)	Senior 'boss-boys' (cents/shift)
A	1962	44-54	90- 95
B	1964	52-65	115-120
D	1965	61-76	148-168

NOTE: In the stope gang, excluding the supervisors and mechanical workers, 50% were in grade 4, 40% in grade 3, and 10% in grade 2.

APPENDIX 11. ANNUAL COST PER WORKER OF FOODSTUFFS SUPPLIED FREE, 1936-69

Date	Black (rands)	White[a] (rands)	Index in real terms[b] (1936 = 100) Black	White
1936	12·26	1·8	100	100
1946	26·22	2·24	150	123
1956	39·68	6·14	148	219
1969	56·30	9·72	155	257

[a] It is not clear whether or not these figures include the subsidies on lunches for some officials (see p. 57), but it is unlikely that they do for the 1969 cost works out at little more than 3 cents a shift.
[b] Using retail price index with 1938 as base year.
SOURCES: G.M.E. Annual Reports and T.C.M. Annual Reports.

APPENDIX 12. HOUSING SUBSIDY FOR WHITES,[a] 1965

Type of housing	Area (sq. ft.)	Rent paid	Economic rent[b] (rand per month)	Subsidy
Cottages and flats[c]	1,200	10·0	51·0	41·0
Junior standard staff houses[d]	1,500	12·6	65·0	56·4
Senior standard staff houses[e]	1,700	14·0	115·0	101·0
Senior officials' houses[f]	1,800–2,000	15·0	130·0	115·0
Assistant mine manager's house	2,400	20·0	n.a.	n.a.
Mine manager's house	3,500–5,000	20·0	350·0	330·0

[a] On the new mines of one group.
[b] The amount that would cover cost and interest, amortising over 15 years.
[c] For day's pay men.
[d] For shift bosses and junior officials.
[e] For mine captains, accountants, assistant heads of departments.
[f] For underground managers, reduction officers, engineers etc.

Besides leasing housing, one of the groups also developed a home ownership scheme on its newer mines. This began in January 1957 and at first employees were allowed to buy only mine houses; but later they were allowed to build or buy any house of their choice, the maximum bond allowed being R10,000. Finally four building societies were brought into the scheme and furnished 75% of the deposit. The other 25% was furnished, not by the prospective buyer but by the group's housing company. The buyer was then given a housing allowance by the company of R40 per month for the length of the bond, with a maximum of 20 years. However in spite of all this assistance it was still more economic for an employee to rent a mine house, for thereby he did not incur the various service costs for which, as owner, he would have been liable. Since the beginning of the scheme until the end of 1965 only 320 houses had been bought and of these half were subsequently repossessed by the housing company at a price equal to its original cost (maximum R10,000) plus any improvement, less the cost of repairs needed to make it ship-shape.

APPENDIX 13. ACCIDENT RATES[a] 1952–63

		Welkom (O.F.S.)	Johannesburg (Central Rand)	Heidelburg (East Rand)
Death	1952–57[b]	2·8	1·9	0·7
	1958–63	1·6	1·6	0·9
Accidents	1952–63	70·3	66·8	49·6

[a] Annual rates per 1,000 persons at work in gold mines of the different inspectorates.
[b] The high death rate in the Orange Free State between 1952 and 1957 was due partly to the prevalence of methane gas and partly to the fact that the development stage of mining is more dangerous than when production is fully under way.

SOURCE: G.M.E. Annual Reports.

Appendixes

APPENDIX 14. ANNUAL WASTAGE OF EMPLOYEES IN GOLD MINES,[a]
1916-69

Date	White[b] (%)	Black[c] (%)
1916	3·0	4·6
1926	8·9	3·3
1936	11·2	2·4
1946	14·0	2·3
1956	14·0	2·0
1966	11·5	2·2
1969	14·1	2·0

[a] Wastage is a measure of the proportion of men in the servce of the mines who, for one reason or another, are not at work on an average day.

$$\text{Wastage} = \left(100 - 100 \, \frac{\text{No. of persons at work}}{\text{No. of persons in service}} \right)\%$$

[b] Figures for 1946 exclude those on active military service.
[c] Including Coloured and Indians
SOURCES: G.M.E. Annual Reports and T.C.M. Annual Reports.

APPENDIX 15. DERIVATION OF EARNINGS PER SHIFT WORKED, 1911-69
(See table 7, p. 66)

SOURCES: Annual Reports of the Government Mining Engineer and the Chamber of Mines.
NOTE: White earnings include allowances (e.g. cost of living) but exclude all subsidies (e.g. housing).
   Black earnings take account of the cost of food supplied free but exclude other earnings in kind (e.g. housing).
   For both blacks and whites due allowance has been made for 'wastage', thus the figures reflect average earnings per shift actually worked.

Calculations
1. Total wage bill ÷ total number in service = mean annual wage.
2. Mean annual wage ÷ No. of shifts in a year (i.e. 313) = mean wage/shift.
3. Mean wage/shift ÷ (1 − wastage) = mean wage/shift worked.
4. Similar calculations to obtain cost of food/shift worked.

APPENDIX 16. CASH EARNINGS IN DIFFERENT SECTORS, 1936 AND 1961

	1936				1961			
	Black	Coloured	Indian	White	Black	Coloured	Indian	White
Manufacturing								
R/annum	84	158	120	452	370	566	602	2030
Index[a]	100	188	143	538	100	153	163	549
Construction								
R/annum	90	200	214	560	338	712	770	1926
Index	100	222	238	622	100	210	228	570
Gold mines								
R/annum	68	–	196	786	146	–	504	2478
Index	100	–	288	1156	100	–	345	1697
Agriculture								
R/annum	n.a.	n.a.	n.a.	n.a.	68	132	198	1416
Index					100	194	291	2082

NOTE: Figures for agriculture were obtained by dividing total wage bill by the total number of farm employees including domestic servants but excluding casual employees. Whilst the figures for agriculture may be subject to a considerable degree of error, those for other sectors are probably more accurate. Figures for manufacturing include construction (i.e. 'building and contracting') and refer to private establishments (i.e. state enterprise is excluded).

[a] Black = 100

SOURCES: *Census of Industrial Establishments* (U.G. 20, 1938).
G.M.E. Annual Reports, 1936 and 1961.
Statistical Year Book, 1964. H-22, H-25, H-32, H-46, H-47, H-54.

Appendixes

Name of union	Number of mine[a] employees who were members	%
Day's pay men		
Amalgamated Engineering Union	4,142	10
Amalgamated Society of Woodcutters	496	1
Amalgamated Union of Building Trade Workers of S.A.	566	1
Ironmoulders' Society of S.A.	11	–
Mine Workers Union	13,094	31
S.A. Boilermakers' Iron and Steel Workers', Shipbuilders' and Welders Society	1,479	3
S.A. Electrical Workers Association	1,653	4
S.A. Engine Drivers' and Firemen's Association	2,669	6
S.A. Reduction Workers' Association	1,705	4
Total: Represented by Mining Unions' Joint Committee	25,815	60
Officials[b]		
Underground Officials' Association of S.A.	8,394	20
Mine Surface Officials' Association of S.A.	8,428	20
Total[c]	42,637	100

[a] Gold and coal mines, members of the Chamber.
[b] Until 1969, it was not compulsory for officials to join these associations. The figures provided are of these eligible to join.
[c] In 1964 the total number of whites in the service of the gold mines alone was 45,774, which suggests that some whites did not belong to any of the unions or associations listed.
SOURCE: Figures supplied by the Chamber of Mines.

APPENDIX 18. WORKER DEMANDS AND EMPLOYER RESPONSES 1936–69

Year	Demand, and group making it	Outcome
	A. *Whites*	
1936	M.U.J.C.: 10% increase in minimum wages.	Medical benefit allowance established. Increased holiday allowance.
	M.W.U. threatens to strike on Randfontein mine to enforce the 'closed shop' principle.	G.P.C. issues press statement that its policy remains 'to uphold this principle, and not to interfere with the liberty of the individual in deciding for himself whether he joins a Union or not'.
1937	Strike on Simmer and Jack mine 'for the purpose of focussing attention upon the activities of a newly-formed organisation, alleged to be racial and political in character', i.e. a group of predominantly Afrikaans-speaking workers led by Dr. Albert Hertzog.	G.P.C. reversed its 'open shop' policy; recognised seven main unions and demanded that every white employee, excluding officials, be a member of a trade union.
1938	M.W.U.: May Day and Dingaan's Day be paid holidays.	Refused.
1939	M.U.J.C.: 'concessions'.	Improvements in provident fund and savings fund coupled with agreement that the latter concession would act as a set-off against any cost of living allowance should that be necessary later.
	See 1938	G.P.C. decided that Dingaan's Day be a paid holiday for those whites who could be spared.
1940 (May)	M.U.J.C.: cost of living allowance (c.o.l.a.) to cover rise in c.o.l. since September 1939.	G.P.C. refused, but approached government with request to keep c.o.l. down.
(August)	M.U.J.C.: further request for c.o.l.a.	Refused, but G.P.C. agreed that 1939 increase in savings fund had been absorbed by c.o.l. rise since then; granted further increase in savings fund allowance on same condition. Also

Appendixes

Year	Demand, and group making it	Outcome
		granted R60,000 towards liquidation of Mines Benefit Society's overdraft.
1941	M.U.J.C.: c.o.l.a.	Granted at rate of 1d. (0·8 cents) per shift for each rise of 6 points in Retail Price Index number for food, rent, etc. on Witwatersrand.
	M.U.J.C.: c.o.l.a. should be based on full month rather than days counting for leave.	Agreed: c.o.l.a. increased in proportion 30 : 26.
1942	M.U.J.C.: May Day be a paid holiday.	Refused.
1943	M.W.U.: 30% increase in wages of members.	Refused.
	M.W.U.: applied for appointment of an arbitrator in terms of War Measure No. 9 of 1942.	See 1944.
1944	A board of arbitrators appointed.	Lump-sum payment. Agreement signed for the provision of R200,000 per annum for 5 years for benefits to members of M.W.U., plus R50,000 for immediate use.
1944–5	Following above agreement.	Additional medical benefit allowance at rate of R1·12 per month of service to all except M.W.U. members.
1945	M.U.J.C.: extra week's pay for surface workers going on leave.	Refused.
	Mech. U.J.C.: twice asked that wages of all winding engine drivers be increased.	Discussions proceeding at end of year. See 1946. Refused.
1946	M.U.J.C. increase of 12% in wages of all white mine employees.	c.o.l.a. increased by 15 cents per day, 17·3 cents per shift, but G.P.C. pointed out that position had been under review *before* M.U.J.C. demand.
	See 1945. Discussion with Mech. U.J.C.	Increase in basic pay for journeymen mechanics with 10 years or more service on mines.
	Engine Drivers and Firemen's Association ask for similar service increment.	Agreed.
	Following above increases:	Rise in minimum rates for all officials.

Year	Demand, and group making it	Outcome
1947	M.U.J.C.: Number of requests for improvements in working conditions.	Mostly refused, but improvements in leave pay granted.
	S.A. Reduction Workers' Association: Service increment as above, 1946.	Granted.
1948	M.U.J.C. again asked for improvements as in 1947.	Refused: because of the large increase in working costs that this would entail.
	M.U.J.C. approached the government about the G.P.C. refusal.	Van Eck commission of enquiry into conditions of employment in the gold mining industry appointed.
1949	Devaluation: price of gold rises by 40%. Immediate meeting between M.U.J.C. and G.P.C.: Government makes copies of Van Eck Report on Conditions of Employment available to assist negotiations.	Major agreement: 1. Minimum rate increased by 15%. 2. Three allowances (medical benefit, additional medical benefit, and savings) withdrawn and consolidated into minimum rates. 3. Pension fund established for all day's pay men. 4. £25 cash bonus to all day's pay men with 12 months' service. 5. Overtime increased from 1½ times to twice ordinary rate. 6. 10 years' service increment for work in any Chamber mine (gold or coal) irrespective of occupation. 7. Increased holiday leave allowance. 8. System of monthly meetings between M.U.J.C. and G.P.C. 9. Agreement to examine hours of work. 10. Another day of holiday (New Year's Day) on the basis of Dingaan's Day arrangements. 11. Payment into the provident fund so as to improve lump-sum benefits.

Year	Demand, and group making it	Outcome
1950	Following 1948 request by Mech. U.J.C.	Increases in minimum rates of pay.
	M.W.U.: 15% increase in basic wages.	Refused.
	Engine Drivers and Firemen's Association: 15% increase in basic wages.	Refused.
1951	Following 1949 No. 9.: M.U.J.C. agreed that shorter working week not possible but suggested achieving the same result by granting additional leave.	Introduction of system of voluntary accumulative leave: day's pay men after 312 shifts qualifying for ordinary leave commenced to qualify for extra leave at rate of 6 days per annum. M.U.J.C. agreed not to raise question of hours of work for 5 years.
	Three unions (M.W.U.; Reduction Workers; Engine Drivers and Firemen): general increase of 15% in wages plus further leave.	G.P.C. suggested discussion with M.U.J.C. but three unions refused and applied for Conciliation Board settlement.
	Officials' Association (Surface and Underground): improvement of earnings.	Actual and minimum salaries increased retrospectively from 1 January.
	Underground Officials' Association: consolidation of part of c.o.l.a. into basic salaries.	Refused.
1952	M.U.J.C.: holiday leave allowance for accumulated leave.	Total annual holiday leave allowance increased.
	M.U.J.C.: New Year's Day and Day of the Convenant (formerly Dingaan's Day) be paid holidays like Christmas Day and Good Friday.	Refused: but Coronation Day was observed as a paid holiday like Christmas Day.
1953	M.U.J.C.: renewed demands (refused in 1952) for 5-year service increment to all employees.	G.P.C. increased existing 10-year service increment.
	M.U.J.C.: 'closed shop' agreement be extended to white employees of companies engaged on contract work on the mines.	G.P.C. refused to interfere.
	Surface and Underground Officials: as in 1951, consolidate.	Rules of the officials' pension fund altered such that R20 of the c.o.l.a. be regarded as pensionable emolument.

Year	Demand, and group making it	Outcome
	G.P.C. informed M.U.J.C. of above agreement.	Similar arrangement made for day's pay men.
1955	M.U.J.C.: general increase of 15% in wages. Increase in holiday leave allowances.	G.P.C. offered: rise in actual pay of 17 cents per shift; increased holiday allowance; and R1·00 per shift of c.o.l.a. consolidated into wages.
	Following increases for day's pay men, G.P.C. met Officials' Associations.	Similar increases.
1958	Surface and Underground Officials' Associations: review of salary scales.	Increases in minimum rates granted.
	M.U.J.C. complained that 'mines were employing non-Europeans on work previously and traditionally performed by Europeans'.	Matter carefully investigated and M.U.J.C. 'assured that no attempt had been made, as a matter of policy, to replace Europeans by non-Europeans'.
	M.U.J.C.: Day of the Covenant be a paid holiday.	See 1959.
	Mech. U.J.C.: increase in basic wages.	Agreed.
	Engine Drivers and Firemen: increase in basic wages.	Refused
	Reduction workers: increase in basic wages.	Under consideration at close of the year. See 1959.
1959	Reduction Workers: see 1958. See 1952, and 1958.	Increase in service increment. Day of the Covenant granted as a paid holiday like Christmas Day and Good Friday.
	M.U.J.C. and Officials' Associations: increased leave allowance.	Increased by R5·00 per annum after completion of each 5 years of service.
1960	General review of wages of day's pay men by G.P.C.	Minimum rates increased to R3·20 per shift on surface and R3·50 underground.
1961	Following above increases:	Minimum rates for officials raised.
	M.U.J.C.: hours of work be reduced to 40 hours per week over a period of 5 years with no loss in earnings.	Detailed consideration. See 1962.
	Officials' Associations requested review of pension fund.	Substantial improvements made.

Year	Demand, and group making it	Outcome
1962	Following above: M.U.J.C. met G.P.C.	Substantial improvements in the other pension fund.
	Hours of work: see M.U.J.C. 1961	One day of paid occasional leave for every 23 days worked, other than shifts worked on days of rest.
1963	Surface Officials: asked for 'closed shop' agreement.	Refused, but G.P.C. asked mine managers to encourage surface officials to join the association.
	M.U.J.C.: R1 increase in c.o.l.a.	Refused. Conciliation Board appointed.
	Following repeated requests (1960; 1961, 1962 twice) by M.W.U.; Reduction Workers; Engine Drivers and Firemen.	Additional pay for afternoon and night shifts at rate of 10 cents per afternoon, and 15 cents per night.
1964	Federation of Mining Unions (formerly M.U.J.C.): introduction of a 5-day week.	Under detailed consideration.
	M.W.U.: introduce monthly rates of pay coupled with slight easing of the colour bar.	Introduced, on experimental basis, with government permission, on 11 mines.
1965	'Rebel Miners' opposed experiment. Wild cat strikes. Official commission of enquiry appointed.	Following recommendations of Commission, government halts the experiment.
1966	Officials' Associations (Surface and Underground) make various requests to G.P.C.	G.P.C. agrees, provided basis of productivity bargaining is accepted.
	F.M.U. rejects G.P.C. offer and demands all-round wage increase of R1 per shift.	G.P.C. revises its offer and enters into discussion with F.M.U.
	Wild cat strikes by members of M.W.U. continue.	G.P.C. representatives visit Minister of Mines who requests Industrial Tribunal to investigate alleged grievances in M.W.U.
	'Action Committee' institutes a series of strikes.	Government promulgates Act making such strikes illegal if called for purposes other than those defined in Act.
1967	Discussions between G.P.C. and F.M.U.	Government appoints mediating committee to assist negotiations. Agreement finally reached with effect from 1 June. Chamber agrees to pay monthly rates and Federation,

Year	Demand, and group making it	Outcome
		as a *quid pro quo*, agrees to relax various restrictions in order to increase productivity.
	Review of salaries for officials.	Higher rates as from 1 January 1968.
1968	M.W.U., S.A. Reduction Workers' Association and S.A. Engine Drivers' Foremen's and Operators' Association resign from F.M.U. and form Federation of Mine Production Workers.	G.P.C. recognises F.M.P.W. on the understanding that 'closed shop' agreement still holds.
1969	M.W.U. hits out at gold producers for alleged new attempt to upset job reservation by allowing blacks to 'infiltrate' white jobs of sampling, survey work and ventilation.	G.P.C. rejects 5-day working week because of cost. Holiday allowance for whites increased.
1969	F.M.P.W. announces that it will no longer abide by 30-year-old closed shop agreement which allocated certain occupations to each of the trade unions. It aims to recruit anybody working in mining industries.	Officials' Association persuades G.P.C. to make membership a condition of employment for officials in order to 'prevent poaching'.
	F.M.P.W. continues to press for 5-day week.	G.P.C. agrees to re-open talks on 5-day week. G.P.C. announces substantial increases in white minimum rates as from 1 January 1970 in order to attract staff.

B. *Blacks*

Year	Demand, and group making it	Outcome
1941	African Mine Workers' Union (A.M.W.U.) formed.	
1942		Government passes War Measure 145 making all strikes by black workers illegal in all circumstances.
1943	A.M.W.U. demands higher wages.	Government appoints (Lansdown) Commission to investigate remuneration and conditions of employment of blacks on Witwatersrand gold mines.

Appendixes

Year	Demand, and group making it	Outcome
1944	Lansdown report recommends: 1. c.o.l.a. of 2·5 cents per shift, per black. 2. Boot allowance 30 cents per 30 shifts. 3. Overtime at time-and-a-half rates. 4. Minimum rates of surface workers, 22 cents per shift; minimum rates of underground workers, 24 cents per shift.	Government awards increases of 4 cents per shift to underground workers, 3 cents per shift to surface workers, but no c.o.l.a. Overtime rate increased as recommended. Cost of the increase to be met largely by the government. Government, under pressure from G.P.C., prohibits meetings on mine property and arrests the President of the A.M.W.U.
1946 (April)	A.M.W.U. demands minimum wage of R1·00 per shift and better conditions of work. A.M.W.U. writes to the T.C.M. four times setting forth the demands and requesting an interview.	Chamber of Mines does not reply.
(August)	70,000 blacks strike.	Compounds immediately sealed off under armed guard. Clashes with police who use their guns. Strike leaders arrested. Chamber states its implacable opposition to black trade unionism. A.M.W.U. defeated.
1948	Annual review of black wages by Chamber of Mines.	Principle of progressive service increment introduced. Earnings increased by 2 cents a shift after each period of 270 shifts worked on continuous underground employment.
1949	Price of gold rises by 40%.	Earnings increased by 2 cents a shift (2 cents on surface, 3 cents underground).
1951	Chronic labour shortage.	Minimum pay for underground workers increased from 27 to 30 cents a shift.
1955	Annual review.	Minimum rate for underground 'boss-boys' raised from 36 to 40 cents a shift. Earnings of

Year	Demand, and group making it	Outcome
		all other underground workers varied from a minimum of 30 to a maximum of 44 cents. 'Boss-boys' earnings varied from 36 to 59 cents a shift.
1969	Annual review.	Minimum wage raised from 34 to 40 cents a shift. Also mines now to pay cost of return train fare as well as the incoming journey.

APPENDIX 19. MULTIPLE REGRESSION ANALYSIS OF BLACK LABOUR SUPPLY 1936–62

E_n = Total employment, of all races, in manufacturing industry during the year n.
I_n = Retail price index (1938 = 100).
L_n = Total number of blacks (including non-recruited) from the Cape Province engaged, during the year n, by the gold mines.
M_n = Number of 200 lb bags of maize produced in the Reserves of the Cape Province during the year ended 30 April.
P_n = Number of pass laws (i.e. influx control) convictions during the year ending 31 December.
W_n = Price of wool during the year ended 30 June.

Equation Number	Date	Equation	Multiple correlation co-efficient		R^2
			Uncorrected	Corrected[d]	
1	1936–55[a]	$L_n = 130330 - 0{\cdot}35E_n + 41P_n - 22363\,W_n/I_n$ $[5{\cdot}4]^* \quad [4{\cdot}3]^* \quad [0{\cdot}66]$	·78	·46	·21
2	1940–62[b]	$L_{n+1} - L_n = 4000 - {\cdot}28(E_{n+1} - E_n) + {\cdot}18(P_{n+1} - P_n) - 100{\cdot}6(W_{n+1} - W_n)$ $[{\cdot}99] \quad [1{\cdot}43] \quad [0{\cdot}66]$	·16	·00	·00
3	1940–62[c]	$L_{n+1} - L_n = 5253 - {\cdot}35(E_{n+1} - E_n) + {\cdot}21(P_{n+1} - P_n)$ $[1{\cdot}38] \quad [1{\cdot}83]^\circ$	·18	·00	·00
4	1947–62[d]	$L_{n+1} - L_n = 910 - {\cdot}39(E_{n+1} - E_n) + 2{\cdot}0(P_{n+1} - P_n)$ $[1{\cdot}96]^\dagger \quad [1{\cdot}86]^\circ$	·30	·00	·00
5	1947–62[c]	$L_{n+1} - L_n = 6803 - {\cdot}28(E_{n+1} - E_n) + {\cdot}18(P_{n+1} - P_n) - 103(W_{n+1} - W_n) + 3{\cdot}77(M_{n+1} - M_n)$ $[1{\cdot}23] \quad [1{\cdot}41] \quad [0{\cdot}80] \quad [1{\cdot}16]$	·41	·00	·00

[a] Excluding 1937 and 1946. [b] Excluding 1946. [c] Excluding 1961.
[d] Corrected according to figures in Ezekiel and Fox, *Methods of Correlation and Regression Analysis* (1959), pp. 294–7.
Figures in brackets [ ] are *t* values.
Regression co-efficients significant to the ° = 90%, † = 95%, * = 99% } level

How to read the equations: see Appendix 5.

SOURCES:
E_n: *Union Statistics for Fifty Years*, L-3, and *Statistical Year Book 1964*, L-3.
I_n: *Union Statistics*, H-23, and *Statistical Year Book 1964*, I-13.
L_n: N.R.C. Annual Reports.
M_n: Figures supplied by the Mealie Industry Control Board, Pretoria.
P_n: *Union Statistics for Fifty Years*, F-4, and South African Institute of Race Relations, *Annual Survey*, 1959–62.
W.: *Die Wolboer*, December 1958, and South African Wool Board, *Statistical Review of the South African Wool Clip*, 1959–64.

APPENDIX 20. CHOICE OF TECHNIQUES[1]

Salter's[2] analysis may be carried a stage further in considering the choice of techniques between black and white labour. As with the choice between capital and labour, the shift in the production function may be biased towards one or other, while changes in factor prices will generate pressure to adapt and develop machines and training that allow for substitution of one class of labour for the other. One would have expected that the relative rise in white wages would have led to the development of techniques that were black-labour intensive and white-labour saving. But this pressure has been resisted by the colour bar which places an effective limit on substitution between the two factors. In other words we would argue that while technical progress provides a steady pressure to mechanisation, there is, within this, a bias toward developing techniques that save black labour relatively more than white (see fig. 12).

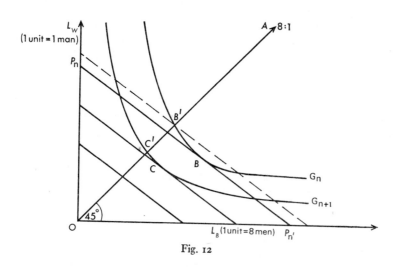

Fig. 12

Assuming that all white labour is skilled and all black labour is unskilled and assuming constant returns to scale, let G_n represent a production function (for any output) relating to black and white labour at time n. $P_n P_n'$ is the price line and OA is the colour bar ray.

Without a colour bar in the mining industry (given the existing training, education and experience of the two groups) the optimum technique, with the given capital, would be at B. However this lies within the 'forbidden' range, to the right of OA, where the employment of the two groups would be in a ratio greater than 8 blacks to 1 white. A second-best solution, for the given output, would have to be found at B'. Over the period n to n+1 a new $L_B - L_W$ production function will develop, not as a result of technical progress but because of the substitution of capital for labour. The same output will be attained with less black and white

---

[1] I am indebted to Professor J. A. Mirrlees for his considerable assistance in clearing my thinking on this matter. He, of course, is not responsible for any errors that may remain.
[2] See p. 83.

labour in the later period. Assuming no change in the price line between the two periods, the industry will focus its attention on substituting capital for labour in such a way that it alters the shape of the production function as shown. In period $n+1$, C would be the optimum combination of the two classes of labour. While not attainable, the shift to C' would be less costly than if the production function had not altered its shape between n and $n+1$. This helps to explain why, in the gold mining industry, although the costs of white labour have been rising relatively to black labour, the industry has laid greatest stress upon the development of techniques which save labour, but which save black labour more than white.

Although it is difficult to distinguish in practice between changes due to technical progress and those due to factor substitution, it seems possible to suggest that much of the mechanisation that has taken place in the gold mining industry is in the nature of adaptations to meet the change in relative capital–labour prices. It is noticeable that these changes have all led to a saving in the use of black labour without immediately affecting 'white' jobs. Such a development, while doing nothing to alter the ratio of black–white employment, has the effect of reducing the costs to the industry of maintaining the ratio by altering the production function so as to minimise the difference between the technical optimum C and the second-best solution C'.

APPENDIX 21. EDUCATION IN SOUTH AFRICA, 1930–60

A. *Extent of education, 1960*

Percentage of each racial group	Over the age of	Black (%)	Coloured (%)	Indian (%)	White (%)
With no education at all	19	64·9	36·2	32·1	2·1
Who have passed standard 5 (at least 7 years of school)	9	11·7	28·9	34·2	84·5
Who have passed standard 10 (at least 12 years of school)	14	0·2	1·0	2·5	22·8

SOURCE: *Statistical Year Book*, 1964, A-32, A-35.

B. *State expenditure per pupil (in rands)*[a]

Year	Black	Coloured and Indian	White	Ratios White:Coloured and Indian	White:Black
1930	2·1	4·6	22·6	4·9:1	10·8:1
1945	3·9	10·8	38·3	3·5:1	9·8:1
1953	8·5	20·2	63·9	3·2:1	7·5:1
1960/1	6·2	(28·3)[b]	(72·3)	2·6:1	11·7:1

[a] The figures have not been corrected to allow for inflation over the years.
[b] Figures in brackets refer to the Cape Province only.

SOURCES: M. Horrell, *African Education* (Johannesburg, 1963), and *A Decade of Bantu Education* (Johannesburg, 1964).

C. *State expenditure per head of population (in cents)*

Year	Black	Coloured and Indian	White	Ratios White:Coloured and Indian	White:Black
1930	21	104	932	9·0:1	44·4:1
1945	60	397	1,446	3·6:1	24·1:1
1953	178	(796)	(2,694)	3·4:1	15·1:1

SOURCES AND NOTES: As for table B.

APPENDIX 22. AGE DISTRIBUTION IN GOLD MINES, 1960

Age group (years)	Black (%)	White (%)
−19	11·3	5·8
20–24	26·7	14·8
25–34	35·8	27·2
35–44	17·1	23·0
45–54	7·3	18·9
55–64	1·5	8·6
65–	0·2	1·6

SOURCE: *Statistical Year Book*, 1964, H-10 and H-15.

APPENDIX 23. TURNOVER

It has been suggested[1] that the concept of turnover as it is usually defined in labour studies is not the same as the measurement of turnover made by social scientists studying worker behaviour under a system of migrant labour. Clack argues that in the older industrial countries turnover is normally highest during the first few weeks or months of employment, and it can be related to differences in age, sex, marital status, skill, type of work, and other characteristics. Under the South African migrant pattern, on the other hand, 'workers are expected to leave their jobs with contractual regularity, and there are stringent administrative and legal controls against irregular job changes'. In other words, Clack submits that, 'the gold mining industry...with its far-flung recruiting machinery processing an annual flow of African workers measured in hundreds of thousands, can be nevertheless said to have a very low rate of labour turnover in the usual sense of the term'. The distinction is a valid one, but for our purposes what matters is a measure of the stability of the labour force. The definition used in the text (p. 97) includes both those who change jobs from one mine to another (internal turnover) as well as those who enter and/or leave the industry as a whole (external turnover).

[1] G. Clack, 'Review of African workers in town', *African Studies*, February 1966 c.

Appendixes

On one gold mine in 1941 the annual turnover of the black labour force, according to place of origin, was estimated to be as follows:[1]

	%
Mocambique	62
Transvaal	104
Cape Province	131
Lesotho	159
Elsewhere	156

APPENDIX 24. RELATIVE WAGES AND EMPLOYMENT RATIOS

Assume a production function of the Cobb-Douglas type

$$Q = AL_b^{\alpha} L_w^{\beta} K^{\gamma}$$

Where Q is output; A is a constant; L_b is black labour; L_w is white labour; K is capital and $\alpha + \beta + \gamma = 1$.

In a competitive situation, equilibrium would be obtained where:

Relative wage rates $\left(\dfrac{\pi_w}{\pi_b}\right)$ = Relative marginal products $\left(\dfrac{\delta Q/\delta L_w}{\delta Q/\delta L_b}\right)$

But $\dfrac{\delta Q/\delta L_w}{\delta Q/\delta L_b} = \dfrac{\beta AL_b^{\alpha} L_w^{\beta-1}K^{\gamma}}{\alpha AL_b^{\alpha-1}L_w^{\beta}K^{\gamma}}$

$= \dfrac{\beta}{\alpha} \cdot \dfrac{L_b}{L_w}$ where $\dfrac{\beta}{\alpha}$ is some constant, c.

Therefore competitive equilibrium would be where:

$$\frac{\pi_w}{\pi_b} = c\frac{L_b}{L_w}$$

Thus as white wages have increased relative to black, one would have expected black employment to have increased relative to white.

APPENDIX 25. MONOPSONISTIC COLLUSION

Elliot J. Berg has shown[2] how Chamberlin's theory of monopolistic competition may be applied to the labour market as a powerful device for understanding the behaviour of wages in those economies where the total labour force is being utilised by only a few big firms. Consider fig. 13.

Suppose that the wage rate being paid in the economy is *OP*. Suppose that an individual firm employs *OA* labour at that wage.

Let S_1 be the supply curve facing that firm if, when it raised or lowered wages,

---

[1] J. S. Ford, 'Scientific management with particular application to a Witwatersrand gold mine', *Papers and Proceedings of the Association of Mine Managers* (T.C.M., Johannesburg 1942–5), p. 924 C.

[2] Elliot J. Berg, *Recruitment of a Labor Force in Sub-Saharan Africa*, Ph.D. thesis, Harvard, 1960, p. 392 D.

184

no other firms followed suit. Let S_2 be the supply curve facing that same firm if, when it raised or lowered wages, the other firms did likewise.

Because there are only a few firms, any employer knows that if he employed more labour he would drive up the wage rate, thus both S_1 and S_2 have marginal charge curves (MCh_1 and MCh_2) which show the addition to total cost of employing one more unit of labour.[1] D is the demand curve, showing the marginal revenue product of labour.

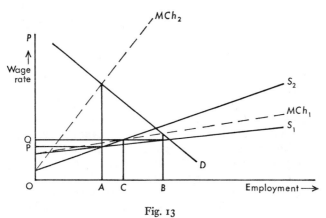

Fig. 13

Now, if when the individual firm raised wages no other firms raised theirs, then it would be profitable for that firm to go on employing labour up to the point OB for which it would have to pay a wage OQ. But if the other firms also raised their wages then the original firm would be faced with a supply curve S_2 and any increase in employment above OA would add more to costs than to revenue.

Then the firm which raised wages from OP to OQ, in the hope of increasing its employment from OA to OB would in fact be worse off (having only managed to employ OC workers) than when it started.

Under these conditions, it is in the interests of each individual firm to eliminate the risks of retaliation by colluding with the other firms in holding down wages at OP, even although this causes a shortage of labour.

APPENDIX 26. THE 8:1 EMPLOYMENT RATIO

Although the ratio $(L_B:L_W)$ for the industry as a whole was remarkably constant, it is worth noting that it varied significantly between mines within the industry. In 1966 for example, when the overall ratio was 8·5:1, a survey of individual mines in one group showed a wide variation in ratios.

It is striking that the size of the ratio tends to be inversely related to the age of the mine. Younger mines generally employed a higher ratio of black:white labour than did the older mines. Thus, as the old mines die out, one would expect the ratio to rise during the 1970s.

Although the ratio varied within the industry and although it was not, every

[1] Richard G. Lipsey, *An Introduction to Positive Economics*, Weidenfeld and Nicolson, London.

Employment ratios on individual mines, 1966

Mine	Vintage (years)	Ratio B:W
A	27	7·3:1
B	10	7·4:1
C	30	8·3:1
D	69	8·3:1
E	19	8·9:1
F	12	9·0:1
G	11	10·7:1
H	14	10·9:1
I	13	11·4:1
J	15	11·4:1

year, exactly 8:1 in the industry as a whole, the analysis (on p. 111 ff.) which hinges on the assumption of a fixed ratio is not thereby invalidated. The argument is concerned with the industry as a whole because it is at that level that wage rates are determined and it is the overall employment ratio that the white trade unions watch. With regard to the variations from year to year the fundamental point is that for 60 years the black–white ratio centred around 8:1 although, over the same period, the ratio of white to black cash earnings increased from 11·7:1 to 20·1:1. In such circumstances the simplifying assumption of a fixed ratio does not seem unduly unrealistic.

APPENDIX 27. THE COLOUR BAR AS A TAX

Suppose that, given the relative wages (π_b and π_w) of black and white labour, the industry would minimise its costs for a given output Q, by employing them in a ratio of $(8+x)$ whites to 1 black, where $x > 0$. Assume that if a colour bar was imposed the ratio would fall to 8:1 but that the total level of employment, E, and the wage rates, π_w and π_b, did not change. Then, with the colour bar, the total labour cost would be:

$$C_1 = \frac{8}{9} . E . \pi_b + \frac{1}{9} . E . \pi_w$$

Without the colour bar, the cost would be:

$$C_2 = \frac{8+x}{9+x} . E . \pi_b + \frac{1}{9+x} . E . \pi_w$$

Cost of the colour bar is:

$$C_1 - C_2 = \frac{E . x}{9(9+x)} (\pi_w - \pi_b).$$

Thus the cost of the colour bar depends directly on the level of employment, the size of x (i.e. the extent to which the employment ratio in the absence of a colour bar was larger than 8:1) and the difference in wage levels between the two groups.

Employers wishing to minimise the costs of the colour bar would therefore seek to reduce the level of employment (e.g. through mechanisation or better management) to reduce x (e.g. by biasing the process of mechanisation so that it is black-labour saving – see Appendix 20), and, if possible, to lessen the gap between white and black wages.[1] It is worth noting that the widening of the wage gap in the gold mines, particularly after the Second World War, will have had the effect of increasing the cost of the colour bar, thus providing an added incentive for employers to mechanise production.

Now let us consider how imposition of this colour bar 'tax' might actually lead to a reduction in the level of white employment on a particular mine. Assuming constant returns to scale, let the price line $P_1 P_2$ be tangential to the isoquant G_1 at point A. Imposition of the colour bar 'tax' will effectively raise the relative cost of employing black labour, thus causing the price line to rotate from $P_1 P_1$ to $P_2 P_2$ which is tangential to the isoquant at B. Substitution of white labour for black will take place (see fig. 14).

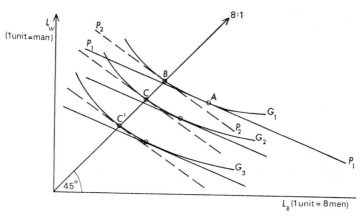

Fig. 14

However, the increased cost also causes a scale effect and the level of output is reduced from G_1 to G_2. Overall employment is thus reduced. The scale effect could be so great (e.g. reducing output from G_1 to G_3) that the final position (C') was such that less whites were employed as a result of the colour bar. By the same token, if C' *was* the final position, abolition of the colour bar could increase white employment.

It is worth noting that if, for some reason, e.g. white trade union pressure, the wages of whites rose relative to blacks the whites could counter the substitution effect by pressing for a colour bar. However their action would reinforce rather than reduce the previous scale effect as fig. 15 makes clear.

For a given gold output G_n, with the relative wage line P_1 the optimum point of production for a given mine would be at A. Trade union pressure raises the white wage relative to the black and the price line swings to P_2. Substitution of black labour for white takes place in the movement from A to B. At the same time

[1] Not, of course, by raising black wages.

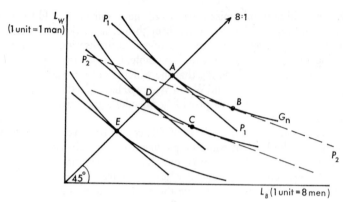

Fig. 15

there is the scale effect from *B* to *C*. To counter the substitution a colour bar tax is imposed so that the price line swings back from P_2 to P_1. (We are assuming constant returns to scale.) Substitution is annulled by the movement from *C* to *D* but the scale effect is from *D* to *E* and acts to reduce overall employment still further.

APPENDIX 28. RURAL EARNINGS

A detailed study of the various rural economies from which the gold mines draw their labour lies beyond the scope of this book. However a considerable amount of research into various parts of the Ciskei and Transkei has been done over the past fifty years. Some of the salient facts about this area, from which the gold mines still draw almost a quarter of their black labour force, are summarised below.

As early as 1914 the economic dependence of the Reserves upon the mines was described, in blunt terms, by missionaries in the Ciskei. 'Is it possible,' they asked, 'that the Government does not realise that the Native territories are in effect being turned into mining villages, and that the mainstay of the population is becoming the wages earned in that industry?...surely [General Smuts] does not accept the ridiculous popular fiction that the Native goes to the mines only when he wants to marry or to pay *lobola* for an additional wife...At the present time, for parts of the year, there are large areas in the Native districts where the sustenance of the whole community is dependent upon the money from the mines.'[1]

A decade later Dr. James Henderson of Lovedale found after careful research that Africans in the Ciskei were desperately poor, and their position in 1925 was he estimated worse than it had been fifty years earlier.[2]

A quarter of a century later another detailed study, the *Keiskammahoek Rural Survey*[3] undertaken by Professors Lindsay Robb, Hobart Houghton, Monica Wilson and others, provided further evidence of poverty. Professor Hobart Houghton summed up the economic situation as follows, 'Productivity is generally

---

[1] Editorial, *Christian Express*, March 1914.
[2] *South African Outlook*, August 1928, November 1929.
[3] *Keiskammahoek Rural Survey 1947–1951* (4 Vols.), Shuter and Shooter, Pietermaritzburg, 1952 B.

so low that the population is wholly unable to support itself from activities within the district. It is dependent upon imports to the area for all its clothing and manufactured articles, and a very large part of its food. Apart from a small quantity of wool, it is only *labour* that can be exported to pay for the imports. Remittances from emigrant workers in the industrial centres support the economy of the reserve to the extent of almost 50 per cent of its total cash income. Without the earnings of the emigrants the population of the district would starve.'[1]

It was found that, in the area investigated, 29% of the married men were without fields.[2] In the Ciskei as a whole the total number of landless families was officially estimated to be 13,000.[3] For those without land the situation was one of grinding poverty. In a study of landless villagers in 1961 Hobart Houghton found that the median *per capita* income in the village was R1·75 per month from all sources, including remittances sent home by migrant workers and the value of vegetables grown for home consumption. The cost of providing each person with minimum food required for healthy life was calculated at the prices then ruling to be R5·00 a month.[4]

In the Transkei the position is much the same. The following table shows the mean annual income, of a family of five persons, gained from farming.

Family farming income

	Value of produce[a] (rands)			Index[b] in real terms
Date	Consumed	Sold	Total	
1931	27·8	8·1	34·5	100
1941	27·0	8·5	35·5	95
1951	33·4	12·9	46·3	78

[a] The Tomlinson Report figures, for 1951, were calculated on the basis of 6 per family and so, for comparison, were multiplied by 5/6.
[b] The real earnings were calculated using the retail price index with 1938 as the base year. The real earnings were then converted into an index taking 1931 as 100.

SOURCES: *Report of Native Economic Commission*, 1930–2, p. 275; *Report of the Witwatersrand Mine Natives' Wages Commission*, p. 17; *Verslag van die Kommissie vir die Sosio-Ekonomiese Ontwikkeling van die Bantogebiede binne die Unie van Suid Afrika* (Tomlinson Report), vol. 10, chap. 24, p. 21.

Even allowing for errors in the basic statistics as well as in the use of the price index, the evidence points clearly to a substantial decline, over the period 1931–51 in the rural earnings. Since 1952 the people of the Transkei do not appear to have become any better off.[5]

[1] D. Hobart Houghton, *Life in the Ciskei*, South African Institute of Race Relations, Johannesburg, 1955, p. 36 B.
[2] *Keiskammahoek Rural Survey*, vol. 4, p. 128 B.
[3] *Report of the Witwatersrand Mine Natives' Wages Commission*, U.G. 21/1944, para. 150.
[4] D. Hobart Houghton, *S.A.J.E.*, September 1961 C.
[5] G. L. Rutman, *S.A.J.E.*, March 1968 C.

APPENDIX 29. LABOUR PRODUCTIVITY, 1911–65

Date	No. of tons hoisted per day per man at work underground	Index (1936 = 100)
1911	0·677	85
1916	0·620	78
1921	0·631	79
1926	0·778	98
1931	0·750	94
1936	0·795	100
1941	0·876	110
1946	0·390	112
1951	1·003	126
1956	1·038	131
1961	0·987	124
1965	1·233	155

NOTES: After 1965 figures are not available; cf. H. H. McGregor, *J. of S.A. Inst. of Mining and Metallurgy*, 1970 C.

SOURCES: G.M.E. Annual Reports.

APPENDIX 30

In the Gold Mines
by
B. Wallet Vilakazi

Roar! and roar! machines of the mines,
Roar from dawn till darkness falls;
I shall wake, Oh, let me be!
Roar, machines, and never stop
For black men groaning as they labour,
Tortured by their aching muscles,
Gasping in the reeking air
Poisoned by the dirt and sweat –
(Shake, shake you haunches, clammy, wet!)

Shout, old boy! It's far away,
So far away where you were smelted,
Where the furnace made you strong;
Coals were left and you were sent.
We watched you cross the mighty seas;
Then puffing engines, hot with fire,
Brought you here to us to Goli...
Then the moment came: you called!
Rock-rabbits at your summons swarmed.

Those rabbits, each and all were black;
Their tails were clipped, you trapped each one,
And deep in a pit you drained their strength.
Turn round and round you iron wheels,
For us you're meant, for us you're here;
You had no choice, you had to come;
And now you roar, revolve and toil,
Till, thrown away, worn out, you rot
On some neglected rubbish plot.

Quite often, passing on the road,
I turn to look at you and wonder
If you, as well, are going to breed,
Increase and multiply; No! No!
And yet we are brothers, we like you
Grow old and rusty in the mines.
Our strength soon goes, our lungs soon rot,
We cough, we try to rest, we die...
But you are spared that coughing, why?

I heard it said that in the pit
Are very many black men's tribes;
It's they who raise the great white dumps
That so amaze their ancestors.
They said, one day a siren screeched
And then a black rock-rabbit came,
A poor dazed thing with clouded mind;
They caught it, changed it to a mole,
It burrowed, and I saw the gold.

Then swarms of moles went burrowing deep,
And soon there rose the great white hills;
The holes were deep, the hills were high,
Sandhlwana hill's not higher now.
Sweating, I climb and reach the top
And watch the dust; like smoke it drifts,
That wind-blown dust of fine white sand;
I see it swirl beneath my feet
And all the earth is covered with it.

Roar! and roar! machines of the mines,
Louder still and louder roar;
Drown our voices with your uproar;
Drown our cries and groans of pain
As you eat away our joints.
Jeer, machines, yes, jeer and mock us,
Let our sufferings cause you laughter;
Well we know your terrible powers,
We, your slaves, and you our masters.

O

We agreed to leave our kraals,
In herds we came, castrated cattled;
We left our mealies, milk and beer
To eat this lumpy porridge here.
Now we are 'boys', and men no longer
And all our world is upside down;
At dawn we're roused to stand in lines...
Have you seen buried men survive,
Walking and seeing and staying alive?

Roar! and roar! machines of the mines;
I am awake, I do not dawdle,
I am going underground,
And here's my pick to strike the rock.
And you, above, though hearing nothing,
Will know I'm toiling for the white man,
Sweating at the white man's work,
Because the trolleys are in sight,
Heaped with stones, some blue, some white.

My brother is with me, carrying
His pick and shovel on his shoulder,
And, on his feet, are heavy boots.
He follows me toward the shaft;
The earth will swallow us who burrow
And, if I die there underground,
What does it matter? Who am I?
Dear Lord! all round me, every day,
I see men stumble, fall and die.

When first I travelled to the mines,
No great white hills of sand were here
Whose tops I'd stretch my neck to see...
And then, one day I journeyed home –
What did I find? Dry mealie stalks
And empty huts. I scratched my head,
Asked for my wife, and her relations;
'Oh', they said, 'go ask the white man...'
I said no more. I went away.

Roar! and roar! machines of the mines;
As far away as Germiston
The noise you make must vex my soul
And echo in my ears
Like distant bells of booming brass.
They speak to me of splendid homes,
Of men made rich because of me,

Made richer by my poverty;
A bloodless used-up ox am I!

Growl more softly, you machines;
Because the white men are as stone,
Can you, of iron, not be gentler?
Hush your roaring in the mines
And hear what we would say to you
Or else we may not care for you
When that far day, now hidden, dawns,
And we, at last, will cry: machines!
You are ours, the black men's, now!

Take care! Though now our arms are weak,
Once they had power; then skies were dark,
Then earth was torn, then nations reeled;
The Great White Queen lost many sons,
Paul Kruger's children too we slaughtered;
Then we, the conquerors were defeated.
And now I dream, Oh thing of Iron,
Dream this land, my father's land
Shall be my father's sons' again.

But now I have no place to rest
Though wealth is everwhere around me;
Land that my fathers sowed is bare
And spreads untilled before my eyes;
And even if I had some wealth,
This land my father's fathers owned,
I have no right to buy nor hold.
Father above, fathers below,
Can you not end my wretchedness?

There, in my fathers' resting place,
Where our ancestral spirits dwell,
They say your powers are unrivalled
When you talk with the Almighty
Who judges no man by his colour.
Soon my blood will drain away,
Dried by the sun, lost in the earth;
I toil and pray to you, Oh Spirits!
But never have my prayers been answered.

Every day this land of yours
Is seized and spoiled by those who rob us;
These foreign breeds enrich themselves,
But all my people and myself

Appendixes

Are black, and, being black, have nothing.
Above the pit the grass is green,
As bright and fresh as clear blue skies;
We gaze, and cry out 'Woe!' but cries
Of 'Woe' and 'Woe' remain unanswered.

Roar! and roar! machines of the mines,
Our hands are aching, always aching,
Our swollen feet are aching too;
I have no ointment that might heal them –
White man's medicines cost money.
Roar machines, but don't disturb me;
Well I've served the rich white masters,
But Oh, my soul is heavy in me!

Roar less loudly, let me slumber,
Close my eyes and sleep and sleep
And stop all thinking of tomorrow.
Let me sleep and wake afar,
At peace where my fathers' spirits are
And where, no more, is earthly waking.
Let me sleep in arms long vanished,
Safe beneath the wood's green pastures.

Originally published by the Witwatersrand University Press, Johannesburg, in 1945 as 'Ezinkomponi' in *Amale 'Zulu* by B. W. Vilakazi (Bantu Treasury Series No. 8). Translated by F. L. Friedman.

BIBLIOGRAPHY

ABBREVIATIONS

A.E.A.	American Economic Association
A.E.R.	American Economic Review
C.C.T.A.	Commission for Technical Co-operation in Africa South of the Sahara
C.N.A.	Central News Agency
E.J.	Economic Journal
I.L.R.	International Labour Review
J.A.H.	Journal of African History
J.P.E.	Journal of Political Economy
M.L.R.	Monthly Labor Review
Q.J.E.	Quarterly Journal of Economics
S.A.I.R.R.	South African Institute of Race Relations
S.A.J.E.	South African Journal of Economics
S.A.M. and E.J.	South African Mining and Engineering Journal
S.Y.B.	Statistical Year Book
U.G.	Union Government

A. GOVERNMENTAL AND OTHER INSTITUTIONAL PUBLICATIONS

Bechuanaland, *Report on the Census of the Bechuanaland Protectorate, 1964* (Campbell), Francistown.

Chamber of Mines of South Africa (1889–96, Witwatersrand Chamber of Mines, 1897–99, Chamber of Mines of the S.A. Republic; 1900–53, Transvaal Chamber of Mines; 1954–66, Transvaal and O.F.S. Chamber of Mines), *Annual Reports,* 1889–1969.

1897. *Evidence and Report of the Industrial Commission of Enquiry into the Mining Industry,* Witwatersrand Chamber of Mines, Johannesburg.

1943. *Statements of Evidence submitted by the Gold Producers Committee to : The Commission appointed to enquire into the remuneration and conditions of employ-ment of Natives on Witwatersrand Gold Mines,* Johannesburg.

1946. *Tribal Natives and Trade Unions. The Policy of the Gold Mining Industry,* Chamber of Mines, Johannesburg, November.

1947. *The Native Workers on the Witwatersrand Gold Mines,* P.R.D. No. 7, Johannesburg.

1952. 'The story of the Transvaal Chamber of Mines', *The Mining Survey* September.

Bibliography

1954. 'The native mineworkers of Southern Africa', *The Mining Survey*, March.

1955. 'Transportation and the gold mining industry', *The Mining Survey*, June.

1956. 'How the Chamber of Mines serves the mining industry', *The Mining Survey* VII, September.

n.d. *In the Common Interest*, P.R.D. Series No. 94, Johannesburg.

Commission for Technical Co-operation in Africa South of the Sahara (C.C.T.A.),

1955. *Inter African Labour Conference*, 4th session, Beira, vol. 2.

1961. *Migrant Labour in Africa South of the Sahara*, No. 79, Abidjan.

Copperbelt of Zambia Mining Industry (1956–63, Northern Rhodesia Chamber of Mines), 1957–69. *Yearbook*, 1956–68, Kitwe.

International Labour Office, 1958. African Labour Survey, Geneva.

1958. 'Interracial wage structure in certain parts of Africa', *I.L.R.* LXXVIII, July.

1962. 'Report of the Commission appointed under Article 26 of the constitution of the International Labour Organization to examine the complaint filed by the Government of Ghana concerning the observance by the Government of Portugal of the Abolition of Forced Labour Convention, 1957 (No. 105)', *Official Bulletin* XLV, April.

1967. *Report to the Government of the United Republic of Tanzania on Wages, Incomes and Prices Policy* (Turner), Government Printer, Dar es Salaam.

1968. *Minimum Wage Fixing and Economic Development*, Geneva.

1969. *Report to the Government of Zambia on Incomes, Wages and Prices in Zambia : Policy and Machinery* (Turner), The Cabinet Office, Lusaka.

Malawi, 1936. *Report of the Committee appointed by His Excellency the Governor to enquire into Emigrant Labour*, 1935, Zomba.

Native Recruiting Corporation, 1933–70. *Annual Reports*, 1933–70, Johannesburg.

Northern Rhodesia, 1954, *Report of the Board of Inquiry appointed to Inquire into the Advancement of Africans in the Copper Mining Industry in Northern Rhodesia* (Forster), Lusaka.

Northern Rhodesian Chamber of Mines, *see* Copperbelt of Zambia Mining Industry.

Nyasaland, 1936. *Report of the Committee appointed by His Excellency the Governor to enquire into Emigrant Labour, 1935* (Lacey), Zomba.

South Africa, 1919. *Report of the Low Grade Mines Commission* (Interim), U.G. 45, Cape Town.

1920. *Report of the Low Grade Mines Commission* (Final), U.G. 34, Cape Town.

1922. *Report of the Mining Industry Board* (Solomon), U.G. 39, Cape Town.

1926. *Report of the Economic and Wage Commission, 1925* (Clay), U.G. 14, Cape Town.

1932. *Report of the Low Grade Mines Commission*, U.G. 16, Pretoria.

1932. *Report of Native Economic Commission, 1930–1932* (Holloway), U.G. 22, Pretoria.

1941. *Third Interim Report of the Industrial and Agricultural Requirements Commission* (van Eck), U.G. 40, Pretoria.

1944. *Report of the Witwatersrand Mine Natives' Wages Commission on Remuneration and Conditions of Employment of Natives on Witwatersrand Gold Mines, 1943* (Lansdown), U.G. 22, Pretoria.

1946. *Report of the Committee on Gold Mining Taxation* (Holloway), U.G. 16, Pretoria.

1946. *Report of the Mine Workers' Union Commission of Enquiry, 1946* (Williamson), U.G. 36, Pretoria.

1948. *Report of the Natives Laws Commission, 1946–48* (Fagan), U.G. 28, Pretoria.

1950. *Report of Commission on Conditions of Employment in the Gold Mining Industry* (van Eck), U.G. 28, Pretoria.

1951. *Report of the Mine Workers' Union Commission of Enquiry* (De Wet), U.G. 52, Pretoria.

1951. *Report of the Commission on Native Education, 1949–51* (Eiselen), U.G. 53, Pretoria.

1955. *Report of the Commission of Enquiry for the Socio-Economic Development of the Bantu Areas within the Union of South Africa* (Tomlinson), U.G. 61, Pretoria.

1955. *Verslag van die Kommissie vir die Sosio-Ekonomiese Ontwikkeling van die Bantoegebiede binne die Unie van Suid Afrika* (Tomlinson), full version, duplicated, Pretoria.

1958. *Report of the Commission of Enquiry into the Policy Relating to the Protection of Industries* (Viljoen), U.G. 36, Pretoria.

1965. *Verslag van die Kommissie van Ondersoek Insake Proefnemings op Sekere Myne* (Viljoen), Pretoria.

South African Bureau of Census and Statistics, 1937–64. *Industrial Census, 1935/6–1961/2*, Pretoria.

1957. *Labour Turnover*, Special Report 215, Pretoria.

1960. *Labour Statistics in the Building Industry* (1946–59), Special Report 235, Pretoria.

1960. *Union Statistics for Fifty Years, 1910–1960*, Pretoria.

1961. *Labour Statistics in the Engineering Industry* (1955–9), Special Report 242, Pretoria.

1961. *Labour Statistics in the Printing and Newspaper Industry* (1955–9), Special Report 245, Pretoria.

1961. *Labour Statistics in the Motor Industry* (*1955–1959*), Special Report 246, Pretoria.

1962. *Labour Statistics in Commerce* (*1955–1959*), Special Report 248, Pretoria,

1964 *Labour Statistics: Labour Relations, Trade Unions* (*1959/60–1961/62*), Special Report 263, Pretoria.

1964. *Financial Statistics of Gold and Coal Mining Companies for the Years 1960/61–1962/63*, National Accounts & Finance Memorandum 37, Pretoria.

1964. *Labour Statistics in the Building Industry, 1963*, Special Report 269, Pretoria.

1964. *Labour Statistics: Labour Relations, Trade Unions, 1961/62–1963/64*, Special Report 277, Pretoria.

1965. *Report on the Revised Monthly Sample Survey of Employment and Salaries and Wages in Manufacturing and Construction, 1964*, Special Report 280, Pretoria.

1966. *Labour Statistics in the Printing and Newspaper Industry*, Special Report 293, Pretoria.

Bibliography

1966. *Labour Statistics in the Engineering Industry*, Special Report 294, Pretoria.
1966. *Labour Statistics in the Building Industry*, Special Report 295, Pretoria.
1964–8. *Statistical Year Book* (1964–8), Pretoria.
South African Department of Information, n.d. *The Progress of the Bantu Peoples towards Nationhood*, Pretoria.
South African Department of Mines, 1937–69. *Annual Report of the Government Mining Engineer, 1938–1968*, Pretoria.
South African Government Miners' Training Schools, 1936–66. *Annual Reports, 1936–1966*, Johannesburg.
South African Institute for Medical Research, n.d. *South African Institute for Medical Research, 1913–1963*, Johannesburg.
South African Railways and Harbours, 1936–66. *Report of the General Manager, 1936–1966*, Pretoria.
South African Social and Economic Planning Council, 1946. *The Native Reserves and their Place in the Economy of the Union of South Africa* (van Eck), Report No. 9, U.G. 32, Pretoria.
1947. *Economic Aspects of the Gold Mining Industry*, Report No. 11 (van Eck), U.G. 32, Pretoria.
Transvaal, 1903. *Report of the Transvaal Labour Commission*, Johannesburg.
1908. *Minutes of evidence to the Mining Industry Commission* (with appendices), T.G. 2, Pretoria.
1908. *Report of the Transvaal Indigency Commission, 1906–08*, T.G. 13, Pretoria.
1908. *Report of the Mining Industry Commission, 1907–08* (Stockenstroom), Pretoria.
Transvaal and (after 1953) O.F.S. Chamber of Mines [T.C.M.], *see* Chamber of Mines of South Africa.
United Kingdom, 1960. *Basutoland, Bechuanaland Protectorate, and Swaziland: Report of an Economic Survey Mission* (Morse), H.M.S.O., London.
United Nations Economic Commission for Africa, 1963. *Economic and Social Consequences of Racial Discriminatory Practices*, New York.
United Nations Economic Commission for Africa; Food and Agricultural Organization, 1964. *Report of the UN/ECA/FAO Economic Survey Mission on the Economic Development of Zambia* (Seers), Ndola.
United States Council of Economic Advisors, 1962. *Economic Costs of Racial Discrimination in Employment*, Washington.
United States Department of Labor, 1952. *Negroes in the United States: Their Employment and Economic Status*, Bulletin No. 1119, Washington.
1960. *Excerpts from Notes on the Economic Situation of Negroes in the United States*, Washington.
1963–5. *Manpower Report of the President and a Report on Manpower Requirements, Resources, Utilization and Training*, Washington.
1963. 'Educational attainment of workers, March, 1962', *M.L.R.* LXXXVI, May.
1963. 'Economic status of non-white workers, 1955–1962', *M.L.R.* LXXXVI, July.
1964. 'Geographic mobility and employment status, March 1962–March 1963', *M.L.R.* LXXXVII, August.
United States Advisory Commission on Farm Labor, 1959. *Report on Farm Labor*, Public Hearings, Washington, 5 and 6 February.

United States President's Commission on Migratory Labor, 1951. *Migratory Labor in American Agriculture*, Washington.

Witwatersrand Native Labour Association, 1904–70. *Annual Reports*, 1904–1969, Johannesburg.

1959. 'Organization of migrant labour in the South African mining industry', *Bulletin of the Inter-African Labour Institute* (C.C.T.A.) VI.

World Council of Churches, 1970. *Fetters of Injustice: Report of the Ecumenical Consultation on Ecumenical Assistance for Development Projects*, W.C.C., Geneva.

Zambia, 1954. *Report of the Board of Inquiry Appointed to Inquire into the Advancement of Africans into the Copper Mining Industry in Northern Rhodesia* (Forster), Government Printer, Lusaka.

1966. *Report of the Commission of Inquiry into the Mining Industry, 1966* (Brown), Government Printer, Lusaka.

B. BOOKS AND PAMPHLETS

Agricola, Georgius, 1912. *De Re Metallica*, translated by Herbert Clark Hoover and Lou Henry Hoover, The Mining Magazine, London.

Anonymous, 1959. *African Farm Labour: A Survey*, S.A.I.R.R., Johannesburg.

Anonymous, 1959. *The Economic Development of the 'Reserves': The Extent to which the Tomlinson Commission's Recommendations are being Implemented*, S.A.I.R.R., Johannesburg.

Baldwin, Robert E., 1966. *Economic Development and Export Growth: A Study of Northern Rhodesia, 1920–1960*, University of California Press, Berkeley.

Becker, Gary S., 1957. *The Economics of Discrimination*, University of Chicago Press, Chicago.

1964. *Human Capital*, National Bureau of Economic Research, New York.

Benson, Mary, 1966. *The Struggle for a Birthright*, Penguin Africa Library, London.

Beveridge, W. I. B., 1950. *The Art of Scientific Investigation*, Vintage Books, New York.

Black, Duncan, 1939. *The Incidence of Income Taxes*, Macmillan, London.

Boulding, Kenneth E., 1955. *Economic Analysis* (3rd edition), Hamish Hamilton, London.

Bowen, William G., 1964. *Economic Aspects of Education*, Princeton University, New Jersey.

Bradley, Philip D. (ed.), 1959. *The Public Stake in Union Power*, University of Virginia Press, Charlottesville.

Brinton, Crane, 1952. *The Anatomy of Revolution* (revised edition), Vintage Books, New York.

Burn, Duncan (ed.), 1958. *The Structure of British Industry*, C.U.P., Cambridge.

Busschau, W. J., 1936. *The Theory of Gold Supply*, O.U.P., London.

1950. *The Measure of Gold*, C.N.A., South Africa.

Cartter, Allan M., 1959. *Theory of Wages and Employment*, Richard D. Irwin, Homewood.

Cartwright, A. P., 1962. *The Gold Miners*, Purnell and Sons, London.

Chamberlin, Edward, 1938. *The Theory of Monopolistic Competition* (3rd edition), H.U.P., Cambridge, Mass.

Bibliography

Clarke, W. M., 1967. *The City in the World Economy*, Penguin, Harmondsworth.
Davies, Ian, 1966. *African Trade Unions*, Penguin Africa Library, London.
Davies, Jack L., 1969. *Gold: A Forward Strategy*, Essays in International Finance No. 79, Princeton.
Davis, J. Merle (ed.), 1933. *Modern Industry and the African*, Macmillan, London.
Dean, Edwin, 1966. *The Supply of African Farmers: Theory and Measurement in Malawi*, North Holland Publishing Co., Amsterdam.
Descloitres, R. 1967. *The Foreign Worker*, O.E.C.D, Paris.
De Kiewiet, C. W., 1941. *A History of South Africa*, O.U.P., London.
De Kock, Alan, 1965. *Industrial Laws of South Africa*, Juta and Co., Cape Town.
Doxey, George Victor, 1961. *The Industrial Colour Bar in South Africa*, O.U.P., Cape Town.
Duffy, James, 1959. *Portuguese Africa*, H.U.P., Cambridge, Mass.
Dunlop, John T., 1950. *Wage Determination under Trade Unions*, Basil Blackwell, Oxford.
   (ed.), 1957. *The Theory of Wage Determination*, Macmillan, London.
Dunlop, John T. and Diatchenko, V. P. 1964. *Labor Productivity*, McGraw-Hill New York.
Education Panel (The 1961), 1963 and 1966. *Education for South Africa*, First and Second Reports, Witwatersrand U.P., Johannesburg.
Elkan, Walter, 1956. *An African Labour Force*, East African Institute of Social Research, Kampala.
   1960. *Migrants and Proletarians*, O.U.P., London.
Ellis, H. S. (ed.), 1948. *Survey of Contemporary Economics*, Richard D. Irwin (for A.E.A.), Homewood.
Ellis, H. S. and Metzler, L. A. (eds.), 1950. *Readings in the Theory of International Trade*, Allen and Unwin (for A.E.A.), London.
Elton Mills, M. E. and Wilson, Monica, 1952. *Land Tenure*, Keiskammahoek Rural Survey, vol. 4, Shuter and Shooter, Pietermaritzburg.
Ezekiel, Mordecai and Fox, Karl A., 1963. *Methods of Correlation and Regression Analysis* (3rd edition), Wiley, New York.
Fawzi, Saad El Din, 1957. *The Labour Movement in the Sudan 1946–1955*, O.U.P., London.
Fisher, Lloyd H., 1953. *The Harvest Labor Market in California*, H.U.P., Cambridge, Mass.
Fisher, Malcolm R., 1966. *Wage Determination in an Integrating Europe*, A. W. Sijthoff, Leyden.
Frankel, S. Herbert, 1938. *Capital Investment in Africa*, O.U.P., London.
   1967. *Investment and the Return to Equity Capital in the South African Gold Mining Industry 1887–1965*, Basil Blackwell, Oxford.
Franklin, N. N., 1948. *Economics in South Africa*, O.U.P., Cape Town.
Friedman, Milton, 1953. *Essays in Positive Economics*, University of Chicago Press, Chicago.
Galbraith, J. K., 1967. *The New Industrial State*, Hamilton, London.
Gayer, Arthur D., 1937. *Monetary Policy and Economic Stabilization*, Adam and Charles Black, London.
Ginzberg, Eli, 1956. *The Negro Potential*, Columbia U.P., New York.

Gluckman, Max, 1941. *Economy of the Central Barotse Plain*, Rhodes-Livingstone Paper No. 7, Livingstone.

Greene, Lorenzo J. and Woodson, Carter G., 1930. *The Negro Wage Earner*, Association for the Study of Negro Life and History Inc.

Gregory, Theodore, 1962. *Ernest Oppenheimer and the Economic Development of Southern Africa*, O.U.P., Cape Town.

Guillebaud, C. W., 1966. *An Economic Survey of the Sisal Industry of Tanganyika* (3rd edition), James Nisbet and Co., London.

Hailey (Lord), 1957. *An African Survey* (revised), O.U.P., London.

Hall, A. R., 1954. *The Scientific Revolution 1500–1800*, Longmans Green, London.

Hancock, W. Keith, 1937. *Survey of British Commonwealth Affairs*, vol. 2, part 2, O.U.P., London.

Harris, Marvin, 1958. 'Portugal's African "Wards": a first hand report on labor and education in Mozambique', *American Committee on Africa*.

Hartmann, Heinz, 1962. *Enterprise and Politics in South Africa*, Princeton University, New Jersey.

Harbeler, Gottfield, 1962. *Money in the International Economy*, Hobart Paper, No. 31, Institute of Economic Affairs.

Henderson, Vivian W., n.d. 'The economic status of Negroes', *Southern Regional Council*.

Hepple, Alex, 1959. *Poverty Wages: the Shame of Low Wages in South Africa*, Wages Committee, Johannesburg.

1966. *South Africa*, Pall Mall Press, London.

n.d. *The African Worker in South Africa: A Study of Trade Unionism*, The African Bureau.

Herskovits, Melville J. and Hernitz, Mitchell, 1964. *Economic Transition in Africa*, Routledge and Kegan Paul, London.

Hicks, J. R., 1963. *The Theory of Wages* (2nd edition), Macmillan, London.

Hiestand, Dale L., 1964. *Economic Growth and Employment Opportunities for Minorities*, Columbia, New York.

Hobson, John A., 1926. *The Evolution of Modern Capitalism* (4th edition), George Allen and Unwin, London.

Holloman J. F., Knox J., Mann J. W. and Heard K. A. (eds.), 1964. *Problems of Transition*, Institute for Social Research, Durban.

Horrell, Muriel, 1950–70. *A Survey of Race Relations in South Africa: 1948–1969*, S.A.I.R.R., Johannesburg.

1959. *Racialism and the Trade Unions*, S.A.I.R.R., Johannesburg.

1959. *The Economic Development of the 'Reserves'*, S.A.I.R.R., Fact Paper No. 3.

1960. *The 'Pass Laws'*, S.A.I.R.R., Johannesburg.

1961. *South African Trade Unionism*, S.A.I.R.R., Johannesburg.

1963. *Legislation and Race Relations*, S.A.I.R.R., Johannesburg.

1963. *African Education; Some Origins and Development until 1953*, S.A.I.R.R., Johannesburg.

1964. *A Decade of Bantu Education*, S.A.I.R.R., Johannesburg.

1968. *Bantu Education to 1968*, S.A.I.R.R., Johannesburg.

1969. *South Africa's Workers; their Organizations and the Patterns of Employment*, S.A.I.R.R., Johannesburg.

Bibliography

Horwitz, Ralph, 1967. *The Political Economy of South Africa*. Weidenfeld and Nicolson, London.
Houghton, D. Hobart, 1955. *Life in the Ciskei: A Summary of the Findings of the Keiskammahoek Rural Survey, 1947–51*, S.A.I.R.R., Johannesburg.
1960. *Economic Development in a Plural Society*, O.U.P., Cape Town.
1967. *The South African Economy* (2nd edition), O.U.P., Cape Town.
Houghton, D. Hobart and Walton, Edith M., 1952. *The Economy of a Native Reserve* (Keiskammahoek Rural Survey, vol. 3), Shuter and Shooter, Pietermaritzburg.
Hunter, Guy (ed.), 1965. *Industrialization and Race Relations*, O.U.P., London.
Hunter, Monica, 1936. *Reaction to Conquest*, O.U.P., London.
Hurwitz, Nathan, 1964. *The Economics of Bantu Education*, S.A.I.R.R., Johannesburg.
Hutchinson, T. W., 1964. *'Positive' Economics and Policy Objectives*, G. Allen and Unwin, London.
Hutt, W. H., 1964. *The Economics of the Colour Bar*, André Deutsch, London.
Ilersic, A. R., 1959. *Statistics* (12th edition), H.F.L., London.
Jackson, J. A. (ed.), 1969. *Migration*, C.U.P., Cambridge.
Jeppe, E. Biccard, 1946. *Gold Mining on the Witwatersrand*, Transvaal Chamber of Mines, Johannesburg.
Katzen, Leo, 1964. *Gold and the South African Economy*, A. A. Balkema, Cape Town.
Kuper, Hilda (ed.), 1965. *Urbanization and Migration in West Africa*, University of California Press, California.
Lebergott, Stanley, 1964. *Manpower in Economic Growth*, McGraw-Hill, New York.
Lerner, Abba P., 1953. *Essays in Economic Analysis*, Macmillan, London.
Lipsey, Richard G., 1966. *An Introduction to Positive Economics* (2nd edition), Weidenfeld and Nicolson, London.
Lorimer, Frank and Karp, Mark (eds.), 1960. *Population in Africa*, Boston U.P., Boston.
Lystad, Robert A. (ed.), 1965. *The African World*, Pall Mall Press, London.
Mackenzie, J., 1871. *Ten Years North of the Orange River*, Edmonston and Douglas, Edinburgh.
Marris, Robin, 1964. *The Economic Theory of Managerial Capitalism*, Macmillan, London.
Marshall, Ray, 1965. *The Negro and Organized Labour*, Wiley, New York.
Mason, P., 1970. *Patterns of Dominance*, O.U.P., London.
Mayer, Philip, 1961. *Townsmen or Tribesmen*, O.U.P., Cape Town.
Mphahlele, Ezekiel, 1959. *Down Second Avenue*, Faber and Faber, London.
Mushkin, Selma J., 1962. *The Economics of Higher Education*, U.S. Department of Health, Education and Welfare, Washington.
National Bureau of Economic Research, 1962. *Aspects of Labour Economics*, Princeton U.P., Princeton.
Naudé, Louis, 1969. *Dr. A. Hertzog, Die Nasionale Party en Die Mynwerker*, Nasionale Raad, Pretoria.
Norgren, Paul H. and Samuel, E. Hill, 1964. *Toward Fair Employment*, Columbia U.P., New York.

Norman-Scoble, C., assisted by Cordon-Lloyd, R., 1956. *Law of Master and Servant in South Africa*, Butterworth, Durban.

Northrup, Herbert R., 1944. *Organized Labor and the Negro*, Harper and Bros., New York.

Orwell, George, 1957. *Selected Essays*, Penguin, Harmondsworth.

Paton, Alan, 1964. *Hofmeyr*, O.U.P., Cape Town.

Pauw, B. A., 1963. *The Second Generation*, O.U.P., Cape Town.

Perlman, Richard (ed.), *Wage Determination Market or Power Forces?* D. C. Heath and Co., Boston.

Phelps Brown, E. H., 1962. *The Economics of Labor*, Yale U.P., New Haven.

Reader, D. H., 1961. *The Black Man's Portion*, O.U.P., Cape Town.

Reder, M., 1957. *Labor in a Growing Economy*, Wiley, New York.

Rees, Albert, 1962. *The Economics of Trade Unions*, C.U.P., Cambridge.

Reynolds, Lloyd G. and Gregory, Peter, 1965. *Wages, Productivity and Industrialization in Puerto Rico*, Irwin, New York.

Reynolds, Lloyd G. and Taft, Cynthia, 1956. *The Evolution of Wage Structure*, Yale U.P., New Haven.

Richards, Audrey I., 1939. *Land, Labour and Diet in Northern Rhodesia*, O.U.P., London.

Roberts, Margaret, 1958. *Labour in the Farm Economy*, S.A.I.R.R., Johannesburg.

Robinson, E. A. G. (ed.), 1964. *Economic Development for Africa South of the Sahara*, Macmillan, London.

Robinson, Joan, 1933. *The Economics of Imperfect Competition*, Macmillan, London.

Rothschild, K. W., 1956. *The Theory of Wages*, Basil Blackwell, Oxford.

Routh, Guy, 1965. *Occupation and Pay in Great Britain 1906–60*, C.U.P., Cambridge.

Roux, Edward, 1964. *Time Longer than Rope* (2nd edition), University of Wisconsin Press, Madison.

Sachs, E. S. (Solly), 1957. *Rebels' Daughters*, MacGibbon and Kee, London.

Salter, W. E. G., 1960. *Productivity and Technical Change*, C.U.P., Cambridge.

Sampson, Anthony, 1956. *Drum*, Collins, London.

Schapera, Isaac, 1947. *Migrant Labour and Tribal Life*, O.U.P., London.

Schultz, Theodore W., 1963. *The Economic Value of Education*, Columbia U.P., New York.

Schumpeter, Joseph A., 1954. *History of Economic Analysis*, O.U.P., New York.

Simons, H. J. and R. E., 1969. *Class and Colour in South Africa 1850–1950*, Penguin, Harmondsworth.

Skinner, Walter R., 1965. *Mining Year Book*.

Smith, Adam, 1776. *The Wealth of Nations* (1st edition).

Southall, Aidan (ed.), *Social Change in Modern Africa*, O.U.P., London.

Spooner, F. P., 1960. *South African Predicament*, Jonathan Cape, London.

Sterner, Richard, *et al.*, 1943. *The Negro's Share*, Harper and Bros., New York.

Stigler, George J., 1946. *Domestic Servants in the United States 1900–1940*, National Bureau of Economic Research, Occasional Paper No. 24.

Tawney, R. H., 1961. *The Acquisitive Society*, Fontana, London.

Thomson, E. T. (ed.), 1939. *Race Relations and the Race Problem*, Durham, N. Carolina.

Bibliography

Tinley, J. M., 1942. *The Native Labor Problem of South Africa*, University of North Carolina Press, Chapel Hill.

Transvaal Strike Legal Defence Committee, 1924. *The Story of a Crime*, Johannesburg.

Turner, H. A., 1965. *Wage Trends, Wage Policies, and Collective Bargaining: the Problems for Under-developed Countries*, C.U.P., Cambridge.

University of Natal, Department of Economics, 1950. *The African Factory Worker*, O.U.P., Cape Town.

Van der Horst, Sheila T., 1942. *Native Labour in South Africa*, O.U.P. London. 1964. *African Workers in Town*, O.U.P., Cape Town.

Van Sickle, John V., 1943. *Planning for the South*, Vanderbilt U.P.

Von Weizsäcker, C. F., 1964. *The Relevance of Science*, Collins, London.

Walker, Eric, 1957. *A History of Southern Africa*, Longmans Green, London.

Walker, Ivan L. and Weinbren, Ben, 1961. *2,000 Casualties*, South African Trade Union Council, Johannesburg.

Weaver, Robert C., 1946. *Negro Labor*, Harcourt, Brace and Co.

Wilson, Francis and Perrot, Dominique (eds.), 1972. *Outlook on a Century: South Africa 1870–1970*, Lovedale Press.

Wilson, Godfrey, 1941–2. *An Essay on the Economics of Detribalization in Northern Rhodesia*, Rhodes-Livingstone Institute, Livingstone, parts 1 and 2.

Wilson, Godfrey and Monica, 1945. *The Analysis of Social Change*, C.U.P., Cambridge.

Wilson, Monica, 1959. *Communal Rituals among the Nyakusa*, O.U.P. London.

Wilson, Monica and Mafeje, Archie, 1963. *Langa*, O.U.P., Cape Town.

Wilson, Monica and Thompson, Leonard (eds.) 1969–71, *The Oxford History of South Africa*, vols. 1 and 2, Clarendon Press, Oxford.

Wootton, Barbara, 1962. *The Social Foundations of Wage Policy* (2nd edition), Unwin University Books, London.

Wright, D. McCord (ed.), 1956. *The Impact of the Union*, Kelley and Millman, New York.

Yudelman, Monty, 1964. *Africans on the Land*, H.U.P., Cambridge, Mass.

C. ARTICLES, PAPERS AND CHAPTERS IN BOOKS

Allen, V. L., 1963. 'Management and labour in Africa', *The Listener*, 15 August.

Allport, Gordon W., 1964. 'The force of racial differences in human relations', reprinted from *Religious Education*, January–February.

Anderson, C. B., 1961. 'The organisation and management of the gold mining industry in South Africa', Address before the 7th *Commonwealth Mining and Metallurgical Congress*, Johannesburg, 11 April.

Anonymous, 1952. 'African labour for the mines' (three articles), *S.A.M. and E.J.*, 15 November, 22 November and 20 December.

Anonymous, 1963. 'Education: an advantage for a lifetime', *Occupational Outlook Quarterly*, December.

Anonymous, 1964. 'The London gold market', *Bank of England Quarterly Bulletin*, March.

Anonymous, 1969. 'Inside the Anglo power house', *Financial Mail*, Special Supplement, 4 July.

Arrow, K. J. and Capron, W. M., 1959. 'Dynamic shortages and price rises: the engineer-scientist case', *Q.J.E.* LXXIII, No. 2.

Baliol-Scott, V., 1956. 'Labour for the Union's gold mining industry', *S.A.M. and E.J.* LXVII, 30 March.

Barker, Anthony, 1970. 'Community of the careless', *South African Outlook*, April.

Batchelder, Alan B., 1964. 'Decline in the relative income of Negro men', *Q.J.E.* LXXVIII, November.

Bauer, Peter T., 1959. 'Regulated wages in underdeveloped countries', *The Public Stake in Union Power*, Philip D. Bradley, University of Virginia Press, Charlottesville.

Becker, Gary S., 1960. 'Investment in education', *A.E.R.* L, May.

1964. 'Economic discrimination', *International Encyclopeadia of Social Sciences*.

Becker, Gary S. and Chiswick, Barry R., 1966. 'Education and the distribution of earnings', *A.E.R.* LVI, Papers and Proceedings, May.

Berg, Elliot J., 1961. 'Backward sloping labor supply functions in dual economies – the Africa case', *Q.J.E.* LXXV, August.

1965. 'The development of a labor force in sub-Saharan Africa', *Economic Development and Cultural Change* XIII, July.

1965. 'The economics of migrant labor systems', *Urbanization and Migration in Africa*, ed. Hilda Kuper, University of California Press.

Black, R. A. L., 1956. 'Bright future with more mechanisation and automation forecast for S.A. Mines', *Mining and Industrial Magazine* XLVI, May.

1956. 'Mine management in South Africa', *S.A.M. and E.J.* LXVII, 30 November.

1956. 'Mining group management in South Africa', *S.A.M. and E.J.* LXVII, 14 December.

Black, R. A. L. and Edwards, Tom, 1956. 'The Economics of full mechanization and automation in the mining industry', *S.A.M. and E.J.* LXVII, 28 December.

1957. 'The possibilities of full mechanization and automation in mining', *S.A.M. and E.J.* LXVII, 4 January.

BLAINEY, G., 1965. 'Lost causes of the Jameson Raid', *The Economic History Review*, Second Series XVIII, December (misprinted as August).

Blumer, Herbert, 1965. 'Industrialization and race relations', *Industrialization and Race Relations*, ed. Guy Hunter, O.U.P., London.

Browne, G. W. G., 1943. 'The production function for South African manufacturing', *S.A.J.E.* XI, December.

Busschau, W. J., 1960. 'The world's greatest goldfield', *South Africa Today*, September.

1967. 'Future trends in gold production', *Kyklos* XX, Fasc. 3.

Carr, W. J. P., 1962. 'Laws and regulations relating to the employment of the Bantu in the urban areas', *Journal of the S.A. Institute of Personnel Management*, January.

Clack, Garfield, 1966. 'Review of "African workers in town" by Sheila T. van der Horst', *African Studies* XXV, February.

1966. 'The nationalisation of South African trade unions', *Cambridge Research*, January.

Bibliography

Curtis, J. F., 1952. 'African labour at Rand Leases (v) G.M. Co. Ltd.', *S.A.M. and E.J.* LXIII, 4 October.

De Villiers, W. J., 1962. 'Key to native wage increases', *Optima* XII, December.

De Vyver, Frank T., 1960. 'S.A. labor relations', *Labor Law Journal*, September.

Dewey, Donald, 1952. 'Negro employment in Southern industry', *J.P.E.* LX, August.

Diamond, Charles, 1968. 'The native grievances inquiry 1913–1914', *S.A.J.E.* XXXVI, September.

Eckstein, Otto and Wilson, Thomas A., 1962. 'Determination of money wages in American industry', *Q.J.E.* LXXVI, August.

Elkan, W., 1959. 'The persistence of migrant labour', *Bulletin of the Inter-African Labour Institute* (C.C.T.A.) V, September.

1959. 'Migrant labour in Africa: an economists' approach', *A.E.R.* XLIX, May.

Enke, Stephen, 1962. 'South African growth: macro-economic analysis', *S.A.J.E* XXX, March.

Ewing, J. M. M., 1934. 'Witwatersrand mining policy: the dominant factors', *S.A.J.E.* II, June.

Falcoln, M., 1946. 'Aspects of organization in the Witwatersrand gold mining industry with special reference to labour', *Journal of the Chemical Metallurgical and Mining Society of South Africa* XLVII, August.

Farrell, M. J. and Jolly, A. R., 1963. 'The structure of the British coal mining industry in 1955', *Journal of Industrial Economics* XI, July.

First, Ruth, 1961. 'The gold of migrant labour', *Africa South in Exile* V, April–June.

Frankel, S. Herbert, 1935. 'Return to capital investment in the Witwatersrand gold mining industry 1887–1932', *E.J.* XLV, March.

1960. 'The tyranny of economic paternalism in Africa: a study of frontier mentality 1860–1960', *Optima*, special supplement, December.

Glick, Paul C. and Miller, Herman P., 1956. 'Educational level and potential income', *American Sociological Review* XXI, June.

Gluckman, Max, 1961. 'Anthropological problems arising from the African industrial revolution', *Social Change in Modern Africa*, ed. Aidan Southall, O.U.P., London.

Graaff, J. de Villiers, 1962. 'Alternative models of South African growth', *S.A.J.E.* XXX, March.

Grubel, Herbert B. and Scott, Anthony D., 1966. 'The international flow of human capital', *A.E.R.* LVI, Papers and Proceedings, May. See also subsequent discussion, by Weisbrod and others, in the same issue.

Gugler, Josef, 1968. 'The impact of labour migration on society and economy in sub-Saharan Africa: empirical findings and theoretical considerations', *African Social Research*, No. 6, December.

Gulliver, P. H., 1965. 'Anthropology', *The African World*, ed. Robert A. Lystad, Pall Mall Press, London.

Handy, L. J. and Turner, H. A., 1966. 'Absenteeism in the mines', *New Society*, 7 April.

Hansen, W. Lee, 1963. 'Total and private rates of return to investment in schooling', *J.P.E.* LXXI, April.

Hanson, D. F., 'Induction training of the Bantu', *Journal of the S.A. Institute for Personnel Management*.

Harris, Marvin, 1959. 'Labour emigration among the Moçambique Thonga: cultural and political factors', *Africa* XXIX, January.

1960. 'Reply to A. Rita-Ferreira', *Africa*, XXX, July.

Hayes, Marion, 1962. 'A century of change: Negroes in the U.S. economy: 1860–1960', *M.L.R.* LXXXI, December.

Hicks, J. R., 1955. 'Economic foundations of wage policy', *E.J.* LXV, September.

Hill, F. G., 1948. 'Social service on the gold mines – personnel management essential for complete success', *Papers and Discussions of the Association of Mine Managers of the Transvaal, 1942–1945*, T.C.M., Johannesburg, vol. 2.

Hoernlé, A., 1938. 'Native education at the crossroads', *Africa* XI, October.

Horwood, O. P. F., 1962. 'Is minimum wage legislation the answer for South Africa?', *S.A.J.E.* XXX, June.

Houghton, D. Hobart, 1961. 'Land reform in the Bantu areas and its effect upon urban labour', *S.A.J.E.* XXIX, September.

Hume, Ian, 1970. 'Notes on South African wage movements', *S.A.J.E.* XXXVIII, September.

Hurst, H. R. G., 1959. 'A survey of the development of facilities for migrant labour in Tanganyika during the period 1926–1959', *Bulletin of the Inter African Labour Institute* (C.C.T.A.) VI, July.

Kantor, B. S., 1970. 'The gold agreement and the future of gold', *South African Banker* LXVII, February.

Katzen, L. B., 1961. 'The case for minimum wage legislation in South Africa', *S.A.J.E.* XXIX.

Keat, Paul G., 1960. 'Long-run changes in occupational wage-structure: 1900–1956', *J.P.E.* LXVIII, December.

Kerr, Clark; Harrison, H.; Dunlop, J. T. and Myers, Charles A., 1930. 'Industrialism and industrial man', *I.L.R.* LXXXII, September.

Kidd, B., 1903. 'Economic South Africa', *Christian Express*, May (reprinted from *The Times*).

Kilby, Peter, 1965. 'Review of "African workers in town" by Sheila T. van der Horst', *E.J.* LV, December.

Knight, A. S. *et al.*, 1942. 'Methods of breaking and handling ore in East Geduld', *Association of Mine Managers of the Transvaal: Papers and Discussion, 1939–41*, Johannesburg.

Knight, John B., 1964. 'A Theory of income distribution in South Africa', *Bulletin of the Oxford University Institute of Economics and Statistics* XXVI, November.

Knowles, K. G. J. C. and Robertson, D. J., 1951. 'Differences between the wages of skilled and unskilled workers, 1880–1950', *Bulletin of the Oxford Institute of Statistics* XIII, April.

Koch, H. C., n.d. 'The organization of the South African gold mining industry', revised version of a lecture in Stellenbosch.

Kops, C. W., 1939. 'Witwatersrand gold mines employees provident fund', *S.A.J.E.* VII, March.

Kotze, Robert, 1933. 'The gold mining position: a review of the report of the Low Grade Ore Commission, 1930–32', *S.A.J.E.* I, June.

P

Bibliography

Lester, Richard A., 1946. 'Shortcomings of marginal analysis for wage-employment problems', *A.E.R.* xxxvi, March.

Lewis, W. A., 1954. 'Economic development with unlimited supplies of labour', *The Manchester School of Economics and Social Studies* xxii, May.

Liberal Party of South Africa, *Transkei Liberal News*, especially June 1964.

Lomas, P. K., 1958. 'African trade unionism on the Copperbelt of Northern Rhodesia', *S.A.J.E.* xxvi, June.

Lomax, K. S., 1950. 'Coal production functions for Great Britain', *Journal of the Royal Statistical Society*, Series A, cxiii.

Lombard, J. A., 1964. 'The determination of racial income differentials in South Africa', in *Problems of Transition*, ed. J. Knox, J. W. Mann and K. A. Heard, Institute for Social Research, Durban.

Malherbe, Etienne G., 1965. 'Manpower training: educational requirements for economic expansion', *S.A.J.E.* xxxiii, March.

McCormick, Brian, 1959. 'Labor hiring policies and monopolistic competition theory', *Q.J.E.* lxxiii, November.

McGregor, H. H., 1970. 'Manpower utilization in South Africa with special reference to the mining industry', *Journal of the South African Institute of Mining and Metallurgy*, June.

Machlup, Fritz, 1968. 'The price of gold', *The Banker* cxviii, September.

Markham, Jesse W., 1950. 'Some comments upon the north–south differentials', *Southern Economic Journal*, January.

Martin, John, 1929. 'Group administration in the gold mining industry of the Witwatersrand', Address delivered before the *Economic Section of the British Association for the Advancement of Science, Johannesburg*, August.

Mincer, Jacob, 1958. 'Investment in human capital and personal income distribution', *J.P.E.* lxvi, August.

Mitchell, J. Clyde, 1961. 'The causes of labour migration', *C.C.T.A.*, No. 79, Abidjan.

Mohlabi, F. R., 1971. 'Moral Effects of the System of Migratory Labour on the Labourer and his Family', *Migrant Labour and Church Involvement*, Mapumulo Consultation.

Moore, William E., 1964. 'The adaptation of African labor systems to social change', *Economic Transition in Africa*, ed. Melville J. Herskovits and Mitchell Hernitz, Routledge and Kegan Paul, London.

Mouly, Jean, 1967. 'Wage determination: institutional aspects', *I.L.R.* xcvi, November.

Newman, Dorothy K., 1965. 'The Negroes journey to the city', *M.L.R.* lxxxviii, May and June.

Nieuwenhuysen, J. P., 1964. 'Economic policy in the Reserves since the Tomlinson Report', *S.A.J.E.* xxxii, March.

1965. 'Prospects and issues in the development of the Reserves', *S.A.J.E.* xxxiii, June.

Oi, Walter Y., 1962. 'Labor on a quasi-fixed factor', *J.P.E.* lxx, December.

Oppenheimer, Harry, 1952. 'The future of the gold mining industry', *S.A.J.E.* xx, March.

Panofsky, Hans E., 1961. 'The significance of labour migration for the economic welfare of Ghana and the Voltaic Republic', *C.C.T.A.*, No. 79, Abidjan.

Payne, A. E., 1937–8. 'Transport of ore underground', *Association of Mine Managers of South Africa : Papers and Discussions*, Johannesburg.

Phelps-Brown, E. H., 1949. 'Equal pay for equal work', *E.J.* LIX, September.

1957. 'The meaning of the fitted Cobb-Douglas function', *Q.J.E.* LXXI, November.

Piercy, Mary V., 1960. 'Statutory work reservation—requirement of a static or of an expanding economy', *S.A.J.E.* XXVIII, June.

1960. 'Statutory work reservation in the Union of South Africa', *S.A.J.E.* XXVIII, September.

Prest, A. R. and Turvey, R., 1965. 'Cost-benefit analysis: a survey', *E.J.* LXXV, December.

Pursell, Donald E., 1958. 'Bantu real wages and employment opportunities', *S.A.J.E.* XXXVI, June.

Read, C. L., 1933. 'The union motive and the Witwatersrand gold mines', *S.A.J.E.* I, December.

Read, Margaret, 1942. 'Migrant labour in Africa and its effects on tribal life', *I.L.R.* XLV, June.

Reder, M. W., 1955. 'The theory of occupational wage differentials', *A.E.R.* XLV, December.

1964. 'Wage structure and structural unemployment', *Review of Economic Studies* XXXI, October.

Reuter, Ed. B., 1939. 'Competition and the racial division of labor', in *Race Relations and the Race Problem*, ed. E. T. Thomson, Durham, N. Carolina.

Reynolds, Lloyd G., 1948. 'Economics of labor', *Survey of Contemporary Economics*, A.E.A., Philadelphia.

Richards, C. S., 1968. 'Review of S. H. Frankel's *Investment and the Return to Equity in the South African Gold Mining Industry 1887–1965*', *S.A.J.E.* XXXVI, December.

Rita-Ferreira, A., 1960–1. 'Comments on labour emigration among the Moçambique Thonga by Marvin Harris', *Africa* XXX, April 1960; and XXXI, January 1961.

Rivlin, Alice M., 1962. 'Research in the economics of higher education', in *The Economics of Higher Education*, ed. Selma J. Mushkin, Washington.

Robertson, H. M., 1934–5. '150 years of economic contact between Black and White', *S.A.J.E.* II, December 1934; and III, March 1935.

Ross, Arthur M., and Goldner, William, 1950. 'Forces affecting the inter industry wage structure', *Q.J.E.* LXIV, May.

Rottenberg, Simon, 1952. 'Income and leisure in an underdeveloped economy', *J.P.E.* LX, April.

1953. 'Wage effects in the theory of the labor movement', *J.P.E.* LXI, June.

Rouch, Jean, 1961. 'Second generation migrants in Ghana and the Ivory Coast', in *Social Change in Modern Africa*, ed. Aidan Southall, O.U.P., London.

Rutman, Gilbert L., 1968. 'The Transkei: an experiment in economic separation', *S.A.J.E.* XXXVI, March.

Schultz, Theodore W., 1961. 'Education and economic growth', in *Social Forces Influencing American Education*, The 60th Yearbook of the National Society for the Study of Education, Part II, ed. Nelson B. Henry, Chicago University Press, Chicago.

1961. 'Investment in human capital', *A.E.R.* LI, March.

Schultz, Theodore W., Becker, Gary S. *et al.*, 1962. 'Investment in human beings', *J.P.E.* LXX, special supplement, October.

Scully, G. W., 1969. 'Interstate wage differentials: a cross section analysis', *A.E.R.* LIX.

Seers, Dudley, 1963. 'The limitations of the special case', *Bulletin of the Oxford University Institute of Economics and Statistics*, XXV, May.

Simons, H. C., 1944. 'Some reflections on syndicalism', *J.P.E.* LII, March.

Simons, H. J., 1961. 'Death in South African mines', *Africa South in Exile* V, July–September.

Steenkamp, W. F. J., 1963. 'Bantu wages in South Africa', *S.A.J.E.* XXXI, June.

1965. 'In quest of aims and norms for minimum wage fixing in terms of the wage act (1925)', *S.A.J.E.* XXXIII, June.

Stigler, George J., 1946. 'The economics of minimum wage legislation', *A.E.R.* XXXVI, June.

Thomas, Dana L., 1969. 'Trading in gold', *Barron's*, 2 June.

Thomson, A. G., 1953. 'Shortage of Native labour in the South African gold mining industry', *Mining Journal* CCXLI, 24 July.

Turner, H. A., 1952. 'Trade unions, differentials and the levelling of wages', *Manchester School of Economics and Social Studies* XX, September.

Turner, Ralph H., 1952. 'Foci of discrimination in the employment of non-whites', *American Journal of Sociology* LVIII, November.

Ulman, Lloyd, 1965. 'Labor mobility and the industrial wage structure in the post war United States', *Q.J.E.* LXXIX, February.

Van den Bogaerde, F., 1962. 'Occupational wage differentials in the South African metal industry', *S.A.J.E.* XXX.

Van der Horst, Sheila T., 1939. 'Review of the Native Farm Labour Committee, 1937–39', *S.A.J.E.* VII, December.

1953. 'The Native in South Africa's industrial revolution', *Optima* III, June.

1954. 'Equal pay for equal work', *S.A.J.E.* XXII.

1957. 'A note on Native labour turnover and the structure of the labour force in the Cape Peninsula', *S.A.J.E.* XXV.

1960. 'The economic implications of political democracy: the road to progress', *Optima*, special supplement, June.

1963. 'Lessons from the South African labour market', *Proceedings of the Central African Scientific and Medical Congress*, Lusaka.

1965. 'The effects of industrialization on race relations in South Africa', in *Industrialization and Race Relations*, ed. Guy Hunter, O.U.P., London.

Van der Merwe, P. J., 1969. 'The economic influence of the Bantu Labour Bureau system on the Bantu labour market', *S.A.J.E.*, XXXVII, March.

Van Velsen, J., 1961. 'Labour migration as a positive factor in the continuing of Tonga tribal society', in *Social Change in Modern Africa*, ed. Aidan Southall, O.U.P., London.

Viljoen, S. P., 1961. 'Higher productivity and higher wages of native labour in South Africa', *S.A.J.E.* XXIX.

Ward, Barbara, 1968. 'We modern tribalists', *South African Outlook*, August.
Watson, William, 1961. 'Migrant labour and detribalisation', *C.C.T.A.*, No. 79, Abidjan.
Wilson, Francis, 1971. 'Farming 1866–1966', *Oxford History of South Africa*, vol. 2, ed. Monica Wilson and Leonard Thompson, Clarendon Press, Oxford.
Wolfe, Alvin W., 1963. 'The African mineral industry: evolution of a supra-national level of integration', *Social Problems* XI, Fall.

D. UNPUBLISHED MATERIAL

Berg, Elliot J., 1960. *Recruitment of a Labor Force in Sub-Saharan Africa*, Ph.D. thesis, Harvard.
Bolitho, E. J., 1937. *A Short History and Details of the Government Miners' Training Schools*, Johannesburg.
  1947. *The Government Miners' Training Schools: An Outline of Two Vocational Training Schemes*, paper delivered to a Conference on Silicosis, Pneumoconiosis and Dust Suppression, London.
Camerer, R. A., 1965. *Economic Consequences resulting from Mine Closures in the Marginal Mines Region*, being Part 1 of the Marginal Mines Research Unit Report, Johannesburg.
Clack, Garfield, 1962. *The Changing Structure of Industrial Relations in South Africa with special references to Social Factors and Social Movements*, Ph.D. thesis, London School of Economics.
Coleman, Francis L., 1965. *The Technological Development of the Northern Rhodesian Copperbelt, 1899–1960, with particular reference to the Nchanga Mine*, Ph.D. thesis, University of Edinburgh.
Daubresse, Henry J. C., 1960. *Native Labour in the Belgian Congo*, M.Sc. (Econ.), London School of Economics.
Denoon, Donald, 1965. *Reconstruction in the Transvaal 1900–1905*, Ph.D. thesis, Cambridge.
Diamond, Charles R., 1969. *African Labour Problems on the S.A. Gold Mines with special reference to the Strike of 1946*, M.A. thesis, Cape Town.
Fleischer, A. C., 1954. *Social and Administrative Problems of Labour Migration in South Africa*, B.Litt. thesis, Oxford.
Fry, James, 1970. *The Turner Report—a Zambian View*, University of Zambia.
Gilman, Harry J., 1963. *Discrimination and the White-Nonwhite Unemployment Differentials*, Ph.D. thesis, Chicago.
Giuliano, Sara, 1965. *L'accueil des travailleurs Italiens à Genève*, Travail presenté à l'Ecole de Service Social de Genève en vue de l'obtention du diplôme, Geneva.
Graham, Michael Richard, 1964. *The Gold Mining Finance System in South Africa: with special reference to the Financing and Development of the Orange Free State Gold Field up to 1960*, Ph.D. thesis, London.
Hessian, Bernard, 1957. *An Investigation into the Causes of the Labour Agitation on the Witwatersrand, January to March, 1922*, M.A. thesis, University of the Witwatersrand.

Bibliography

Helman, C., 1971. *The Agro-Economic Development of the Lowland Region of Lesotho*, M.A. thesis, Cape Town.

Jones, J. D. Rheinallt, 1948. *Adoption of Personnel Management to Native Labour Problems on the Gold Mines:* address before the Johannesburg Branch of the S.A. Institute for Personnel Management, Johannesburg.

JRDB/KS/NE, 1945. *An Analysis of Native Labour Requirements in Witwatersrand Reduction Works*, Johannesburg.

Keat, Paul G., 1959. *Changes in Occupational Wage Structure, 1900–1956*, Ph.D. thesis, Chicago.

Koornhof, P. G. T., 1953. *The Drift from the Reserves among the South African Bantu*, D.Phil. thesis, Oxford.

Landes, William, 1965. *An Economic Analysis of Fair Employment Laws*, paper to Columbia University Labor Workshop, 2nd draft, March.

Menell, C. S., 1961, *The Changing Character of the South African Mining Finance Houses in the Post War Period*, M.A. thesis, Wharton.

Meyer, F., 1965. *A Survey of Past and Future of Heavy Industry in the Republic of South Africa*, speech at Kelvin House, Johannesburg, 9 September.

Moore, A. A., 1931. *Mining Problems*, Ballinger Papers, Memo, Cape Town, April.

National Institute for Personnel Research, 1956. *Factors affecting the Popularity of Mines and the Mining Industry: A Study of Native Attidudes on Four Mines of the Central Mining and Investment Group*, South African Council for Scientific and Industrial Research, Johannesburg.

Ould, C. R., 1964. *General Smuts's Attitude to White Labour Disputes between 1907 and 1922*, M.A. thesis, University of the Witwatersrand.

Reynolds, Norman, 1969. *A Socio-Economic Study of an African Development Scheme*, Ph.D. thesis, Cape Town.

Zeman, Morton, 1955. *A Quantitative Analysis of the White–Nonwhite Income Differentials in the United States*, Ph.D. thesis, University of Chicago, September.

INDEX

Absenteeism, 124
accidents, 20–1, 49, 167; causes, 21, 93, 96; compensation, 50; rate, 21–2, 167, 192
age of workers, 96, 183
agriculture: in California, 71, 152; earnings in, 4, 169; farms and farmers, 1, 75, 81, 86, 114; labour, 1, 81, 86, 148; land tenure, 121, 123, 134; *see also* Bantustans; rural incomes
Anderson, C. B., 30
Anderson, P. H., 30
Anglo-Boer war, 4, 45
Angola, 69, 129
Austria, 72

backward sloping supply curve, 75–6
Ballingall, H. C., 31
Bantustans (reserves), 3, 130, 131, 134, 146–7, 148, 153, 188; *see also* Ciskei; Transkei
Barotseland, 70, 128, 130, 132
Bemba, 132
Berning, F. S., 30
Berstein, B. L., 31
Biesheuwel, Dr S., 95n
Blakeway, R. E. M., 31
Botswana, 69, 70, 71, 73, 88, 128, 130, 133
Braceros, 71, 152
Brakpan, 84
British Somaliland, 87
Buckle Commission, 149
Busschau, Dr W. J., 31
B$_8$W units, 111–12, 143

California, 71, 152
Cape Province, 70, 71, 81, 181, 182, 184
Cape Town, 138
Central Rand, 167
centripetal *v.* centrifugal forces, 121
Chamber of Mines, xi, xii, xv, 3–5, 10–11, 20, 27–8, 32, 45–6, 50–3, 69–81, 87, 91–2, 95–6, 101, 110, 114–18, 143, 147, 150, 154–5, 170; Gold Producers Committee, 28, 47–8, 52, 76, 171–9; Rand Mutual Assurance Company, 50; recruiting organisations (N.R.C. and W.N.L.A.), 4–5,

49, 68, 72–3, 81, 88, 105–6, 127–9; Technical Advisory Committee, 106
Chinese labour, 4–5, 7–8, 45
Ciskei, 71, 85, 133, 134, 135, 138, 188–9
civil service, employment in, 148
civilised labour policy, 11–12
coal mining, 16, 22, 27, 70, 71, 117n, 170
Cobb–Douglas production function, 43, 184
collusion, 33, 40, 101–2, 184–5
Commonwealth, South African withdrawal from, 106
competition, 90, 111, 142, 184; for labour, 73–5, 101, 114, 147
conditions of work, 20–2, 171–9
Congo, 124, 125, 149
construction industry, 148, 169
contract labour, *see* migrant system of labour
convicts, earnings of, 163
co-operative scheme, 52
copper industry, 125
Copperbelt, 69n, 99, 101, 119, 124, 125, 126, 137
Cornwall, 50
currency, xvii–xviii
current terms, xviii, 55

Dahomeyans, 152
death, 4, 5, 95, 167, 192
decision making, workers' participation in, 151
depression, 125, 137
diamond mining, 1, 6, 7, 22, 57; illicit diamond buying, 6
discipline among workers, 100
Dow Report, 122

earnings
allowances: active service, 52–3, 163–4; breakdown of, 164; cost of living, 9, 47–8, 164, 171, 174–5; leave, 47–9, 62, 164, 171–5
breakdown of, 164
changes in, 4, 8, 10, 45–6, 55, 75, 107, 132, 141–2
Coloured, 163
compared with earnings in: agriculture, 4,

213

Index

Index

Index